Family Afloat

by Jim Toomey

Two Years Sailing the World with
Two Kids and Two Captains

MARINER
STUDIOS

Copyright ©2022 by Jim Toomey

All rights reserved.

No part of this publication may be reproduced, stored in a retrieval system or transmited in any form or by any means, electronic, mechanical, photocopying, recording or otherwise without the prior permission of the publisher or in accordance with the provisions of the Copyright, Designs and Patents Act of 1988 or under the terms of any licence permitting limited copying issued by the Copyright Licensing Agency, except in the case of brief quotations embodied in critical articles and reviews.

First edition June 2022

Original Lagoon 450 floorplan © Groupe Beneteau.

Published by: Mariner Studios, LLC
http://www.marinerstudios.com

ISBN: 978-0-578-38505-1

1 2 3 4 5 6 7 8 9 10

Family Afloat

Other Books by Jim Toomey

Evolution Is Hard Work!
If You Can't Beat 'Em, Eat 'Em
The Adventures of Superfish & His Superfishal Friends
Onward and Downward
Happy as a Clam
Tales from the Deep
Lunch Wore a Speedo
Here We Go Again
Think Like a Shark
Never Bite Anything That Bites Back
Discover Your Inner Hermit Crab
Confessions of a Swinging Single Sea Turtle
Sharks Just Wanna Have Fun
Yarns and Shanties
In Shark Years I'm Dead
Planet of the Hairless Beach Apes
Surfer Safari
A Day at the Beach
Catch of the Day
Shark Diaries
Greatest Hits & Near Misses
Surf's Up
Greetings From Sherman's Lagoon
Another Day in Paradise
An Illustrated Guide to Shark Etiquette
Poodle: The Other White Meat
Ate That, What's Next?

For Valerie,
Thanks for making life an adventure.

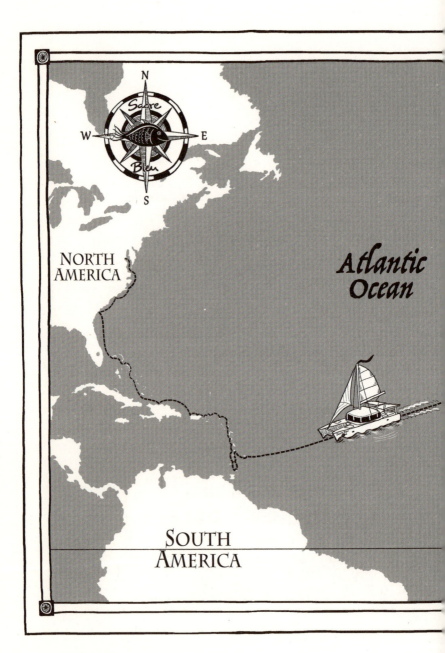

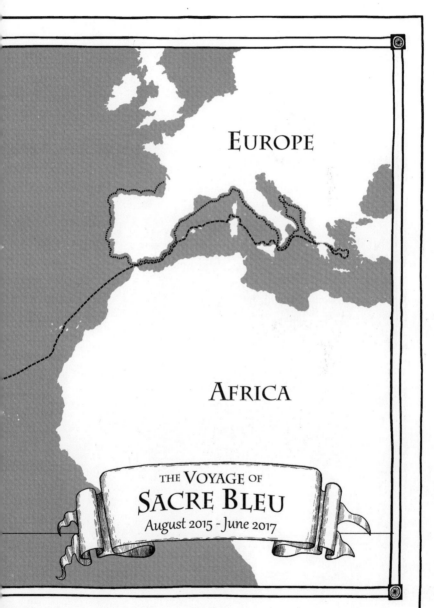

Contents

1 It All Began at a Dead End 1
   Annapolis, Maryland 1

2 Shedding Our Terrestrial Footprint 8
   Annapolis 8

3 The Commissioning 25
   Les Sables-d'Olonne, France 25

4 The Adventure Begins 31
   Les Sables-d'Olonne, France 31

5 'Round the End of the Earth 54
   Costa de Galicia, Spain 54
   Back in Spanish Waters 69

6 A Tax Haven with Monkeys 74
   Gibraltar 74

Contents

7 The Mediterranean: In Poseidon's Realm 81
    Spain 81
    France 92
    Monaco 96
    A Quick Trip Home 99
    Return to Monaco 101

8 Winter in the French Riviera 103
    Antibes, France 103
    Another Trip Home 119

9 Back on the Blue 122
    Italy 122

10 Young Countries, Ancient Histories 159
    Croatia 159
    Montenegro 174

11 Ouzo with a Side of Meltemi 179
    Corfu, Greece 179

12 Turning West 201
    Ios, Greece 201

13 Islands and Volcanoes 210
    Kefalonia, Greece 210
    Stromboli, Italy 215
    Castellammare del Golfo, Sicily 221
    Olbia, Sardinia 225

14 Cruising to Crossing: A New Plan 229
    Alghero, Italy 229
    Gibraltar 235
    Morocco 236

Contents

15 The Transatlantic: If You're Lucky It's Boring...... 239
    Stage I: To the Canary Islands 239
    Stage II: The Big Hop 248

16 The Caribbean: Island-Hopping South.................267
    Barbados 267
    Martinique 270
    Home for the Holidays 275
    Return to Martinique 276
    St. Vincent and the Grenadines 277

17 The Caribbean: Island-Hopping North. 282
    Back to Martinique (Again) 282
    Dominica 284
    Guadeloupe 286
    Antigua and Barbuda 289
    The British Virgin Islands 292
    Puerto Rico and the Virgin Islands 295
    The Dominican Republic 296

18 The Bahamas: The Ultimate Infinity Pool 299
    Great Inagua 299
    Long Island 302
    Exuma Cays Land & Sea Park 305
    Nassau 306

19 Homeward Bound...309
    The Eastern Seaboard 309
    The Chesapeake Bay 313

Afterword 316

Acknowledgements

If not for the dedication and talent of the following people, I would have given up on this book a long time ago. I wish to thank Sandra Olivetti Martin, at New Bay Books, who helped me refine the manuscript line by line into a more readable personal memoir. Sandra's patience and eye for detail are boundless, and her love of books and reading were a guiding force. I would also like to thank Max Regan, at Hollowdeck Press, who played an invaluable role helping me weave my ship's log entries into a compelling narrative, providing advice on structure and character development. Max convinced me I could write this book and that it was a story worth telling. Thank you, Max. Lisa Birman's keen eye for grammar, tense, punctuation and syntax elevated this book to a new level. And thank you, Sheldon Studios, for suggesting a few hundred more corrections just when I thought I had finished the book. I also owe a debt of gratitude to certain dedicated test readers who had the courage to take on my manuscript in its early stages and provide critical feedback, namely Slade Mead and his brother, Winter.

I would also like to thank the people who played a key role in the actual journey this book was written about. We hosted many guests onboard *Sacre Bleu*, but for purposes of brevity and simplicity, we did not name any in this book. For the transatlantic voyage, our insurance company required us to have a third adult onboard to help stand watch. For the four-day Gibraltar-to-Canary Islands leg, Carl Reale stood the third watch, and for the nineteen-day Canary-to-Barbados leg, Don Ferguson joined us. They both quickly proved themselves worthy sailors and shipmates, and their good nature helped us pass the many long hours of ocean crossing. Will Franke, and Paul and Will Fenn joined us in the The Bahamas for our three-day crossing to Charleston. Thanks, guys, for your help.

Finally, we never would have set out on our journey if we hadn't found a loving home for our pets. I wish to thank Adam Whitaker and his daughter, Saylor, for taking our family dog, Belle, into their home. The love and patience they showed were extraordinary and provided us peace of mind during our cruise. I would also like to thank Amelia Johnson for taking care of Munchkin the hamster, and later, Snowball and Squirt.

1

It All Began at a Dead End

Annapolis, Maryland
October 2, 2014

"We've never had a sniper in the bathroom before!" Valerie exclaimed.

An Annapolis SWAT Team sniper knelt by our open bathroom window, his laser-scoped Remington .308 rifle trained on a hijacked airport shuttle. Pursued by the Maryland State Police, the hijacker had driven down our dead-end street where the chase ended in a standoff 50 feet from our front door.

Our twelve-year-old daughter, Madeleine, was watching the drama in our bathroom from the hallway. William, our nine-year-old son, was so engrossed in a video game that he had not noticed the armed sniper walking through the house. Nor had he heard the screeching tires when the hijacked airport shuttle landed at the end of our driveway. Coincidentally, the video game he was playing, Tom Clancy's "Rainbow Six," features commandos dressed in black jumpsuits and Kevlar vests just like the officer in our upstairs bathroom.

"Hey, William," I said, tapping him on the shoulder, "'Rainbow Six' has come to your bathroom." He was in the middle of a kill and didn't dare take his eyes off the screen. "William, there's a guy from a police SWAT team on the second floor," I prodded. "Look!"

His eyes widened as I led him past the front window at the sight of a dozen Maryland State Police cruisers, their flashing blue lights illuminating the trees and houses in the dark night. Just ten feet from our door, a policeman wearing body armor stood in our front yard aiming his service revolver at the shuttle bus. Another one was sheltered behind our car in the driveway holding a shotgun at the ready.

The panicked driver floored the accelerator, but the hijacked shuttle was not budging. The rear tires had been stripped off and the bare wheels were kicking up sparks against the pavement. A special operations armored vehicle with a gun turret rammed the back of the shuttle bus, smashing its rear window as the two vehicles lurched forward together. William was impressed.

"I bet that doesn't happen in St. *Didier*," I said to Valerie over coffee the next morning. St. Didier, population 2,200, was her hometown in the Beaujolais region of central France where her father had been a policeman. If the standoff had happened there, it would have been appropriate to offer everyone a glass of wine afterward.

"Yeah. Thank goodness it ended peacefully," Valerie said as she sipped her coffee. "I can't believe William lost interest in the whole thing after fifteen minutes."

"The real world just isn't as exciting as a video game," I said with a resigned sigh.

"We both know it could be."

"Yeah, I know. We've been down this road before."

"There's nothing keeping us here," she declared.

Valerie was once again turning the conversation to breaking free to sail around the world. The idea intrigued me, but it was not the right time in my life to drop out and take a year off. I was just hitting a groove. Life seemed to be just fine, just the way it was.

"We do have a few little things keeping us here," I said to Valerie. "The kids have school, their friends, their sports…William has Boy Scouts…And we have our friends…your commitments, my commitments." Valerie rolled her eyes. I continued: "What do we do with the house? The cars? And Belle. What about Belle?" Belle was the family dog, a Vizsla we had adopted from a rescue shelter two years earlier. She had separation anxiety and got upset whenever we walked out the door, even to retrieve a package. I could not imagine walking out the door for an entire year.

"You can draw your comic strip anywhere," Valerie declared in a fit of passion. Valerie frequently gets passionate, but unlike me, she can turn it on and off. She can scream at me in the kitchen for using the wrong knife and then calmly ask me to step aside while she gets the correct knife out of the drawer. I try not to get overly emotional because I continue to feel those emotions all day and all night and into the next day—possibly for weeks.

"People don't just buy a boat and sail away," I tried to reason. "It's not that easy."

"We'll take boating courses, talk to people, read books," Valerie said. "This town's full of sailors."

Annapolis, which advertises itself as "America's Sailing Capital," is an undeniably nautical town. Need a new sail? Three sail lofts within a ten-minute drive of downtown can sew one up for you. How about a gudgeon for your transom? No problem. At least a dozen marine suppliers in the downtown zip code can sell you one. Don't know what a gudgeon is? Ask anybody in line at City Dock Coffee. You'll get four or five people answering, each adding their nuance. You might even start an argument. On any given summer night the sidewalks are filled with Naval Academy midshipmen in their summer whites, the harbor is a forest of sailboat masts, and the yacht club cannons can be heard starting regattas. At the open-air theater by the waterfront, the players have grown accustomed to stopping the action and dialog, sometimes in mid-sentence, for the duration of a ship's horn.

Despite all of the sailing culture around us, we rarely got out on the water. We had sailed more regularly some years ago, but now that we had children and other commitments, we had no time for it. We didn't own a boat at the time, never went out on other peoples' boats, and didn't belong to a yacht club. On weekends, we did yard work. Valerie worked part-time in the boating industry, as many do in Annapolis, but she was in marketing and rarely went near an actual watercraft. However, her job did put us in touch with many people who were knowledgeable about ocean sailing, and we explored the idea of an extended family cruise one email at a time.

"You've been talking about doing this ever since I've known you!" Valerie exclaimed.

It's true. I have always loved ships and the sea. When I was a boy, the ocean was far more fascinating than any of Hollywood's science fiction. The dinosaurs in *Jurassic Park* were big, but whales are bigger. The aliens in *Star Wars* were weird, but deep-sea anglerfish are weirder. The highlight of my childhood summers was the week my family spent on the Delaware shore, where I sat on the beach for hours transfixed by the ocean, looking for any sign of life—a fin or a splash. I knew that under all that featureless blue, faithfully reproduced on maps as more featureless blue, an entirely different world lay hidden from view, waiting for an intrepid explorer to unlock its mysteries. It is a world with mountains and valleys, forests and meadows, and creatures great and small whose evolutions did not answer to gravity. It is a world still largely unexplored.

Of all the animals in the sea, sharks obsessed me. They have been put on this planet to keep us humble. Almost every one of my school projects that started with crayons or clay ended with a shark. Over time, my sketches evolved into a cartoon shark named Sherman and eventually into a career. I began drawing the daily newspaper comic strip *Sherman's Lagoon* in 1991, and by 2014, I was syndicated in over 150 newspapers with 22 books in print.

Back in the day, I would draw the comic strip on paper and overnight the physical artwork to my syndicate in New York on a weekly basis. In 2000, once I started drawing on a digital tablet and emailing digital files, I never set foot in an art supply store again. My office became a laptop computer. Not only was my job portable, it was one of those rare jobs that could be done in advance. Theoretically, if I wanted to trek the Andes for a month, all I had to do was draw a month's worth of comic strips, hit the send button and hit the road. Before children, I occasionally took advantage of this freedom. Once the kids arrived, I stopped thinking about freedom.

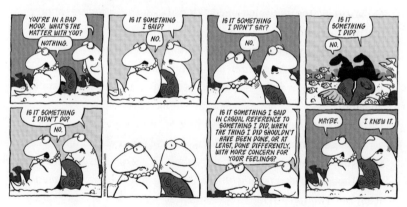

My comic strip Sherman's Lagoon.

"What about the kids?" I asked Valerie. "We don't know anything about homeschooling."

"We have friends who do it. It's not rocket science, especially at their age," she insisted.

Madeleine was a twelve-year-old with a soul that was much older. Patient and thoughtful, she can immerse herself in a project for hours, completing a thousand-piece puzzle in a single sitting. She loves animals and loves to draw them in meticulous detail. She'll sketch every follicle on a mountain lion, every feather on an owl, every fold in a seahorse. When Madeleine and I ride in the car together, we typically do not say a word the entire trip, and neither of us feels awkward about the silence. We are both lost in our thoughts, and we understand that about each other. Why disrupt a good thought with idle chitchat? She is also painfully shy. For better or for worse, Madeleine got my personality.

William, nine years old, came into this world a freshly minted soul who could not contain his curiosity. A car ride with William is guaranteed to be entertaining because his train of thought follows no route or schedule. He might ask a question about dragonfly aerodynamics followed by one about George Washington's teeth. He is a builder. On the floor throughout the house lurk sharp Lego pieces ready to throw themselves under a bare foot. William was obsessed with the sinking of the *Titanic* and cultivated an encyclopedic knowledge of this famous maritime disaster.

"There's no better time than now," Valerie said as we finished breakfast. "Once Madeleine hits high school, it'll be impossible to tear her away from her circle of friends and go on a family adventure."

"You don't think William's too young?"

"He's old enough to appreciate it," Valerie responded. "And they're both comfortable on a sailboat."

Though we never made time for boating ourselves, we did impose it on our children. With two summers of junior sailing under their belts, they had both developed enough boat sense…we told ourselves. Madeleine had taken to dinghy racing well and even placed in a few regattas and won a trophy. William cared less about trophies and enjoyed sailing for the independence it gave him.

"What has happened in the past twelve months that changed your life?" asked Valerie.

"Not much," I admitted. Time was passing without many highs or lows to measure it by.

"If we drop out for a year, I bet most people won't even notice we were gone," Valerie declared.

"I'll miss career opportunities."

"You might actually get *better* at what you do. Telling ocean stories *is* your career."

"Mom and Dad aren't going to be around much longer," I persisted.

"But we can't plan our lives around that," said Valerie. She was right. My parents' imminent passing had been a ticking time bomb for years.

"Have you considered how much this will cost?" I continued, grasping for a new angle.

"Maybe a lot. So what?"

"Well…if we get a decent rent on the house, it might not be all that bad," I said, more to myself than to Valerie. I was warming to the concept. I was ready to start a spreadsheet.

Valerie was right, I concluded. We had hit a Goldilocks moment: the kids were old enough, but not too old. There was no better time. After putting my wife off since the early days of our marriage, I relented.

"Hey, guys, we've got a serious question for you," I announced to Madeleine and William at the dinner table that night. "We're thinking of going on a family adventure." I got no reaction from the kids. They had already been on a few of our family adventures, which frequently involved piling into the minivan and driving until William threw up.

"For a whole year," Valerie added.

"A *year*? Huh? Where?" asked Madeleine.

"We don't know yet," I said.

"We're going to live on a boat," said Valerie.

"Whaddaya think?" I asked the kids with a wide grin.

Dead silence.

"Are we taking Belle? What about Munchkin?" asked Madeleine when she found her voice.

"We'll find somebody to take care of them. They'll both be here when we get back," Valerie said, being overly optimistic about hamster lifespans.

2

Shedding Our Terrestrial Footprint

Annapolis
October 4, 2014

As Valerie and I spun out our plan on the kitchen table, we narrowed the world of possibility to three regions. The first was the Caribbean. We could start in our own backyard, sail south to the Bahamas and work our way down island along the crescent-shaped Caribbean chain as far as Trinidad, then visit different destinations on our return trip north. Dozens of islands in the Caribbean beckoned, each with a unique culture, and lots of beaches and coral reefs and warm water we could enjoy as scuba divers, paddle boarders, and amateur treasure hunters. On the downside, the Caribbean has hurricanes. Hurricanes are a thousand miles wide, and anywhere from ten to sixteen named storms pass through this part of the world every hurricane season. If we spent a year there, an encounter was inevitable.

The Galapagos Islands was another farther paradise. We would sail through the Caribbean and the Panama Canal, out to Cocos Island, and then on to the Galapagos. But getting to the Galapagos Islands requires nine hundred miles of open-ocean sailing. This idea most resembled my preconception of an epic adventure, complete with life-threatening scenarios that are much better watched on reality television than experienced in reality. As first-time ocean sailors, we concluded, we weren't ready to cast off the lines and just keep sailing over the horizon. This plan also lacked an exit strategy. What would we do after the Galapagos? Turn around and sail back across all that open ocean and through the Canal again? Continue sailing west another three *thousand* miles to the next closest destination, French Polynesia? Buy a house and adopt a tortoise?

Then we imagined ourselves in the Mediterranean: cradle of Western civilization, cornucopia of culture, birthplace of pizza. The more we researched this itinerary, the more it appealed. Valerie could be closer to her family in France, and for the kids the cruise would be an immersive course in language, culture, history, religion, cuisine, antiquities, contemporary geopolitics—the list goes on and on—not to mention sailing, oceanography, geography, and astronomy. For me, every few miles of coastline would bring a different variety of wine and cheese. We could start in France with Bordeaux, pass through the Garnachas of Spain, followed by Portugal and its wonderful Ports, then on to the Barolos of Italy. We would have to pair all that wine with food. Sailing the Med amounted to circumnavigating a five thousand-mile-long buffet. I would put on fifty pounds and possibly need heart bypass surgery by the time I waddled off the boat, but it seemed a small price to pay.

The Mediterranean has no hurricanes, but I discovered, much to my surprise, it does have winter. How bad can winters be on the palm-lined boulevards of the French Riviera or sun-soaked Capri? From the safety of land, Mediterranean winters are merely bone chilling and damp. From a sailor's perspective, winter brings violent storms that churn the sea into a field of angry, confused waves that stalk small boats and swallow them whole. The Phoenicians, the Romans, the Greeks, and countless other ancient mariners learned this the hard way. Whatever sailing sense we possess today comes at the expense of generations of these brave souls who ventured out to sea in search of fish, fortune, or a fight and frequently never returned. Instead of a hurricane plan, we would need a winter plan. We would have to find a safe harbor and settle down for the months of November through March. But five months in a Mediterranean seaport didn't sound so bad. We began to look at the winter plan not as a disruption but as the perfect intermission to our nomadic adventure.

October 9, 2014

October in Annapolis brings crisp breezes, falling leaves, and the Annapolis Boat Show, one of the largest displays of watercraft and accessories on the planet. We attended the 2014 boat show with a mixture of trepidation and glee. It was going to be the biggest shopping spree of our lives, yet we knew so little about what we had to buy.

At the top of our list was the boat itself. We weren't merely shopping for a vehicle that could transport us safely and reliably. We were looking for a space where we would live as a family for a year and share the experiences of our new lives. We had to balance all the technical considerations that accompany a boat purchase with the emotions that come with choosing a new home. This was no ordinary move. We were trading a 3,800 square foot house with four bedrooms, four baths, and…I don't know how many closets because I've never counted them all…for a fiberglass box with roughly 500 square feet of interior space, a considerable part of which is devoted to machinery and electronics I did not understand.

We wanted a catamaran because we liked the extra room the twin hulls provided and the fact that most of the living space of a catamaran was high above the waterline as opposed to the down-below arrangement of a monohull (single-hulled) sailboat. Catamarans range from high-tech, carbon-fiber racing machines that skate on hydrofoils, to floating condominiums, laden with frills, that push walls of water in front of them like snowplows. Tradeoffs had to be made. What did we value more: speed or comfort? Fast boats are wonderful for getting from A to B, but speed comes with a price. Fast boats have narrower hulls, are more cramped inside, and to save weight they have fewer luxuries, like, say, toilets.

We decided we didn't need fast. On a typical day we might sail 20 or 30 miles and settle in for the night on anchor or in a marina. At those distances, another two knots of boat speed wouldn't make much of a difference in our transit time. In addition to offering more finished space and creature comforts, slower boats are generally more stable, and stability is critical with catamarans. When a monohull sailboat gets knocked down in a storm, even to the point of turning upside down, it tends to eventually right itself because, thanks to its keel (the big, heavy fin attached to the bottom of the hull), upright is its most stable position. Any sailor will tell you that a catamaran has two stable positions: upright and upside down. Fast cats, being lighter with bigger sails, are more prone to capsizing.

Valerie tends to be a discerning shopper who contemplates a purchase methodically, carefully, slowly but surely, the way lichens might contemplate jumping to a new rock. However, in choosing our boat, she was uncharacteristically compulsive. "I love this boat!" Valerie exclaimed to me, the sales rep, and everyone else inside the boat.

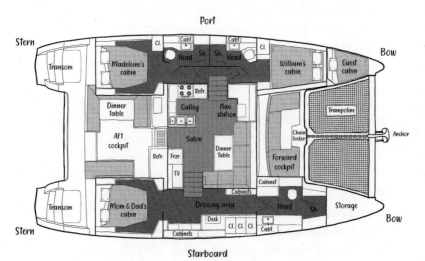

The floor plan of the Lagoon 450.

The Lagoon 450 catamaran is 45 feet long by 25 feet wide, with two hulls and a large platform in between. It has all the amenities of a small house, including two reefers (refrigerators), a freezer, a water maker and a flatscreen TV. You board at the transom steps (rear face of the hull), which lead to the aft cockpit (exterior seating area) under a roof, that features a dining table surrounded by settees and a reefer. As you move forward, a sliding door in the aft cockpit opens into the salon (living room), with the galley (kitchen) to port (the left, looking forward) and a second dining table and settee to starboard (the right, looking forward). On either side of the salon, short stairways lead down to the hulls, where the cabins are located. The port hull holds two cabins and two heads (bathrooms), while the entire starboard hull is devoted to one large owner's cabin with a larger head, closets, and a desk. Back out in the aft cockpit, exterior stairways on both sides lead up to the flybridge (elevated steering area), with helm (steering wheel), engine controls and navigation electronics. The boat also comes with a mast and lots of ropes and pulleys that make sailboats go. We didn't pay much attention to that stuff.

For years we had been saving a nest egg to buy a second home someplace—maybe a ski condo, maybe a beach house—but we could never decide what or where. In twenty minutes that debate was over, and our new lives as a cruising family had begun.

Skeptical that anyone could decide to buy a new 45-foot catamaran after a twenty-minute walkthrough, the Lagoon salesman was nevertheless happy to start the paperwork. Our next step was a test drive, or what is referred to in the industry as a sea trial. We couldn't hop on one during the show, but there was a fully rigged Lagoon 450 sitting in his charter operation in Puerto Rico, so we shook hands and made plans to fly there later in the year. We were making big decisions quickly, and for me the extra time was a welcome delay.

With the boat selected, our focus turned to filling it with gear. As we wandered the aisles of the boat show, we evaluated every purchase according to three guiding principles: Did we need it? Could we afford it? And most importantly, where would we put it? At the top of our shopping list was safety equipment. We definitely needed it. At the boat show there was an entire circus tent devoted to safety equipment, and the choices were mindboggling. Should we buy every safety gadget on the shelf? Were we bad parents if we subjected our children to risks when a little more money could mitigate those risks? What if the worst happened? What if one of the kids fell overboard? That circus tent had a several-thousand-dollar answer for every anxiety we felt.

When I was a boy, safety gear consisted of an orange life jacket and a whistle. But boat safety, like most everything else in recent years, has moved to technology. As with any technology, safety gear has the shelf life of bananas. If you have yesterday's safety gear, you've missed out on the more feature-packed safety gear that just came out this morning. For those of you foolish enough to have bought your safety gear this morning, a firmware upgrade is available that will make your safety gear almost as good as the gear that will be released tomorrow. Sooner or later we had to make the commitment, so we purchased two items that are standard equipment on any offshore cruise: an EPIRB (emergency position indicating radio beacon), a small, floating device that when immersed in water automatically transmits a mayday signal; and a six-person, auto-inflating life raft, in case the boat sinks before anyone responds to your mayday signal. The life raft, when packed, is about the size of a large suitcase, and on most sailboats, our new Lagoon included, there is a dedicated space for it. Both items passed our three-part test. With any luck, our safety gear would sit unused and become more obsolete with each passing day. It is the one purchase for which you hope you don't ever get your money's worth.

Anchors, on the other hand, are an investment that we hoped would prove their worth daily. Who knew that anchors come in so many shapes and sizes? The Danforth, the Delta, the Spade, the plow, the kedge, the mushroom, the grapnel, the Bruce, and a dozen more, each one designed for specific bottom conditions. The anchor salesman quickly set us straight: "A Bruce is fine for a sandy or muddy bottom," he cautioned, as he dragged a miniature Bruce anchor through his tabletop sandbox. "However, a rocky bottom requires a different kind of anchor. You might need 'The Claw' for rocky bottoms. What kind of bottom are you likely to encounter where you're going?"

That was a very good question, and one I had not considered. I discreetly pulled out my cell phone and performed a quick internet search of "Mediterranean bottoms." After scrolling past all the adult websites, I determined that we would eventually need all 14 kinds of anchors. However, the Spade anchor met more of our needs in the part of the world we planned to cruise. Pound for pound, it was the best deal we got all day.

As we filled our new boat with more and more gear, we strictly followed our three guiding principles: buying only what we needed, what we could afford, and what had room for. We were judicious, circumspect, and selective. That is, until we walked into the toy tent. On display were folding bicycles, stand-up paddleboards, fishing gear, dive gear, underwater cameras, solar-powered blenders and more. On land, many of these items are considered weekend warrior closet clutter, but on a cruising boat, we reasoned, they played a utilitarian role. Dive gear is a nice luxury for exploring the coral reefs, but it is a necessity for working on a boat under the waterline or unfouling an anchor. Bicycles serve as the primary mode of transportation in ports of call without taxis, buses or rideshare services. Fishing is also more than recreation on a boat, especially on long ocean passages where a rod can provide a welcome change to the menu, or in an emergency, a sustainable food source. We could not think of a utilitarian role for the paddleboard, and after a while we gave up justifying our toys and just bought them without thinking of where we would put them.

We went on to look at single-sideband radios, water makers, solar panels, wind generators, satellite phones, forward-scanning transducers, digital barometers, first aid kits, sail-repair kits, blocks, tackles, shackles and turnbuckles.

"Looking for a drogue?" a salesperson asked.

"I've never used one before." I responded vaguely, trying not reveal that I didn't know "drogue" was a word.

"It's like a parachute that slows your boat down in big waves."

"Sounds like something we'll need. You know, I'm taking my family on a blue-water cruise in a few months." I said this casually, as in, "We do expeditions like this all the time. Next year, we'll be tagging emperor penguins in Antarctica."

"Have you done much open-ocean, heavy-weather sailing?"

"No."

"Have you done much heavy-weather sailing?"

"No."

"Have you done much sailing?"

"Some."

Spending a new car's worth of money at the boat show was easy. Harder was planning our homeschooling curricula for William and Madeleine, going into fifth and seventh grades. How to put a year of school in a box? We needed a low-tech program that was not reliant on the internet, since internet, and even electricity, was a big unknown. Books, though they are bulkier than laptops and iPads, are failsafe. In the end, we chose a curriculum that used storytelling as a teaching tool because it would allow the kids to work independently while we were busy driving the boat, making meals, fighting pirates, or whatever else boat parents did. Our children would learn their history from fictional characters who lived in the era they were studying. They learned geography from an explorer who had to acquire local knowledge to solve mysteries. Math was the one subject that required technology, with the instruction enhanced by interactive CD-ROMs that did not rely on an internet connection.

We also wanted to encourage the fun side of learning for the kids. We aspired to be a Corps of Discovery, like Lewis and Clark, or Darwin and his ship HMS *Beagle*, or Cousteau and *Calypso*, outfitted with state-of-the-art home schooling gadgets that could help our children shed light where there was dark and probe the deepest mysteries of the planet. With the entire online retail world at our computer keyboard, we tried search terms such as "astronomy" and "oceanography" and watched our screen fill with merchandise. Soon the boxes were piling up on the doorstep. We bought an inexpensive telescope that transported us about a hundred feet closer to the heavens, and a $30 USB-based microscope that transmitted magnified images onto a computer screen. We bought a compact piano keyboard that, when connected to an iPad, provided endless piano lessons. We stocked up on robotics kits, chemistry sets, and arts and crafts supplies, which all seemed like a bargain compared to the EPIRB we just bought. By the end of the outfitting process, I had surrendered to Valerie's philosophy. This trip was going to cost a lot. So what?

October 19, 2014
Surprisingly, a license is not required to operate a private boat in U.S. waters. We live in the Land of the Free, and anyone can damn well buy a boat and drive away in it. But as we planned to sail a big ocean in a relatively small boat with two young children, we wanted to become better sailors.

In my younger years, I'd gained most of my sailing experience on a rented sailboat doing daytrips and the occasional weeklong charter. Charters provide all the benefits of cruising with none of the hassles, like boat maintenance and dealing with marine contractors, valuable experience that comes only from owning a boat. When we lived in San Francisco, we frequently rented small sailboats and set out on the Bay, with its strong winds, heavy seas, fast-moving commercial traffic and rocky bottom. The San Francisco Bay made me a sailor. Before I could rent a sailboat at my sailing club there, I had to take a few classes and pass an on-the-water test, which I failed on my first try. Back in those days, Valerie was happy to accompany me on my sailing adventures, but I was the one packing the cooler and the foul weather gear.

Fifteen years and two children later, we still considered ourselves amateur sailors. The occasional weekend excursions and charters had been fun, but they had not given us any of the skills necessary for long-distance cruising: navigation, anchoring, heavy weather sailing, to name a few. Valerie and I needed to find a way to get more sailing experience quickly. Fortunately, in Annapolis, that's easy. One or two emails are all it takes to find a racing boat needing a crewmember. Competing in regattas compresses the sailing experience into a rapid-fire stream of short, intense exercises. A crew might tack and jibe, trim sails, set and douse sails more in a three-hour race than on a three-day run to Bermuda.

October 25, 2014
The Halloween Howl was the last regatta of the year for the junior sailing fleet in Annapolis, and wind conditions were ideal. The youngest sailors, including our children, sail an Optimist, a sailboat the size of a bathtub. Madeleine's ability to focus was an asset in regattas, where the slightest change in sail shape or ripple on the water can signal a wind shift and a change in tactics. She finished in the top third of the fleet that day, happy with her season. Madeleine seemed to have caught the sailing bug. William was competing in a different fleet for younger sailors, and his sailing bug had crawled off and was nowhere to be found. After these last regattas, the junior fleet sailed across the harbor, where Halloween candy awaited them. In this regatta, William led the pack. With the right motivation, he showed potential.

During these last few warm weeks of fall, Valerie and I tried to get on the water as frequently as possible. I had become a volunteer with the U.S. Naval Academy's Offshore Sail Training Squadron, a program that was training hundreds of midshipmen to sail and had a need for adult supervision that far outstretched its fulltime coaching staff. I spent my weekends on one of the Academy's big sloops, with a midshipman crew and a more experienced naval officer, learning the nuances of offshore sailing, like the ability to recognize a fishing boat from a tugboat at night based on its navigation lights. Valerie was taking classes at a local sailing school that included practical lessons on the water. She was also volunteering for any sailing opportunities that would arise at the office, which were many, considering she worked for a sailboat manufacturer.

Developing sailing skills is only half the game. We also had to confront our fears about the cruel and unrelenting sea. Thousands of years of folklore and superstition have given the ocean a reputation as a dark netherworld populated with monsters possessed with the intelligence, motivation and means to chase you down and devour you. Some of that superstition is rooted in reality; the ocean is a dangerous place.

Storms were at the top of my list of frightful encounters. I have a visceral fear of big waves, their roar and their power. It's not an irrational fear. It's not like I'm afraid of cracks in the sidewalk. Big waves are dangerous. But, if I were ever to grow into a real sailor, I would have to find a way to get beyond this fear. With the help of books, seminars, and long discussions with experienced sailors, Valerie and I learned that weather is a manageable risk, as opposed to, say, pirates, giant whirlpools, krakens and rogue waves. Weather forecasting has vastly improved over the years, and the latest information is readily available on the internet. If there was any doubt about the weather conditions, we would wait it out. That is the most important lesson of all: Never be on a schedule. As a family that has never functioned well with schedules, we could embrace this golden rule.

Pirates ranked second on my list of fears. Today's pirates are not Johnny Depp in mascara and dreadlocks but ruthless criminals who pack automatic weapons and prowl the lawless ocean. We've seen their often-murderous predations on the news, with ships, captains, and cargos held for ransom. Certain hotspots, like the Red Sea, the Gulf of Aden, the Strait of Malacca, and a handful of other places can be dangerous even for large commercial ships, but the chances of a pirate encounter outside of these known trouble areas is almost zero. We read about cases, mostly in the Caribbean, of private boats being robbed while the owners were away. On land, we call this burglary. It is an opportunistic crime, and we take precautions to minimize these opportunities. We packed away the remote danger of piracy lest it become an obsession.

The topic of piracy led us to a related discussion about whether we should carry a firearm onboard. That answer was an easy "no." I had last shot a real gun—one that shoots bullets, not paintballs or staples—at summer camp when I was twelve years old. When I look in the mirror, I do not see James Bond. Having a gun on the boat would make us *less* safe, not more. Guns also cause headaches in customs, and many countries deny entry if a firearm is onboard.

Finally, for some historical perspective and inspiration, I dusted off classics I had not opened since college: Melville's *Moby Dick*, Dana's *Two Years Before the Mast*, Slocum's *Sailing Alone Around the World*, and London's *Sea Wolf*. Time-tested literature, I figured, would make my new life's challenges seem small. Did Captain Ahab worry about pirates? Heck no.

December 12, 2014

The aquamarine-blue Caribbean Sea stretched out below us as we dropped through the clouds. I was already thinking like a sea captain, taking note of the sea state and how the wind seemed to be raging in some parts of the ocean, kicking up white caps and blowing spray, while other areas appeared to be calm as a koi pond. As master and commander of my vessel, I would have to make the decision whether to take my family out to sea in these conditions. My new responsibilities were beginning to weigh on me.

Our final approach into Puerto Rico took us over Castillo San Felipe del Morro and Old San Juan, past the luxury hotels that line the beach along the north coast, and over verdant fields of sugarcane dotted with palm groves and tin-roofed stucco homes. We had arrived in a completely foreign environment, exotic and tropical, and dropping into a new world on an airplane still evoked a childish thrill in me. Would I grow tired of traveling after a year of it?

That night over mofongos and Medalla beers, we rehearsed the questions we were going to ask the Lagoon salesman we'd last seen at the Annapolis Boat show two months earlier. "How does she handle upwind?" "Does she make a lot of leeway?" I've never been comfortable referring to a boat as a "she." It seems too old salt.

On the other hand, calling a boat "it" doesn't sound any better, so I gave in to nautical tradition. "How often do you scrape her bottom?" Sometimes boat gender gets awkward.

The next morning we met, climbed aboard a Lagoon 450 and set a course for nearby Palomino Island, a tiny island with a few-dozen palm trees and a tiki bar. The three of us settled into the flybridge to learn about the workings of the boat before taking turns at the helm. The Lagoon 450 is 45 feet long, 25 feet wide, 75 feet high, 4.5 feet deep and weighs 16 tons. It's like driving a tennis court. We tried raising the sails, dropping the anchor, launching the dinghy, and running the generator, gradually managing to handle this giant machine all by ourselves.

I don't think our Lagoon rep expected to close a sale that day, and we probably caught him off guard when Valerie said, "We'll take it," as if she were buying a pair of shoes. (I've seen her take longer to buy a pair of shoes.) She knew how much wiggle room we had, which was not much. Catamarans are always in demand. Most of the charter boats here in the Caribbean are cats, and every few years a hurricane comes along and wipes out a significant part of the fleet.

We signed a contract. The next day, in a factory in Belleville-sur-Vie, France, a Lagoon 450 began its journey along an assembly line with delivery scheduled for late July 2015. Up to that point, we could have easily hit the undo button and returned to our old lives. Most of our other purchases were refundable boating supplies. Now, we had a contract and a substantial deposit. Now we were committed. Valerie had been committed from the start, but I had to come to terms with the fact that profound life change was now irreversibly set in motion. I found a quiet spot alone, outside of the sales office, and gave myself a pep talk: Yes, it's a big boat, and yes, it's a lot of money. So what? I cried a little bit and I shook it off. That's when things got fun.

Later that afternoon, spirits high, we boarded a flight back home. Brochures spread across our tray tables, we considered curtains, upholstery colors, wood finishes and all the other options on our new home. Valerie and I could not agree on a single element of the decor.

Valerie: "Do you like the 'sea foam green' or 'stormy gray' upholstery?"

Jim: "'Stormy gray.'"

Valerie: "I like 'sea foam green.' Let's go with 'sea foam green.'"

Jim: "Then why did you ask?"

Valerie: "Because you were supposed to say 'sea foam green.'"

We compromised with the standard configuration: taupe cushions, off-white curtains and a natural wood finish.

January 1, 2015

Our Year of Change began over a quiet dinner at home. Working backward from late July, we calculated when to begin shedding our terrestrial footprint: when to sell the car, place the pets with loving families, find a renter for the house, put our belongings in storage, and throw away that fruitcake that's been in the freezer for years. We would sell the car at the beginning of summer and make the house available for rent the first of August. Insurance policies would have to be modified, and a property management company would have to be engaged. Most of the items amounted to simple business transactions, but more difficult tasks lay ahead. We had enough time to do it all, but just barely.

Over the next six months, we evaluated every element of our lives and put it in one of three categories: leave it behind, manage it from a distance or take it with us.

I have difficulty saying goodbye. When I drop, say, a worn pair of socks in the trashcan, I hear a tiny voice crying: "You're just…*throwing me away*?" An awkward moment passes. I cast a grief-stricken glance towards the trashcan, and I see a pair of socks that are older than my children, socks that got me through my first job interview, socks that I have just betrayed. I put them back in my drawer and try to pretend it never happened. With this profound sense of *till death do us part*, I scrutinized the contents of my closet shelves and was forced to make difficult decisions: my childhood Snoopy blanket, my Camp St. Charles Seahawk award, my beloved brick from my elementary school that has since been torn down. I was going to Europe and they weren't. In leaving behind my golf clubs, tennis racket, camping gear, and mountain bike, I had to further reckon with the fact that my life was going to be very different on a boat.

Valerie, unlike me, is a shedder and does not form sentimental attachments to material items. Take, for example, my white elephant of a sportscar. She sold it in a single email. Gone. Two sentences and an emoji closed the deal.

Leaving behind also meant reading the fine print on the contracts for club memberships and cell phone plans, for they all had to go. Once we finally realized what we had gotten ourselves into, it was simply a matter of throwing money at it until it went away. Eventually, my feeling of letting go was not grief so much as ouch.

Other items we could easily eliminate; we simply needed a compelling reason to do it. We held a yard sale and got rid of our collection of CDs, sold books we had read, children's clothing that no longer fit, and toys they no longer played with. It was the kind of purge we would have had if we were moving. Come to think of it, we were.

I resigned my board position at a nonprofit where I had long been a member. Did that create chaos and soul searching within the group? No, much to my chagrin. They found somebody to replace me in minutes. My regular golf foursome found a new fourth. My seat at poker night? Taken before the potato chip bowl was empty. The gaping hole I thought I was leaving behind in my world was filled before I could turn around and wave goodbye.

Many parts of our lives could be easily managed from a distance, especially finances. Banking, bills, and taxes were already online. Since Valerie was an E.U. citizen, we had always maintained a modest bank account in France for visits to her family. We simply had to wire money from our U.S. account into our French account and voila: we could use a European credit card and a European mobile phone and avoid foreign transaction fees and long distance charges. We found a renter for the house and hired a management company to keep the tenant happy. Most importantly, I could draw my daily comic strip from anywhere, even a life raft if necessary.

In the take-with-us category, clothing was the major item. Packing for a weekend getaway is about all I can manage. For a one-year expedition over a range of climates, I packed for two weekend getaways, one in summer and one in winter, which still left our bed covered with clothing three feet deep. I found room in the duffel bag for a few favorite T-shirts and one suit and tie for the odd formal occasion, and I put the rest into bins to store in the garage.

Other take-along items included tools and kitchen items specific to boat needs, photography and dive gear, and even ordinary office supplies. European printer paper won't fit our printer, European electronics require a different connection, and online shopping requires a fixed delivery address. Amazon will not deliver to a sailboat anchored in a cove in Greece. We had to think of—and find space for—everything we might need but couldn't buy locally.

Then there was Belle, our four-legged bundle of love and anxiety. Here was a member of the family who loved us unconditionally, and who wanted to follow us everywhere, and we had to leave her behind. Knowing this, and knowing that she didn't know, broke our hearts every day leading up to our departure. Fortunately, one of Madeleine's friends, who loved Belle, was willing to take her in (Thank you, Saylor and Adam.)

Madeleine's hamster, Munchkin, came with a cage and wheel and enough food to keep a hamster spinning on its wheel for at least a year, if said hamster even lived that long. After interviewing several candidates, Madeleine designated one of her seventh-grade classmates as custodian, with regular Instagram photos being a requirement in the agreement. (Thank you, Amelia.) Once the pets found secure, loving homes, Madeleine gradually came around to the idea of a family adventure.

July 5, 2015
For my father's 91stst birthday, the four of us made the short drive to the assisted living community where he and my 89-year-old mother lived. Telling Mom about our plan was one of the most difficult conversations I had ever had. Weeks before, when I told her we were going away for a year, a smile immediately appeared on her face. "Oh, that's wonderful!" she had said. "The kids will love it and remember it their entire lives." She was supremely unselfish and wished us only the best, but I knew beneath that smile she was heartbroken.

When I said goodbye to Mom, I was confident I would see her again. When it was time to say goodbye to Dad, I was just as confident I wouldn't. "Getting old isn't for sissies," Dad would always say during our visits. Because he was struggling with multiple health issues, he had been moved to a hospital-like facility at the assisted living community, where he was confined to bed.

Valerie and the kids kissed him on the forehead and left us alone. I touched his shoulder and his eyes opened. There was so much I still wanted to say, but I did not know where to begin and decided silence was more appropriate.

Dad always had great aspirations for me. Only, they were different from mine. I come from four generations of mechanical engineers, and though I went on to earn my college degree in engineering, I eventually pivoted and became a cartoonist. Yet he, like mom, had always supported my career choice. Dad would always ask me how the "cartoon business" was going, as if I were at the helm of a cartoon empire. Behind his pragmatic demeanor, an exterior hardened by a world war and decades of running his own business, was an abiding love for his children. Typical for his generation, he would reveal his deeper feelings only with subtle expressions: a smile, a wink, an understatement that, if you knew the man, spoke volumes. As a lifelong student of his character, I always strived to match his understatement, but on this day I didn't. With a kiss on his forehead and a tear in my eye, I said goodbye.

3

The Commissioning

Les Sables-d'Olonne, France
July 10, 2015

We began our sailing adventure with an ocean crossing the easy way—in a commercial jet. After a long flight to Paris and a short commuter hop, we met our boat in Les Sables-d'Olonne, a beach town on the Atlantic coast of southwestern France and the launching point for the nearby Lagoon catamaran factory. Our boat show purchases and other gear were waiting for us in a shipping container that Valerie had arranged to arrive in Les Sables when we did. The day before, our new catamaran had been delivered to a nearby boatyard, and a work crew had already started preparing the boat for launch. We found an apartment overlooking the entrance to the harbor, with a balcony where I could watch boats, big and small, leave the safety of port and disappear over the horizon. In just two weeks' time, we would be doing the same.

We had left our comfortable lives behind and were now officially nomads, scrambling to adjust to our new lives of continuous disruption and change. I was trying to fit entire workdays into smaller blocks of time here and there, writing and drawing the comic strip, while

Valerie worked the phones and email in her native French, making arrangements with the marine contractors that would help with commissioning the boat. Madeleine and William, now severed from their internet connection, took to beachcombing in front of the apartment, an encouraging sign that they could embrace the real world as their playground when left with no alternative.

Our new boat was sitting in a boatyard across town, but it was already getting dark and we would have to wait till tomorrow to see her. She was our boat, and we had no regrets, but she still had no name, so we spent our first heady night in the apartment deciding what to call her. I leaned toward the classical, like *Nautilus* or *Oceanus*, or perhaps *Tangaroa*, the Māori god of the sea. Valerie thought it sounded stuffy. Madeleine wanted to combine the boat brand with my comic strip and call her *Sherman's Lagoon*, which I thought was clever, but it was vetoed by Valerie and William. William campaigned heavily for the *Olympic*, *Titanic*'s sister ship that never sank. As with both of our children and the dog, Valerie and I finally flipped a coin for naming rights. I won, which meant that I had a choice between naming the boat or having an enjoyable trip on a boat named by my wife.

Valerie hit on *Sacre Bleu* for two reasons. She pointed out that I frequently use colorful language when things go wrong. *Sacre Bleu*—in French, a minced oath standing in for *sacré dieu*, or "sacred God"—would be a tribute to Belgian cartoonist Hergé's character, Captain Haddock, from the series *The Adventures of Tintin*, who thought up gentle ways *not* to use bad words. Also, the literal translation, "sacred blue," refers to our new lives on the blue part of the map and my love of the ocean.

The next morning, we assembled our folding bikes, which we had retrieved from the shipping container, and pedaled through morning rush hour to the boatyard to meet *Sacre Bleu*. There she was, our bright white, brand-new catamaran, the only recreational boat in a dusty yard full of rusty, overworked fishing trawlers. The mast had not yet been stepped (installed), and she still lacked a boom (horizonal spar on the mast) and rigging, not to mention sails, so our new home looked very much like a work in progress. The deck was a good twelve feet off the ground, and we all took turns climbing the ladder tilted up against the stern to get our first peek at the interior. Inside, a mildly toxic, fresh resin smell permeated the air, and on every surface a fine film of factory dust had settled.

Valerie and I were overjoyed to be finally standing on the magic carpet that was going to take us on the ride of our lives. Madeleine and William, eyes wide and mouths agape, looked around in silence. "We're *all* going to live *here* for a year?" asked Madeleine, hoping to open a door and discover much larger room with a couch and an entertainment center inside. We instructed the kids to pick their cabins, and they both chose the slightly larger aft cabin. Madeleine pulled age rank, though William maintained he had called dibs first. It was our first conflict; now our boat felt like home.

The following day, we returned to watch a gigantic travel lift pick up our new 16-ton baby and gently set her free in the ocean. The mast, boom and sails had been installed, and *Sacre Bleu* was beginning to look like a proper sailboat. We started the twin diesel engines, and Valerie took the helm and drove her on her maiden cruise—the quarter-mile run from the boatyard to a dock we shared with a dozen other new Lagoon catamarans.

We were warned that a mid-July commissioning was dangerously close to the August holiday, when all of France goes on vacation. Just as you don't want to buy a car built on a Friday, in France, we were told you don't want to commission a boat in late July. One of the French contractors explained the national phenomenon by pointing out careless work, shrugging his shoulders and repeating the phrase *mois d'août* (translated month of August and pronounced mwah doot). "Mois d'août!" he exclaimed as he gestured at a small machine screw lying on our deck, left behind by a contractor who was apparently too preoccupied with his upcoming vacation in St. Tropez to pick up his screws. I found that it was not that the craftsmanship suffered, but that it became increasingly difficult to get work done. Businesses stopped taking orders, and their delivery and installation dates slipped into

September. We would have to keep every contractor on task or risk spending all of August stuck at the dock.

The ship chandlery (nautical hardware store) was a five-minute walk from the dock, and we made that walk so many times and got so friendly with the owner, Willy, that by the second week we were inviting him to the boat for happy hour. Instead of slowing down for the inconvenience of paying, Willy opened a credit account and saved all the pain for the last day. We could walk past customers waiting in line, wave a $50 stainless steel shackle, say "put it on our tab, Willy," and stroll out. We felt important. When the time came to settle the invoices, Willy pulled out a shoebox and an adding machine, and we realized how our importance had grown.

Every morning for the two weeks of commissioning, the four of us rode our bikes from the apartment to the boat, where we began our day of meeting contractors, attempting projects, abandoning projects, running up the tab at Willy's, and finding new hiding places to store new supplies and gear that we were just discovering we needed. Most components on the boat were factory installed, but we had ordered enough modifications and add-ons to keep the contractors coming and going, measuring and cutting, texting and smoking well into a third week. The rest of the time we explored farther and wider on our folding bicycles, following bike paths that took us out of town and into the countryside. We were beginning to feel comfortable, as if Les Sables-d'Olonne were just another neighborhood in Annapolis—a neighborhood with a lot more cafes where the patrons seem to drink wine at all hours of the day.

When it came time to emblazon our boat with its name, the kids—who'd lost out on naming rights—had plenty to say. They thought a fish graphic on the side of the boat was great. I admit, I sold it pretty hard. Since drawing fish cartoons is my only marketable skill, a fish cartoon is my answer to just about everything. Most of my *Sherman's Lagoon* characters are walleyed and pear shaped, and that, Valerie and the kids told me repeatedly, was *not* the kind of fish they wanted. Soon, vinyl decals on our hull proclaimed the name

Sacre Bleu, along with our new mascot, a fish inspired by an ancient Roman mosaic.

July 26, 2015
At the end of our second week, we moved out of the apartment and onto the boat, officially becoming a family afloat, departing a world of abundance and privacy and entering a world of scarcity and space shared not only with each other but also with a bevy of workers.

By the end of the third week, the contractors had made *Sacre Bleu* seaworthy. Instead of a conventional boom, we installed a wider "canoe" boom that provided a safe perch for crew to climb up and fold the mainsail, an ideal task for our children. We added an extra reefer in the exterior dining area so that we would never be too far from a chilled bottle of wine. Our new water maker gave us an infinite supply of freshwater from the ocean. A WI-FI booster antenna mounted to the top of the mast would help us find a signal from a greater distance. With wine, water and WI-FI, nothing was holding us back.

However, we did not yet feel any great impetus to cast off the lines and float away. We had finished our own preparations—provisioning, stowing gear, and, literally, learning the ropes—and we were now officially over-preparing, a process with no defined end. I could've spent the rest of the summer tethered to the wharf in Les Sables, like a baby in the womb, our dock lines providing the last bond to my secure little world. In any direction we walked we found a restaurant that served a casual, exquisite and inexpensive meal. The farmers market looked like a food museum, with dozens of individual vendors offering the full spectrum of France's glorious cuisine from dozens of varieties of cheese to breads and pastries of all shapes and sizes to seafood right off the boat. Valerie and the kids had established a daily routine of going to the beach, a broad stretch of bright white sand populated with a diverse cast of vacationers, from families to fashionistas. I tinkered with boat stuff, and I had plenty to tinker with. It was my new garage.

I mentioned to Valerie that we already seemed to have found our groove. She pointed out that without forward movement it's not a groove, it's a hole. This continued until a representative from the factory showed up at the dock and told us we had to leave to make room for more boats. We would have to do what we planned: Sail the wide ocean.

In the light of the morning sun, I fired up the two 57 horsepower diesel engines, Valerie and the kids unfastened the dock lines, and we slowly worked our way out of the basin of Les Sables. *Sacre Bleu* was no longer a plan, it was a reality. Or rather, it was the beginning of a yearlong plan that would gradually unfold into reality in ways we could not anticipate or control. With the right frame of mind, a plan that does not go to plan can be called an adventure, but most adventures achieve adventure status in retrospect. Adventures, in the moment, when no happy ending is in sight, evoke emotions like fear, frustration, boredom and terror, emotions that we try to avoid in our everyday lives. Plans, on the other hand, are perfect in their unexecuted form and bring pure happiness.

I had been planning this trip my entire life. As a boy, I had spent hours studying maps, drawing and erasing the track I would sail around the world, passing my pencil line through exotic destinations like Zanzibar and Rarotonga and dreaming of the adventures I would have there. The thought that we were about to sail into this dream made me both giddy and terrified.

4

The Adventure Begins

Les Sables-d'Olonne, France
August 7, 2015

The kids playing on shore waved at us as we followed the long breakwater of Les Sables harbor, past our former apartment, the open sea stretching out before us. As we made our way along the rocky seawall we passed an inbound cargo ship, and a crewmember looked down and waved. This "small" ship weighed about 15,000 tons, roughly a thousand times more than *Sacre Bleu*. We were entering the Realm of the Giants, populated by giant ships as well as giant seas. Technically, at sea we were equals, both subject to the same Rules of the Road. In reality, we were like a mouse crashing the elephants' ball. Being small requires carefully assessing each move, determining an endpoint, waiting patiently for the opening and committing.

Our endpoint today would be the harbor town of Saint-Martin-de-Ré, on Île de Ré, an island 27 miles to the southeast. With moderate seas and a 15-knot westerly breeze in the forecast, this maiden voyage promised to be an easy first dance; we would cover the distance in four to five hours. Yet in these heavily trafficked waters of Europe, the environment changes quickly, so one of us had to be on constant watch. Off our starboard bow, Valerie spotted a container ship, plodding along at a deceptively slow pace. In fact, it was moving three times faster than us, and it passed safely in front.

In the Realm of the Giants

Now that we were in the open sea, our home was moving, pitching and rolling in the waves. We discovered that all the decorative flairs we had added, like the orchid and the bowl of seashells, had to be stowed. The interior went utilitarian in the first half hour.

As I stood on the bridge scanning the infinite horizon before me, I was both relieved and anxious. My depth sounder passed through 300 feet, reminding me that as we ventured farther, we were not only putting more water behind us but also more water below. The vast, empty sea tempts a comparison to the desert, but boats do not travel on a two-dimensional plane, they travel over a deep ocean. Like airplanes that constantly fight the forces of nature to stay aloft, boats must continuously fight the same forces to stay afloat, and the seafloor is littered with many that lost.

The Adventure Begins

Weather would play an enormous role in our new lives as wind travelers. Strong wind and heavy seas require focus, vigilance, and careful adjustment of the boat and the plan. Riding on the inexhaustible sea, propelled by temperamental winds, we would have to continuously measure their moods and marshal just enough of their forces to take us a few miles and gently set us down. I took comfort in the fact that people have been getting in boats to cross the water and start new lives for thousands of years, and most were far less prepared and equipped than we were.

I drove the boat while Valerie raised the mainsail and unfurled the genoa (the large triangular sail forward of the mast) with the help of the kids. We settled into a close haul (a point of sail at an angle closest to the wind), putting us on a course for Île de Ré. Most of the hoisting (raising) and trimming (adjusting) of sails on a boat the size of *Sacre Bleu* is done with electric winches, since the forces are so great. Despite this modern twist on an ancient practice, working the sails is still labor intensive. In hoisting the mainsail, for example, three different lines (on a boat, a line is a rope with a purpose) must be faked (coiled in figure-eights on deck, ready to run out quickly), while the fourth, the halyard (line used to raise the sail), is loaded into the winch. While I kept the boat headed directly into the wind to keep pressure off the sail, Valerie pressed a foot switch that activated the electric winch and raised the mainsail, while the kids made sure all the lines ran properly. A snag or a tangle could result in a torn sail or worse, for the extremely powerful electric winch can break limbs. All of this ropework under high loads means that hoisting sails on *Sacre Bleu* required all hands on deck.

Once hoisted, the sails filled with wind, and the boat quickened its pace like a galloping horse. Our adventure had begun. I was excited about the year ahead, the destinations ahead, and most of all, the changes ahead.

After five hours of sailing, fighting an army of short, choppy swells, we saw the clock tower of Saint-Martin-de-Ré on the horizon just as the electronic chart promised it would. We had completed our first leg of open-ocean sailing, and a seed of courage germinated in us that day. To keep us on a steady trajectory of confidence building, we needed to encounter conditions that would stretch our abilities just a little bit farther. It was a vulnerable stage of our journey. We had just arrived at the elephants' ball, and we had to get better at dancing without getting squashed.

On the chart, the harbor of Saint-Martin-de-Ré looked like a perfect place to spend our first night, but it was not meant to be. As we approached the mouth of the harbor, we saw an enormous pair of doors blocking the entrance. Massive and ancient looking, with water spilling through the cracks, they resembled castle doors. Checking the cruising guide too late, I learned that in this part of the world the tides have a range of over eight feet. Twice a day the harbor of Saint-Martin-de-Ré closes its nearly watertight doors to prevent it from draining like a bathtub. I took another hard look at my chart and the stops we had planned along the way and learned my first lesson of cruising in this part of the world. We would not be determining our arrival and departure times moving forward. The tide was now in charge.

We changed the plan to anchoring. This was our first anchoring attempt in *Sacre Bleu*, and maybe the fifth or sixth of my entire life. With both engines running, I pointed the boat into the wind, and then I pushed a button that released the chain and dropped the anchor. Our depth sounder read 20 feet, and since we wanted at least a 5-to-1 scope, or ratio between chain length and water depth, I let out about 100 feet of anchor chain. Once we locked the chain, it quickly tightened and the boat stopped abruptly, signaling that our spade anchor had dug into the sandy bottom, just as the salesman promised. It was a textbook anchor set. It was so textbook that we both wondered how it could've gone so well on our first attempt. A *Gendarmerie Maritime* patrol boat—the French equivalent of the Coast Guard—was anchored close by. I was pleased that we had put on a good show for them; I waved, they waved back.

As I was cleaning up the lines on the flybridge, I heard Valerie speaking French at the stern. Three of those friendly gendarmes, all

The Adventure Begins

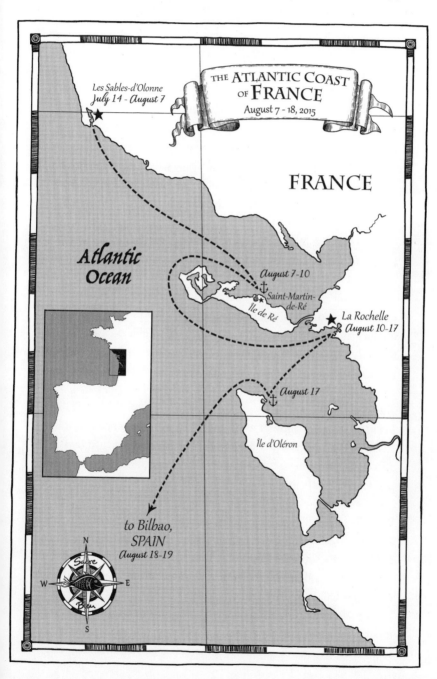

dressed alike in light blue shirts, navy blue pants and baseball caps, were hitching their Zodiac raft to our stern. Valerie invited them to come aboard, her native French taking them by surprise. With the U.S. ensign displayed on our transom, they were expecting Americans. In fact, it was the flag that inspired their visit. They had all visited the U.S. and were eager to try their English on us. Valerie switched to English, and we gave them a quick tour of the boat. Valerie mentioned that her father was a retired gendarme, and it was not long before we were all sitting around the cockpit dining table like old friends. They were a wealth of information on what to see and do and where to eat on the island.

We found room for our folding bicycles on the dinghy and went ashore to see for ourselves some of the sights the gendarmes had recommended. Île de Ré offers enough long, sandy beaches to keep a beachcomber happy all summer. But in our days on the Île, we were to find more to this island than sand. It is home to ten villages, each unique, and miles of bike paths, vinyards and a robust oyster industry that cultivates its harvest in hundreds of floating cages that surround the island.

August 12, 2015

I could have spent another week visiting Île de Ré (on one of our bike rides I saw a splendid golf course) but Valerie was ready to move on after day three. Whether on a bike or not, Valerie always needs forward movement. On the morning of the fourth day, we weighed anchor and set a course for rounding the western tip of Île de Ré and sailing into La Rochelle. The tide table gave us just enough time to sail to La Rochelle and make the last lock opening into the Old Port, which, like Saint-Martin-de-Ré, closes to boat traffic.

Our trip around the western end of the island took us past the Phare des Baleines, or Lighthouse of the Whales, one of the tallest in France. The Phare des Baleines is built like a fortress to withstand the monstrous waves that punish this island during the winter. Unlike the white stucco lighthouses back in America, it looks more like a castle turret. We sailed a little farther along the coast and saw large seawalls lining the beach, placed strategically to keep the marauding winter waves from pushing their way too far inland.

We made the 30-mile sail over choppy, windswept waters in good time, arriving so early we had to hover in a basin with a half dozen other boats waiting for the lock to open. In a large boat, standing still can be more difficult than moving, and I spent the next half hour shifting the two engines into forward and reverse, avoiding contact with the other boats and the concrete seawalls. As we cleared the lock and entered the harbor basin, we saw a dockhand waving his arms and gesturing towards an opening between two boats. The space looked like it couldn't be more than 25 feet wide, and since our boat was 25 feet wide, I wondered whether we would have room for the paint.

This would be my first attempt at a so-called Mediterranean mooring, which is how boats are shoehorned into the crowded marinas of Europe. In a Med mooring, the stern of the boat is fastened to the dock while the bow is secured with an anchor. This arrangement leaves boats very efficiently lined up cheek by jowl like shoes in a closet, with only fenders (handheld rubber bumpers) between. Once the mooring is complete, a passerelle, or gangplank, is dropped from the transom, providing access to the dock.

At the start of the maneuver, the anchor must be dropped at precisely the right place, which can be surprisingly far—sometimes a hundred feet—from the dock. Then the boat is driven in reverse, or backed down, into the slip, all the while letting out more anchor chain. Because the orientation of the rudder and propeller with respect to water flow are reversed, the boat becomes difficult to steer at a time when steering is critical. I needed to back down faster to make the boat more reactive to my steering, which made the maneuver that much more stressful.

During the backing-down process, the anchor must be set by arresting the chain. This ballet is invariably performed while the owners and crews of the neighboring boats are assembled on their decks following every inch of your progress, watching for any contact with their boat. Somehow, we pulled off our first Med mooring and the gallery approved. As the four of us put the finishing touches on the dock lines, we concluded that Med mooring was easier than we thought; or perhaps we had just had some well-timed beginner's luck. Either way, we had done it, and we would be less afraid of it next time.

La Rochelle is a nautical town. The streets are lined with chandleries, marine contractors, nautical flea markets and other businesses devoted to emptying the pockets of boaters. We wanted to stop here a few days into the cruise to pick up what we didn't realize we needed when we were provisioning in Les Sables. Overwhelmed by the selection of sailing merchandise, the shopping strategy changed from need to want. We found a complete set of international maritime signal flags that would be completely useless unless we found ourselves in a naval battle. We didn't need them, but we bought them anyway.

Besides being a nautical supermall, La Rochelle also has a rich history bracketed by the Gauls on one end and the Nazis on the other. The Germans used the harbor as a U-boat base during the Second World War, and so it endured heavy bombing from the Allies. We visited a legacy of the era: a network of underground rooms called Le Bunker that had served as both a refuge from air raids and party room for Nazis. "This isn't ancient history," I said to the kids. "There are people still alive who witnessed this." In Le Bunker, this chapter of history seemed to be still alive as well, suspended in the stale air, the dim light and the graffiti.

Our next excursion was planned for me. I had been an ocean fanatic from the days when I watched *The Undersea World of Jacques Cousteau* on television, and I jump at the chance to see how people make their living from the sea. Valerie arranged a tour of La Rochelle's wholesale fish market, an experience that is free for any hardy souls willing to show up at 5:30 in the morning. There were no taxis to be had at that hour, so Valerie and I assembled our folding bikes and rode five miles through the dark, empty, stone-paved streets. We peddled past a pair of drunk men staggering along, arm in arm, each holding

The La Rochelle Fish Market

an empty bottle and singing. They were just like drunks in a cartoon, until one of them threw up. That never happens in cartoons.

At the fishing docks, we locked our bikes to a lamppost and entered a cavernous warehouse. The air was frigid and damp and smelled of fish and bleach. From sharks to shellfish, hundreds of iced containers filled with a diverse array of mother nature's evolutionary genius was on display, all destined for a plate. Lotte, or monkfish, was the most common catch, numbering in the hundreds, each subtly unique. In other containers sat small sharks and rays, octopuses and squids, eels, shrimp, and a variety of shellfish. Live crabs sitting on ice were lethargic but still moving, perhaps trying to make sense of their surroundings and how they got there. I saw expressions of defeat on their faces: their battle was lost in this contest between fish and fishermen to make each other extinct.

August 17, 2015

The Med mooring process was much easier in reverse. We released the dock lines, nudged our way out of our tight spot between two neighboring boats and hauled up the anchor. With time to kill before the lock opened, we drove *Sacre Bleu* between the medieval towers that flank the entrance into the old port of La Rochelle. During the Hundred Years' War, a 120-foot-long chain curtain was stretched between these two towers every night to keep English ships from sneaking in, and more mundanely, to keep merchant ships from sneaking out without their owners paying their port taxes. There was no chain curtain on this sunny morning, so we took a quick farewell tour through the old port, packed with fishing boats and flanked with ancient buildings.

Then we headed out to sea.

Our destination was Île d'Oléron, a small island about 12 miles south. Sailing conditions were ideal for the two-hour trip: the wind blew at a crisp 15 knots and the seas were flat. All four of us sat on the flybridge, quickly established as our favorite place underway, eyes forward in anticipation of our next stop. It was the kind of togetherness we could never achieve at home. Even the latest, trendiest movie-on-demand would not have compelled the four of us to sit down together on a couch and share a common viewing experience. On *Sacre Bleu*, the horizon was better than television.

August 18, 2015
Our next stop on the horizon was Bilbao, Spain, a 30-hour run across the Bay of Biscay. After five weeks in France, we had decided it was time to move on. Departing at six in the morning would get us to Bilbao around noon the next day, giving us a generous window of daylight in case we arrived early or late. We hoped to avoid nighttime arrivals in unfamiliar ports, and they were all unfamiliar.

Our decision to go to Spain was not driven by any master plan. We didn't have one. Our first stop, Île de Ré, was an easy run from Les Sables and a well-known vacation spot. Our second stop, the city of La Rochelle, offered an ideal contrast to Île de Ré, and it was just far enough away to make a nice day of sailing. We quickly fell into improvising our cruise one destination at a time, staying as a long as we wanted and choosing our next stop only after we were ready for a change.

I spent our time at anchor off Île d'Oléron perusing the user's manual for the satellite-based texting device we had purchased just in case we needed to send a distress signal during our first venture beyond the sight of land. In my old life, it would have taken an actual emergency for me to bother reading a user's manual, but I was shedding my old ways and growing into the proactive role of master and commander. I tested the device by sending a short text to a friend back in the U.S. His reply appeared on my screen moments later. The satellite link worked! I took that as an omen we wouldn't be needing it.

Up early the next morning, we weighed anchor, raised the sails, and enjoyed the day-old baguettes, still delicious, that we bought in La Rochelle. The Bay of Biscay gave us 10-to-15-knot winds from the west, and with the gently rolling seas, the conditions were perfect for a beam reach (a point of sail with the wind at a right angle to the boat).

Madeleine was the first to notice that we were sailing by enormous lion's mane jellyfish, and she snapped photos of them for her home schooling science project called Animals in My Environment. While other homeschoolers' photo albums might boast sparrows and squirrels, I took some pride in knowing our daughter's will feature jellyfish the size of umbrellas.

Sacre Bleu cut through the smooth, rolling seas, driven by her billowing sails. Today, we were beginning to appreciate the carefree frame of mind good sailing conditions could bring. Under well-trimmed sails in a steady breeze and flat seas, our boat can take us as far as we want to go. It is a feeling of freedom like no other. The elemental rush set my mind diving deep into what lay hidden beneath us and the smooth surface of today's sea…

If the Bay of Biscay were drained of seawater, the basin would resemble one side of the Grand Canyon. It is a landscape whales know well but we humans can only imagine. Starting at the shoreline, a continental shelf extends roughly 50 miles off the coast and ends abruptly as the seafloor drops from a depth of a few hundred feet to over 10,000 feet. Carved into this underwater escarpment are deep canyons running towards the shore. Each of these canyons has a name, and a bathymetric chart of the bottom of the Bay of Biscay is peppered with as many proper nouns as a topographic map of Yosemite National Park.

Just offshore near the French-Spanish border—Basque Country— the underwater landscape is dazzling. The Parentis Basin falls off to the Landes Plateau, which ends at the Capbreton Canyon with walls dropping thousands of feet. Unlike the other canyons, the Capbreton Canyon runs almost all the way to shore where, long ago, it is thought to have been connected to an ancient river. Massive ocean swells form in the open Atlantic under nearly continuous westerly winds and roll towards the European coast carrying an astronomical amount of energy. When swells hit shallower water, they slow down, shedding some of their energy as they drag along the seafloor, build in height, and eventually roll over and break on the beach. However, the part of

The Adventure Begins

the swell that rolls in over the deep canyons, like Capbreton, retains most of its energy until it is closer to shore, where it forms a bigger, more powerful wave. As a result, the beach towns along this coast, such as Belharra, France, and Punta Galea, Spain, have become big-wave hot spots for surfers.

Still on a beam reach, the rolling seas were lifting *Sacre Bleu* and gently setting her down again as she plowed on, pushing water out of her way. Suddenly about a dozen Fraser's dolphins appeared on our bow wave like a synchronized swim team. They twisted, jumped, dove deep, then hurled themselves completely out of the water, again and again, like children on a playground. Dolphins seem to be one of the few animals in the wild willing to waste energy on play, although perhaps we are working with a definition of play that's too human-centric. Maybe cows, when they stand in a field, are playing a form of cow chess. Nature holds so many secrets.

The sun sank below the western horizon and darkness fell on the ocean. Valerie and I kept watch on the flybridge while the kids worked on a puzzle in the salon below. Tonight, for the first time on the cruise, we would not be in the safe confines of a port or anchored in a quiet cove. Tonight, we would drive on into the darkness, sails down, motoring, blindly trusting our instruments, confident—but not fully convinced—that there were no objects in our path that could damage the boat.

Valerie and I considered sharing a four-hour watch schedule, with one of us driving while the other slept in the cabin below, but we were both too anxious about this first night under way, so the two of us stayed on the flybridge taking turns driving the boat and napping on the settee beside. The night air was warm, the seas were calm, and the drone of the engines was reassuring, yet sleep did not come easily to either of us. In these small hours of the night, fishing boats are surprisingly active, their navigation lights appearing and disappearing on the horizon around us, yet none coming close enough to require an evasive course change. Like the stars above, time moved slowly, imperceptibly, towards daylight.

Blood-orange twilight filled the eastern sky, lifting the curtain on the darkness around us, revealing a calm sea. Our night watch was over, and we could relax. Valerie went below to get a few hours' sleep, and I let the autopilot drive the boat while I made coffee. The kids would not wake for another two or three hours, so for this sunrise spectacle I was the only one in attendance. Sitting on the flybridge drained of energy, I nursed my hangover from a sleepless night.

Early that afternoon, the coast of Spain appeared on the horizon. This was our first opportunity to practice the nautical tradition of changing the courtesy flag. Because we were a U.S.-registered boat in foreign waters, maritime law requires that we fly the Stars and Stripes on our stern and display the port of registry, Annapolis, Maryland, on the transom. This tells the world that *Sacre Bleu* follows maritime regulations to which the U.S. is signatory, pays taxes to the U.S., and ultimately will be defended by U.S. forces if necessary. The courtesy flag is a handkerchief-sized version of the host country's flag, flown by visiting ships to show respect. On sailboats like ours, it is displayed on the starboard side about halfway up the mast. Madeleine was our official standard bearer, so the honor fell to her to change the French tricolor over to the red-and-yellow ensign of Spain. She performed her responsibility with utmost reverence, except for the giant pink bubble of gum she blew near the end.

We entered the port of Bilbao, and our fatigue shifted to astonishment at the sight of the massive tankers and container ships that surrounded us. An even more humbling spectacle were the 50-foot-high seawalls protecting the port, built with loose concrete blocks the size of minivans. I could not imagine the size of the waves that crashed into these fortifications during a winter storm. We felt like Gulliver arriving in Brobdingnag.

Deeper into the port, where we found a wharf with several sailboats secured to it. We sidled *Sacre Bleu* up against an open stretch of the wharf and cut the engines. The four of us stood on deck sizing up our new surroundings. A row of large, stately homes—terracotta roofed, stucco walled, unmistakably Spanish—overlooked the wharf.

The pedestrians strolling by were predominantly dark-haired and dressed more formally than the French. "Hola!" Valerie shouted to the dockhand helping with our lines. He responded with a string of words that was unintelligible; none of us spoke Spanish. When we left France, we lost our ability to communicate, and we were already getting a sense of how this would make our lives more difficult.

That night, we dove headfirst into the local culture and chose a traditional Basque restaurant for dinner. Strolling in at eight p.m., late for us Americans, we were told that the restaurant opened in another hour. When we came back at nine p.m., all the tables were still empty, but we sat down anyway, famished, cranky, and looking forward to bedtime.

The Spanish eat dinner late because they work late after taking the traditional three-hour siesta in the afternoon. The late dinners were hard enough to adapt to, but the town shutting down for three hours every afternoon was an even more difficult adjustment for our Type A personalities. While the rest of Spain was siesta-ing, we were trying to find boat parts or provisions. Instead, we waited until four o'clock to get anything done.

Spain's food markets offered a wide variety of never-before-seen provisions for the ship's galley. *Pata negra*, or "black leg" ham, is made from black Iberian pigs that free range in ancient oak forests and gorge themselves on a steady diet of acorns. Resembling prosciutto, this black leg ham costs an arm and a leg at $75 a pound. We ventured into one of the shops that sold this luxury lunchmeat and, throwing caution to the wind, ordered a few grams. The storekeeper produced a long, flexible knife, cut a cellophane-thin, translucent slice of greasy succulence, carefully laid it on white butcher paper as if it were a diamond necklace, and then looked at us like a blackjack dealer in Vegas, for a signal that we had the means to buy another slice.

The influences on the cuisine along the coast of Spain range from Moorish to Celtic to Greek and Roman, depending on which invader brought the recipe. The Spanish were also the first Europeans to sample foods from the New World, right from Columbus' boat. New World vegetables such as tomatoes, potatoes and peppers are a staple of many dishes served here, and commonplace in the markets where we bought provisions. For obvious reasons, our provisioning was restricted to coastal towns, so the markets we saw along the way boasted an enormous variety of seafood, particularly octopus, a favorite in this part of Spain.

Back on the boat, after a day of provisioning, we found Madeleine in tears in her cabin. She had gotten an email from her friend that Munchkin the Hamster was now in hamster heaven. One pet down, one to go.

As charming as Bilbao is, after three days, we were feeling the pull to move on. We had read many accounts of families that set out for a yearlong cruise and ended up needing several years to complete it. We didn't want to become that family, so, wherever we stopped, if we found ourselves getting too comfortable, we took it as a sign to leave.

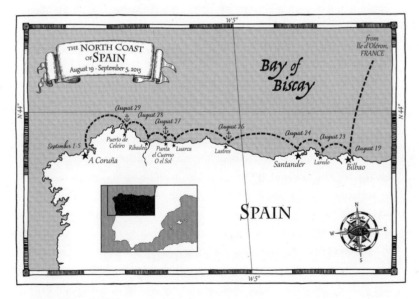

August 24, 2015
Out of Bilbao, we continued west along a cliffy coast marked by small fishing villages with oversized seawalls to protect their fleets from

the violent winter storms. Our destination was Santander, about 25 miles down the coast, just the right distance for a day's sailing. Here, we found an entrance, in contrast to Bilbao's industrial corridor, lined with large, elegant mansions, rolling grass lawns, and well-appointed condominium buildings overlooking white sandy beaches. It was one of those lazy summer days, and we weren't in a hurry, so we anchored off one of the beaches and threw the kids in the water.

We were looking forward to spending the night in this upscale neighborhood when the calm, sunny day suddenly turned dark and threatening. We called the kids, who were some distance away on the paddleboard, to return to the boat. By the time they got back, the wind had picked up and white caps appeared all around us. Before we could worry about where we'd find shelter, a man in a powerboat zoomed up and shouted to us in English, "Follow me."

We tagged along behind our new friend deeper into Santander Harbor. The elegant mansions gave way to a cityscape around us, and we finally came to a marina, where he had a boat slip waiting for us. Señor Arroyo, the driver of the powerboat and, as we would learn, an accomplished yachtsman, tied up close to us and introduced himself. Passing us earlier, he had noticed the port of call on our transom was Annapolis, where he had spent some time as the Spanish exchange officer at the U.S. Naval Academy. He invited us to dinner at his yacht club, the Real Club Maritimo de Santander, where we sampled the local specialty, salt-encrusted cod, or bacalao, and received volumes of local advice on navigating the rugged Spanish coast.

Because we carried our home with us, we had the ability to stop anywhere and stay for a day or three. When we set out for a new destination, we looked for ports or protected anchorages that were an easy afternoon's sail away. This distance was typically 20 to 30 miles, which we could cover in three to five hours of sailing. This was our sweet spot. Frequently, the plan would change, and we would stop short of our original destination or carry on a little farther.

As we sailed along the coast of northern Spain, we encountered our first bout of gale-force winds. We struck sails and took refuge in

Luarca, a small fishing village with characteristically oversized seawalls. Once inside, we realized our mistake. The tiny basin was surrounded by large, steel-hulled fishing trawlers tightly Med moored against the steep concrete wall. We drove in circles inside the small harbor deliberating our next move, as the entire village watched from the docks. Seeing no alternative in Luarca, we aborted and went back out to sea.

As soon as we passed the giant seawall, enormous waves and powerful winds pushed us towards the rocky coast. I jammed both throttle levers forward, pushing *Sacre Bleu*'s two small 57-horsepower diesel engines up to full power. It took every horse we had to drag her through the breaking waves and back out into the open sea. My hands trembled as I gripped the wheel and considered this near miss that could have ended our cruise so early.

We reverted to our original plan of working our way toward Ribadeo. With its protected port a mile up the river Eo, I hoped conditions would be calmer. The open ocean was anything but calm: the wind strengthened, peaking at 55 knots, just nine knots shy of hurricane force. We left the sails down and motored our way up the coast.

As we turned to enter the river, the wind was blowing right on our nose. The channel was marked by red and green buoys, the first navigation markers we had encountered since leaving Les Sables. To my inexperienced eye, the first green buoy seemed very close to land; passing it to the right would put us uncomfortably close to shore. However, I was more concerned about our clearance under the bridge that we were quickly approaching. With a quick look at the chart, I confirmed that the bridge clearance was 90 feet, and our mast height was 75 feet, so we had room to spare, even with the extreme tides. I was lined up with the green buoy, a hundred feet from passing it to our left, when I glanced at the chart and saw I was driving straight into shallows. I slammed the throttle into neutral, and the strong headwind stopped us in our tracks. Only then did I remember that the European buoy system is the opposite of U.S. system. Back home, we follow "red right return," but here in Europe the rule is "*green right return.*"

As we motored up the river and under the bridge, the wind gradually died down to about 35 knots, and the seas laid down to two or three feet. Our situation seemed to be improving, but not yet ideal. We weren't ready to enter the port because the dock lines and fenders were not yet in place. With the seas calmer, we called the kids out of their cabins, and they helped Valerie prepare the boat for docking. While they scrambled to get the boat ready, I drove in circles, a maneuver I seemed to be getting good at. By this time, I had minced all my oaths and used up all my G-rated expletives, and now I had moved on to the more gratifying ones. I studied the entrance, looking over my shoulder as the boat turned in circles, assessing how I could dock a 45-by-25 foot boat in 35-knot winds in a tiny, crowded marina without causing major damage.

Just inside the opening in the seawall, I would have to make a hard left or right turn to avoid hitting the HMS *Pickle*, a wooden tall ship with her crew, attired in period costume, watching at the rails. Which way to turn and where to dock was still undetermined; I was hoping the answers might reveal themselves once we put the plan in motion. In addition to the *Pickle*'s crew, spectators had gathered on the docks to witness this disaster in the making. For the second time that day, we were the best show in town.

On approach, I drove *Sacre Bleu* fast to keep the rudder responsive. The 35-knot wind pushing us from behind was making us go even faster, and I was going to have to form a plan quickly. As we raced through the port entrance, 20 feet from driving into the side of the *Pickle*, I spotted three men waving their arms on a dock to my left. I instantly threw the wheel over to port. The bow swung 90 degrees, just a few feet from the *Pickle* and the eyes of her anxious crew. More than a bit anxious myself, I drove straight for the three men, stopping a few feet short to let the wind blow us gently onto the dock. In a matter of a few tense seconds, we were safely tied up.

That afternoon, glad to be on land, we explored Ribadeo, a small town with an eclectic mix of architecture, mostly contemporary, with some ornate structures built in the last century by local businessmen who clearly had too much money. The winds still raged, and the residents were nowhere to be seen as large objects—a cardboard box, a palm frond, an entire bag of trash—blew through the streets.

August 29, 2015

As we departed Ribadeo, we established a new tradition on *Sacre Bleu*. When we were just far enough away from the marina so that turning back was a major ordeal, we would discover that we still had the marina bathroom key with a ten-euro deposit on it. As our marina bathroom key collection grew over time, Madeleine found ways to work them into her art projects.

Besides bathroom keys, our cruise expenses at this stage of the trip were in line with our expectations. Groceries cost about the same as back home. Though we dined out more often, we found the restaurants less expensive, particularly the wine, which is considered a staple in Europe rather than a luxury or a sin. Fuel was significantly more, but we were using precious little of it in a sailboat. We carried a thousand liters of diesel, and we topped the tanks every couple of weeks. Because we had purchased a new boat, repairs were minimal and covered under warranty. One of our biggest expenses would be paying mechanics for routine maintenance on the diesel engines every two or three months. Other costs decreased. For example, as we became more comfortable with anchoring, we stayed in fewer marinas, with the added benefit that the captain had to execute fewer Med moorings.

September 1, 2015

Downloading the weather report was part of our morning routine, but because we were running along a mountainous coast in this part of Spain, we encountered extremely strong localized winds that no forecast could warn us about. Despite occasional gusts that forced us to reef the mainsail (roll the sail up partially to make it smaller) and anxiously study the chart for alternative ports, the 50-mile run to A Coruña went smoothly. After eight hours of white-knuckle sailing, A Coruña's most prominent feature, a Roman lighthouse called the Tower of Hercules, appeared off our port bow. It is the oldest continuously operating lighthouse in the world (albeit with daily three-hour siesta breaks). We were beginning to enjoy our floating home, our peripatetic lives, and the new experiences that awaited us at every stop.

For shoppers, A Coruña boasts an enormous variety of retail opportunities. After a month living on a boat, Valerie's shopping bug woke like a hibernating bear eager to chase prey in every direction. No sooner had we cinched up the dock lines than she and the kids were off on the folding bikes while I stayed behind to catch up on drawing the comic strip.

My comic strip, *Sherman's Lagoon*, appears in newspapers daily, and my deadlines come weekly. Every Friday, I email my syndicate seven cartoons: six black-and-white cartoons and one color Sunday cartoon. Back in my home studio, before the cruise, creating a week's worth of cartoons was a leisurely process that required a couple of days of writing and a day of drawing, which I accomplished alone in the peace and quiet of a home office. Now that I was working on a boat, sharing a small space with three other people, my creative process had to evolve. On the cruise, I am forced to draw and write cartoons in short time windows whenever the opportunities arises.

Later that evening, we settled into a dinner of local fish and a bottle of Ribeiro wine, an intense, fruity red that went down too easily.

I'm not sure if it was the wine or my sentimentality, which grows with wine, but I hinted that since Munchkin the Hamster had waddled across the rainbow bridge, perhaps Madeleine might consider a replacement rodent. I prattled on about how rabbits bring bad luck to ships, but nautical tradition is silent on the topic of hamsters. My suggestion soon seemed prescient, for as soon as the words left my mouth, Madeleine and William each produced a live hamster from under the table.

On their shopping trip, Valerie and the kids had stumbled onto a pet shop. Out walked William with Snowball, a white Russian dwarf hamster, while Madeleine brought home a taupe-colored version she named Squirt. Snowball blended in perfectly with the ship's white fiberglass, which was almost everywhere, and Squirt blended in perfectly with the taupe-colored upholstery, which was everywhere the fiberglass was not. As soon as the hamsters came out of their cage and got up a head of steam, they tended to vanish, and we would all begin a new round of find the hamster, a game that required sharp eyes and a soft step.

Snowball and Squirt began their cohabitation as civilized roommates, sharing their one-square-foot apartment, taking turns spinning on the wheel and snuggling peacefully in opposite corners. By day three the relationship had gone south, and Squirt had become a territorial brute who tormented the unassertive Snowball with the kind of pathological hatred that is more usual between Yankees and Red Sox fans after a few beers. We needed not one cage, wheel, and water bottle, but two. The urgency was addressed with a quick run to the pet shop on a folding bicycle. We did not have room on the boat for a microwave oven, but now we had two hamster cages.

We also had two happy kids. So much of the hard work on *Sacre Bleu* still had to be done by mom and dad while the kids watched. Snowball and Squirt added a new layer to the family hierarchy. These animals were utterly dependent on their owners, and this gave the kids had a new sense of responsibility.

5

'Round the End of the Earth

Costa de Galicia, Spain
September 5, 2015

For the next three days we anchored in protected coves along the north coast, working our way west until we reached Cape Finisterre, so named by the Romans because they considered it the end of the world. Protected coves were easy to identify on the navigation chart. They were concave land formations with high ground that could protect us from the wind—usually coming from the west—and water shallow enough for anchoring. This stretch of the Spanish coast offers a suitable anchorage every few miles, so at the end of the day, we simply settled into the closest one.

At Finisterre, the coastline abruptly turns south, putting almost a square corner on northwest Spain. From there to the border of Portugal the coastline meanders in and out in the form of four *ría*s, Spanish for flooded valley or estuary. Each ría boasts a unique assortment of fishing villages and secluded coves, making this region of Galicia particularly suited to boat-based adventuring.

Moments after we dropped anchor in the northernmost ría, Ría de Muros e Noia, a fisherman approached us in his small skiff piled high with fish traps. My first thought was that we were anchored in his favorite spot, and he might be angry with us. He came alongside our boat and began laying mackerels on our deck as if he were dealing cards, insisting that we keep them as his gift. Then he gave us a friendly wave and a broad smile and puttered off. Mackerels are a bloody fish and cleaning a dozen of them on the white deck made *Sacre Bleu* look like she had just hosted a gladiator competition. I hoped for sharks, but none showed.

We chose Ría de Muros to see the ruins of Castro de Baroña, an Iron Age settlement. Sitting on a small, rocky promontory on the southern coast of the mouth of the ria, Castro de Baroña is a remarkably well preserved archeological site in a remarkably beautiful setting. We rode the dinghy to the nearby village of Porto do Son, where we tied up to a public dock and wandered aimlessly in the empty streets until Valerie knocked on a random door to ask directions. A very friendly woman answered, and we exchanged polite greetings (we had barely graduated beyond *hola* to *buenos dias*), then pantomimed in dramatic gestures our quest for ancient ruins. As soon as I said "Castro dee BaROH-nah," she lit up and replied "Ah! Castro de Baroña!" pronouncing it completely differently, rolling her r's and putting a lilt in her ñ. Then she pointed to a bus stop across the street, not 20 feet away.

After a series of public buses and hikes through rough, unsigned terrain, we finally broke through the woods and gazed upon an ancient fortress created by Galician warriors.

Collared by breaking waves and connected to the mainland by a narrow isthmus of sand, this whimsical collection of circular stone structures looks more like a Christo sculpture than a fortress built in the first century BC.

We had the entire site to ourselves. There was no trace of modern civilization to be found—no signs, no fences, no restrooms, no gift shop, no other visitors. We felt like archeologists stumbling on the site for the very first time as we climbed through stone walls and trenches, imagining the hail of arrows and spears that must have greeted unannounced visitors like us two millennia ago. Once inside, we found a

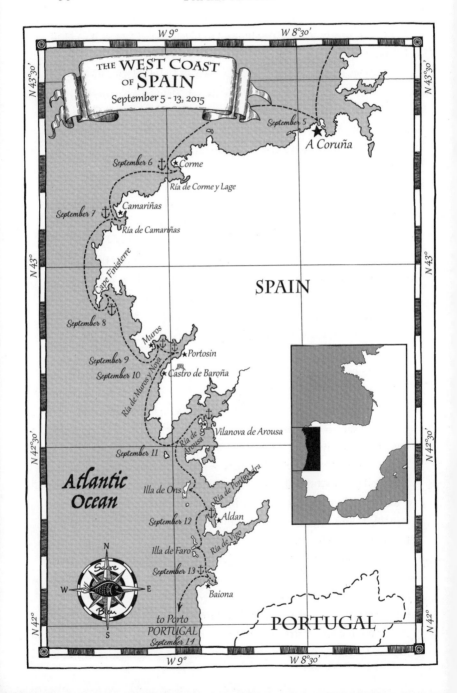

small village of circular, room-sized enclosures built of stone. Back home, had the experiences of this day taken the form of a homework assignment, Castro de Baroña would have been forgotten shortly after the test. Here, on this isolated outcrop, the past opened its doors and let us in for an afternoon. Walking in the footsteps of the ancients, the kids were not mere history students but time travelers.

September 10, 2015
Anchored in Ría de Arousa, the second of the four rias, we woke to the rumble of a diesel engine, which turned out to be a passing fishing boat. Two men on the deck were working the gear, one rolling the trotline into a large wheel and the other pulling live octopuses off the baited hooks as he hauled the line out of the water. The fisherman removing the octopuses from the line saw we were watching him, so he put on a show for us. He pulled the next octopus out of the water, unhooked it, and held it up for us to see. The creature writhed and contorted its eight legs, its body shifting into angry shades of red and orange, like a neon light, as it fought the fisherman's grip. The fisherman produced a short knife, and with a quick jab, the fiery, vibrant, writhing mass was rendered limp and gray. Madeleine was crushed. "Why do we eat octopuses? They shouldn't be food," she said. "It's what fishermen do for a living, Madeleine," I said, trying to comfort her. "It knew," she said, holding back tears. "It knew what?" I asked. "It knew something bad was going to happen to it," she said, as we both watched the fishing boat drive off, hauling in more catch as it went.

We set a course for Illa de Ons, an island in the Atlantic between Ría de Arousa and the next ría south, Ría de Pontevedra. There, we anchored off Playa Area dos Cans, a beautiful strip of white sand, and sent the kids to shore on the paddleboard. Because of its remoteness, Illa de Ons attracts nude sunbathers, and there were several on display in various shapes and sizes. Madeleine and William, having grown up in North America, had never seen a naked, middle-aged human in the wild. Unfortunately, the kids decided to build a sandcastle right next to a group of empty towels that moments later were filled with their owners wearing nothing but sunblock and smiles. William, always in his own world, simply carried on building his sandcastle, while Madeleine clearly wanted to disappear.

The next morning, we set sail for Illa do Faro, another island just south of Illa de Ons. Illa do Faro, or Lighthouse Island, named for its three picturesque lighthouses, is a nature preserve that requires special access permission from the *Reservas de Parques Nacionales*. This simple formality brought a bundle of problems into our lives, any one of which had the potential to derail the entire mission. We needed an internet connection, then we had to send a coherent email in Spanish, naturally, to the parks authority asking for special access to Illa do Faro, then somebody in the parks authority had to pay attention to our request and approve it, then we needed internet service again to receive their approval. This would all have to happen before lunch, otherwise the day would be lost. Amazingly, a permit appeared in our email in-box, and by that afternoon we found ourselves hiking the steep trail up to one of the island's picturesque lighthouses.

On top of the highest peak of Illa do Faro, we took in a panoramic view that included the surrounding islands and their secluded beaches and coves. Suddenly, our perfect anchorage off the sandy beach looked second rate compared to the alternatives we could now take in. We considered moving the boat but decided that our previously perfect anchorage could continue being perfect in our minds if we wanted it that way.

After an early breakfast of homemade bread that was already rock hard, we weighed anchor and set a course for Baiona, a small city at the mouth of the southernmost ria, Ría de Vigo. In March of 1493, the first of Columbus' ships to return from his historic voyage, the *Pinta*, made landfall in Baiona, making its citizens the first on the European mainland to learn about the New World. We spent the night on the dock of Baiona's yacht club, Monte Real Club de Yates. While Valerie and the kids toured a full-scale replica of the *Pinta*, I stayed on *Sacre Bleu* and got caught up with drawing the comic strip. Valerie and the kids reported that *Pinta*, 56 feet by 17 feet, with a crew of 26, was not much bigger than our *Sacre Bleu*, with a crew of four. Like many sailors who came before and after, Columbus concluded that even though his boat was not big, it was big enough.

We were now five weeks into the cruise, and I was discovering aspects of life at sea that I had not anticipated. For example, there is much less routine than I thought. I imagined a steady diet of salted fish and grog, enough idle time to train birds to talk, and the daily grind of swabbing the deck and mending sails. On special occasions, the captain might allow his crew to watch paint dry. That may be life at sea. But we were not at sea, we were coastal cruising. Every day or two, we were dropping into a new port, where we had to locate the new market, find the dairy aisle in the new market, figure out how to incorporate this new cheese in a meal, work the new water hose fitting at the new marina, connect to the new internet, and so on. Life had become a barrage of new experiences, or rather figuring out the new way to do the same old thing over and over. This relentless climb up the learning curve simply to get to where we were the day before was beginning to feel like trudging up the down escalator.

While underway, each of us would gravitate to our favorite spot on the boat and settle into an activity. Valerie or I was usually at the helm, but sometimes not. If there was no boat traffic in view, we let the autopilot drive while we attended to other duties. During these quiet times, I liked to poke around the boat shining a flashlight into dark spaces, behind panels and under floorboards, familiarizing myself with the inner workings of this giant, complicated machine. Valerie liked to read novels, but she would also experiment with boat-specific cuisine, like baking bread in a stovetop skillet or putting anything in the Vitamix and turning it on high. Madeleine spent most of her time in the salon, working on a puzzle or art project, homeschooling, or playing with her hamster. William was most prone to seasickness, and when we were underway, he preferred outdoor spaces with fresh air and a horizon to look at. Settled into an outdoor spot, he would read. William had become an insatiable reader. He had thrown himself into *Percy Jackson & the Olympians* by Rick Riordan, a series of children's adventure books based on Greek mythology, and he gradually became our resident scholar of the ancient world—or at least, a hyper-fictionalized version of it.

Valerie brought her French tradition of sit-down meals to the boat, and lunch and dinner were our designated times to talk about the day's events. This relaxed family time was one of the elements of our new boat life that initially tested my patience, but I eventually saw it as a gift. Sitting down to meals gave us time with the children, discussing the adventures of the day, what we had seen and what we had learned. Meals on the boat and our family meals back in Annapolis were different in two significant ways: nothing competed for our attention—no cell phones, no social media, no television, no pressing business outside of our family circle—and we all had a day's worth of common experiences to share.

On the evening we spent anchored off Illa de Ons, the dinner discussion centered on nudity. Valerie, being French, has always been relaxed about nude sunbathing, though she was not herself a practitioner. In addition to the nakedness on the beach that day, we had also encountered more than a few sailboats with entire crews—not families or couples, mind you, but groups of older and not particularly fit vacationers—in the buff. In Europe, nude is just another wardrobe choice; this notion was evident daily. William questioned the purpose of clothing and thought that we could all save a lot of time and trouble by wearing the same thing every day, or nothing at all, weather permitting. Madeleine did not say a word but spoke volumes with her silence. For her, nudity belonged under a bathing suit.

September 14, 2015

The departure from Baiona marked the end of our time in Spain for now. Just a few miles south lay Portugal, very different from the Spanish coast—no rias, few ports, no protected anchorages in the westerly wind, and miles of wide, sandy beaches. We could not find a good stop midway down the coast, so we decided to sail 60 miles all the way to Porto. This magical city lies where the Douro River meets the Atlantic Ocean. From there, the river meanders inland to form the renowned Douro Valley, home to the world's most famed port wine producers.

Porto's marina is situated just inside the mouth of the river, and though it provides a secure refuge from the punishing ocean waves, getting through those waves is difficult. Large swells rolling in from the open ocean break in the mouth of the river, threatening to turn boats into oversized surfboards. To make matters worse, the entrance of the river is too shallow to pass at low tide, so we had to plan our arrival for high tide, which was 4:40pm that day. To add another layer of excitement to an already tense leg of the journey, a storm was approaching from the north.

We went into heavy-weather mode: the kids were not allowed on deck, and Valerie and I donned inflatable life jackets with six-foot tethers, similar to rock-climbing gear, that allowed us to clip into strong points on the boat built for this purpose.

Ten-foot swells and a powerful wind from the approaching storm forced us to take down the sails and motor carefully through the rough seas, slowing our progress. At 4:40 that afternoon, as the tide was cresting, we were still 15 miles north of Porto. As time marched on, the water at the mouth of the Douro River was getting shallower, the waves bigger, the wind stronger, and the sun lower. I stood on the bridge, my eyes frantically scanning from chart to clock to horizon to wind-speed indicator, looking for some comfort. Powering up the engines was not

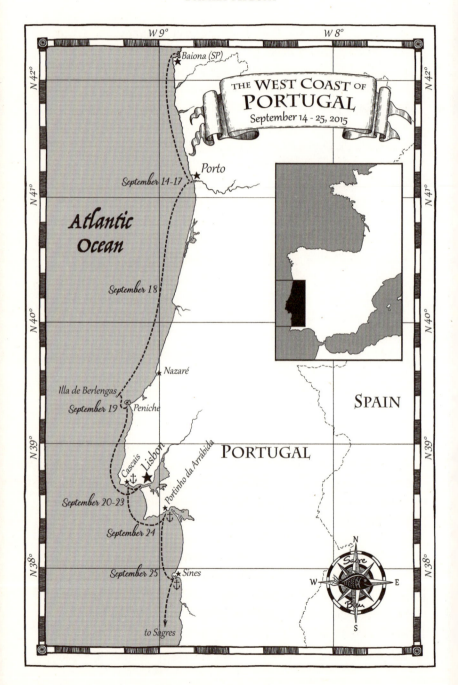

an option; the swell was too big, the ride would become unbearable, and we would damage either the boat or ourselves.

At about 7:45pm, with the sun dipping below the horizon, the two lighthouses that mark the entrance to Porto finally appeared. We were approaching on a course parallel to the shoreline, running with the swell and surfing down the face of the waves as they passed beneath us. Ahead, a rock seawall, perpendicular to shore on both sides of the river mouth, extended a few hundred feet into the ocean. The lighthouses at the ends of the seawalls—a red-and-white-striped lighthouse on the left and a green one on the right—mark the opening. As we got closer, we saw waves crashing into the wall on the north side, creating massive explosions like avalanches in the sky. To make the entrance, we would have to run past the red lighthouse on the north seawall then make a sharp left turn into the river before we got too close to the south seawall.

The sun was now below the horizon and the last glimmers of daylight were quickly fading. From our perspective, we could not see the river opening: instead of two seawalls, there appeared to be one continuous wall of boulders with two lighthouses on it. I simply pointed the boat between the lighthouses, blindly hoping that the opening would reveal itself before we crashed into the rocks. As we zigzagged our way through the sea, the lighthouses would sometimes look as they should (red to the left, green to the right), but at other times they would line up one behind the other or even be reversed.

Approaching the river mouth, we felt the 15-foot swells lifting and dropping us gently, and I did not sense any danger of losing control. In shallower water, however, the waves grew steeper and began to break around us. I had no idea if I could steer *Sacre Bleu* in these conditions because this was a skill I could never have practiced. The opening in the rocks was still not discernable; I simply had to trust my chart and make the commitment. Attempting to turn sideways in the breaking surf would have capsized the boat; trying to reverse our course against the waves would have been futile. The waves were rolling over and breaking all around us, and I still seemed to be driving toward one continuous seawall. Suddenly, the opening appeared. I threw the wheel hard to port. The boat responded instantly. In moments, we were on our way up the calm Douro River. That's when I realized we were coming in on an ebbing tide; I had forgotten to worry about running aground on the sandbar. When you forget to worry, it's time to start worrying.

By the time we tied up in the marina, the sun was long gone, and the lights of Porto were sparkling in the inky waters of the serene Douro River. A faint whistling sound in the rigging of the boats announced the arrival of the storm, and we could hear the thunder of massive ocean waves breaking in the distance.

Six weeks into our crash course in offshore cruising, the professor had dropped the final exam on our desk. With a combination of luck and judgment, we managed to pass. Tonight's arrival was a sober reminder that we could no longer afford to think of ourselves as students of the game. We were now offshore sailors.

The next day brought the full force of the storm's punishing wind and rain. We strolled by the harbormaster's office and saw a notice in the window announcing that the port was closed. We had made it in with only a few hours to spare. Pushing the rain around corners and under awnings, the wind rendered ordinary umbrellas and raincoats useless. Fortunately, because we were sailors, we did not have ordinary raincoats. We stepped into our foul weather gear and knee-high rubber boots and went for a stroll in town, looking like four Maine lobstermen. One indicator that this storm was unusually strong was that every trashcan in the city was overflowing with abandoned, broken umbrellas, creating a tangle of stainless steel and fabric.

Porto boasts the best port wine houses on the planet: Graham's, Offley, Taylor Fladgate, and Sandeman, to name a few. At one of the tasting rooms, we invited the kids to sample the merchandise, and since we were in Europe, nobody took notice. Madeleine refused, but William ventured a sip. I felt a pang of cruelty when his face changed from "How bad can this be?" to "That's the worst thing I've ever tasted."

The next morning, we walked to the beach to see the waves that had been thundering all night. The rain had stopped, but the strong winds continued, and the port was still closed. The waves were breaking far out to sea and storming the beach in massive walls of foamy white chaos. As the swells hit the seawalls at the mouth of the river, they erupted into plumes of spray that towered over the lighthouses, which were themselves two stories high. I could not imagine trying to make the entry in these conditions. We stood on a large rocky outcrop, elevated from the violent surf, and watched in awe as tons of water crashed below us like a liquid train wreck.

September 17, 2015

I was almost as concerned about our departure from Porto as I had been about our arrival. The river was empty of boat traffic, which worried me. Fishermen, tour boat operators, and other locals who make their living on the water are the best source of information for a visiting sailor. Why were they not out on this beautiful Thursday morning? As soon as we left the safety of harbor, I understood why. Massive swells were still rolling in from the ocean, but they were not breaking since it was high tide. I gunned *Sacre Bleu*'s two engines to climb over the oncoming walls of water and slipped out to sea.

As we sailed along the coast toward Lisbon, I kept my eye on the depth sounder, looking for a sudden drop-off. We were approaching the Nazaré Canyon, which, if it were not underwater, would be one of the biggest tourist attractions in all of Europe. Like the Bay of Biscay, the seafloor here is jagged and steep in places, with canyons that rival those of any national park in the American West. The base of the Nazaré Canyon sits at 16,400 feet deep, 10,000 feet deeper than the Grand Canyon, and its walls rise to within a few hundred feet of the water's surface. This submarine gorge cuts horizontally through the continental shelf to within a mile of shore. In the winter, especially, powerful westerly winds send row after row of giant sea swells rolling in over the Nazaré Canyon on their way to the beach. Once the swells reach the end of the canyon, and all that water energy hits the shallows, nightmarishly big waves rise up from nowhere like an angry Poseidon.

Because of this bathymetric oddity, the tiny Portuguese beach town of Nazaré is one of the world's giant wave hotspots, where big-wave surfers come from all over to conquer the Everest of water. It was here in November of 2017 that Brazilian surfer Rodrigo 'Koxa' Augusto do Espírito Santo broke the world record, riding an 80-foot mountain of raging brine into surfing fame.

I handed the watch over to Valerie at two in the morning as we passed Nazaré about five miles off our port side. In our cabin, I laid my head on the pillow, imagining the immense underwater canyon below, hidden in darkness since the beginning of time. I felt the swells, the yet-unformed monsters, rolling harmlessly beneath our keel on their journey to Nazaré beach, where they would rise up and cast their fury onto the rocks like so many countless waves before them. That night, I went to sleep with monsters under my bed—yet another way sailing made me young again.

We arrived at the mouth of the Tagus River at two in the afternoon and started our run up to Lisbon. After we registered at the marina, a customs officer dropped by the boat to do a spot check. While he sat in the cockpit and helped us fill out the declaration forms, the kids brought out the two hamsters and let them crawl all over the table. The official asked with a straight face if we had any animals onboard just as Squirt was crawling across his paperwork. Then he checked the "yes" box.

September 21, 2015

Homeschooling was going well considering it was a new experience for everyone, including the teachers. We were satisfied that the kids were keeping up with their former classmates at Annapolis Middle School. Most of the work was self-paced, and the kids always had the allure of ending their school day when they completed their studies, even if it was before lunchtime.

After they finished their daily reading assignments, Valerie or I would quiz them with the questions provided at the end of the chapter in the textbook. Madeleine was a conscientious student, reading the entire assignment and answering the quiz questions correctly most of the time. William tended to look at the questions first, then try to find the answers in the text, leaving him unfamiliar with the story. This became obvious moments after the quiz began, and we would command him to read the entire assignment over.

Science projects were more engaging and fun for the kids than textbooks. Madeleine was studying chemistry, and her projects involved exercises like combining baking soda and vinegar, resulting in small volcanic explosions. William was studying biology and spent many an afternoon looking at bugs, worms, tiny sea creatures, hamster toes, and anything else he could fit under the USB microscope.

In their free time, William had constructed every possible Lego Mindstorm configuration his kit offered, and he was now improvising. Lego Improvisation #1 was an elevator that transported hamsters from the dinner table to the floor. Setbacks were inevitable, and certain hamsters were stuck in elevators for what seemed like an eternity by human standards, but not, apparently, by hamster standards. If you do not have a particular place to be, then you are not really stuck. It is a philosophy that I would eventually embrace during the cruise, though I will deny that I learned it from a hamster.

While William was pushing the bounds of modular plastic architecture, Madeleine was busy with her new hobby: kirigami, the Japanese art of cutting and folding paper. When I initially referred to it as origami, I was immediately scolded for my ignorance of the Japanese paper arts. Homeschooling seemed to be working in unexpected ways. Madeleine was accumulating a diverse portfolio of kirigami insects, from grasshoppers and butterflies to scarabs, and even mosquitoes.

We celebrated Madeleine's 13th birthday at the Oceanário de Lisboa—the Lisbon aquarium—where we found more odd forms of beauty. This indoor ocean features the usual cast of sea creatures, including sharks, rays, and groupers, as well as a fish that I had never seen in captivity: an ocean sunfish. This alien-looking animal has enormous horse-like eyes and a mouth that is perpetually open in an "o" shape, like the subject in Munch's painting *The Scream*. For a fish, it is not very streamlined. Its amorphous body resembles an omelet, and its horse eyes project an insecure, bashful demeanor, as if it were self-conscious about its lumpy gray body.

Speaking of self-conscious, we now officially had a teenager on the boat. One of the things we all would learn is how our nomadic lifestyle and relentless togetherness as a nuclear family was going to affect this delicate rite of passage

September 22, 2015

The morning after Madeleine's birthday, we cast off the dock lines, said goodbye to Lisbon and headed south along the Portuguese coast. In the following days, we stopped at Cascais, Portinho da Arrábida, Sines, and Sagres, which marked the southwest corner of Portugal and the start of our journey east into the Mediterranean.

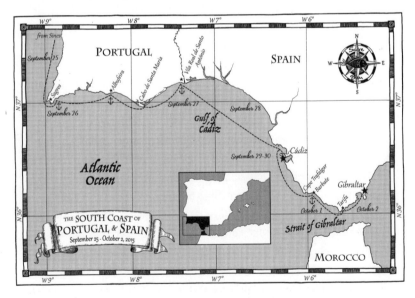

We sailed past miles of sandstone cliffs, isolated beaches, natural stone arches and deep grottoes that make this spectacular southern coast of Portugal more of an aquatic park than a mere beach. On one

appealing stretch, we anchored and sent the kids ashore on the paddleboard to spend the afternoon exploring. Valerie and I opened a bottle of wine and watched as William built a sandcastle and Madeleine poked around in the tidepools with a stick. As I sat on the flybridge savoring the Portuguese Vinho Verde—a crispy, young white wine with a little sparkle to it—I wondered, at what point in my life did playing on a beach stop being fun? As I advanced in age, a full day of childhood happiness had been gradually reduced to a single happy hour.

Back in Spanish Waters
September 28, 2015

After we weighed the anchor the next morning, we dialed in the autopilot to sail a straight line to Cádiz, cutting across the Gulf of Cádiz and the long bight of the Spanish coastline on a course that took us about 15 miles offshore. The winds started light, out of the southwest, perfect for a broad reach (a point of sail between beam reach and downwind), but by midday we were forced to strike sails and motor against a headwind. We typically motored on one engine because it is more fuel efficient. By late afternoon, motoring on one engine, our progress had slowed from six knots to four knots, and our ETA went from 8 pm to 10 pm. Once darkness fell, even stronger headwinds followed, accompanied by heavier seas. Slowed further, I fired up the second engine to keep our ETA at a reasonable 10pm. By 10pm, running full throttle under both engines, we were doing three knots and were still 15 miles from Cádiz. It was going to be one of those nights.

The size of the waves coming at us was difficult to make out, but as each one struck our bow, I could feel the boat come to a complete stop. The rain began: a drizzle at first, then a downpour. Valerie and I sat in the flybridge protected by the enclosed Bimini (canvas canopy) and a plastic windshield, but we were still feeling wet and cold inside what was effectively a tent. By midnight, with three miles between us and Cádiz, our speed had dwindled to a knot and a half, despite running both engines at full throttle. We had two more hours of driving against wind and waves. I could have jogged the distance in thirty minutes.

We were heartened when we saw another set of navigation lights in the distance. "At least there's one other fool out here," I said to Valerie, attempting a smile. As we approached, we realized that other fool was a Spanish Navy frigate. Inching past them, I looked up at the bridge and wished myself onto that ship in a dry and dapper uniform. I would have barked, "Your ship," to the first mate as I retired to the officer's wardroom to enjoy a glass of 20-year-old Cockburn's tawny port before I slipped into my cozy, dry bunk, leaving the night watch to my professional crew. When I came out of my dream, moments later, I found myself still occupying the body of a cold and wet amateur sailor in a small boat on a pitch-black night bobbing in heavy weather off a foreign coast.

As our progress slowed and our arrival time pushed further out, it occurred to me that it was mathematically possible that we might never arrive. We needed a new plan. As usual, we were frantically throwing our Plan B together only after Plan A was in tatters, getting around to reading the parachute instructions as our plane was going down in flames. Going below to study the chart, Valerie found a sheltered cove a couple of miles north of Cádiz where we could anchor. That two miles would save us more than an hour underway in miserable conditions. At three in the morning, settled in the cove, we dropped anchor and fell into bed.

The next day, we moved to the downtown marina and ventured out to see Cádiz on foot. We had to pass through hell to find this patch of heaven, but it now seemed worth it. The imposing Catedral de Santa Cruz de Cádiz presided over a large plaza in the center of town. A climb to the top of its bell tower rewarded us with a 360-degree view of the city and its surroundings, a cityscape of bleached, ornate buildings sparkling like fresh snow in the sun of a cloudless day. We happened to time our visit for a deafening noon bell ringing, leaving all the visitors in the tower fumbling for a way to hold a finger in each ear while simultaneously recording video of the event with their cell phones.

September 30, 2015

Cape Trafalgar, off which the famous 1805 naval battle between the British fleet and the French and Spanish fleets was fought, lies about 30 miles down the coast from Cádiz. Recognizing a teachable moment, I called the kids on deck and explained that *Sacre Bleu* was sailing through hallowed waters, following the same path as the French and Spanish fleets as they slipped out of Cádiz that October morning to make a run for the Mediterranean. "Then they saw trouble on the horizon. Admiral Nelson and his fleet, riding in on a west wind, attacked them!" I exclaimed, gesturing out to sea dramatically. The kids looked in all directions with blank expressions. We were not walking the fields of Gettysburg and stepping into the trenches and over the stonewalls that had once deflected hot, flying lead. Water is water. They were deep into Mario Brothers before the history lecture had ended.

After spending the night on anchor near Barbate, we departed for Tarifa, our last stop on the Atlantic coast. Tarifa is a small town with a large terminal providing regular high-speed ferry service to Tangier, Morocco, less than twenty miles to the south. We were approaching Point Tarifa and the mouth of the Strait of Gibraltar, a sliver of water separating two continents that is the only connection between the Mediterranean Sea and the Atlantic Ocean. Like the mouth of a dragon, this opening is either inhaling or exhaling, and sailors must approach with caution. The relentless wind in Tarifa makes the town a major kiteboarding center in Europe. The same air that shapes trees and reduces flags to tatters makes kiteboarders howl with ecstasy and sailors pale with fear. As we turned the corner at Point Tarifa, the wind hit us like a freight train, and we knew we had to spend the night in a port.

The dock in Tarifa had no empty slips, so we dropped anchor just inside the seawall, where we thought we were out of the way of boat traffic. I was in the middle of making everyone Iberian ham sandwiches when Valerie saw Boatzilla coming straight at us and screamed, "Oh, shit!" A high-speed ferry the size of a shopping mall approached fast on its hydrofoils, and it was too late to do anything but watch and hold our breath as it drew closer and closer, closing in on us like an avalanche. Just as we thought we were going to become roadkill, the giant ferry slowed abruptly, sank off its foils into the water, then harmlessly turned away from us and towards the terminal. Moments later, the harbormaster zipped out in his inflatable boat and informed us that we could not anchor there. "We were just leaving," I said. I cast a fearful eye at the whitecaps just beyond the seawall and gave Valerie a "What now?" look.

Valerie has always lived by the credo *It never hurts to ask*. On a lark, she asked the harbormaster if there was any way that we could tie up at the ferry terminal. He thought about it for a moment and then told us to tie up behind the giant ferry that had almost run us over. In minutes, we were sidled up to a concrete wall just beside the Death Ferry. I could not make the jump onto the dock to tie the boat up, so a nearby policeman volunteered to help. I tossed him a line, and he wrapped it around the bollard a dozen times, then gave us a friendly wave and walked away, leaving no actual knot. Relieved we had a harbor for the night, we stepped off the boat, secured the dock lines and went for a stroll.

The first rule of cruising is never have a deadline, but we now faced one. We had purchased *Sacre Bleu* on July 8, 2015, exactly 84 days prior. This left us only another six days to "export" our boat by bringing it outside the borders of the European Union. Otherwise, we would have to pay a 20 percent value-added tax on the purchase price. The tax amounted to a year's college tuition for both of our children, enough money to prompt me to look at the calendar multiple times daily. Fortunately, Gibraltar lay only 15 miles to the east. Though technically part of the E.U., through the complexities of treaties that only diplomats understand, the British territory counts as non-E.U. with regard to customs and duties. Six days, fifteen miles, and a lot of money at stake. What could go wrong?

The weather forecast called for a levanter, the local name for a powerful wind originating from the eastern Mediterranean, or the Levant. Under certain weather conditions, clockwise winds of a high-pressure system to the north and counterclockwise winds of a low-pressure system in the south work together like colossal gears. Where these opposite-turning gears meet, they push a massive volume of air from the Mediterranean basin into the Atlantic Ocean, and this air tries to pass through the narrow, mountain-lined Strait of Gibraltar like a throng of shoppers forcing its way through the door of a Walmart on Black Friday. Add to this the tide, which tries to push astronomical volumes of water from sea to ocean and back again twice a day, all through this eight-mile-wide opening. At times, the Strait carries a six-knot current, enough to stop us in our tracks. We had to choose our departure time wisely.

What if we got stuck in Tarifa? Airlifting *Sacre Bleu* to Gibraltar by helicopter would cost less than the tax. Sailing there seemed far easier, so we made plans for immediate departure. According to the tide tables, the optimal time to leave was two in the morning. Somehow, I knew the answer was going to be two in the morning. It's never eight-thirty, just after a nice breakfast.

6

A Tax Haven with Monkeys

Gibraltar
October 2, 2015

The alarm sounded, and I crawled out of bed and onto deck while Valerie made coffee. Tarifa was dark and calm, the air chilly and wet and full of night sounds: the beeping sound of a truck backing up, the gentle slap of waves against the concrete bulkhead, the groan of stretching dock lines. In the distance, the low rumble of surf pounding the seawall just outside the port made my stomach sink. Inside the port, a three-quarter moon painted streaks of silver on its serene waters. The Death Ferry's generator hummed, and its empty decks were illuminated, but the monster would sleep for another five hours. By then, we would be long gone.

This morning's journey did not resemble any we had previously attempted. How would the wind, waves and current all play into the next four hours of sailing through the Strait? Could we get carried out to sea? What about the shipping traffic? Why did we buy a sailboat and not a ski condo?

We unfastened the dock lines and motored out through the opening in the breakwater, where we were immediately accosted by a powerful westerly. As we turned east, the instruments indicated that the boat was moving faster over the ground than through the water, a sign that the current was helping us. This was not a surprise since we had carefully timed our departure to take advantage of the flood tide. However, sooner than we expected, our speed over the ground dropped, and we knew it would only be a matter of time before the current would shift from friend to foe.

If you run on a treadmill only looking down at your feet, you might think you're going somewhere, but a glance around the room quickly dispels that illusion. On a boat, in the dark of night, with water flowing by and no reference points around, we were sure we were going somewhere, but the instruments said otherwise. We were using all the horsepower our engines could deliver, fighting a current. As we crawled along at three knots, we knew we had to change the plan. The current usually weakens closer to land, so we gave up on Gibraltar and turned the wheel north towards Spain.

We hugged the Spanish shoreline and continued east in the darkness, keeping a careful eye on the electronic chart for rocks and shoals. The ten-mile stretch of Spanish coastline on our port side is a nature preserve, its sharp silhouette a wall of featureless black even darker than the night sky. Four more hours of careful navigation, blindly at the mercy of our electronics, took us to the Bay of Gibraltar and the lights of the Spanish city of Algeciras. Across the bay, another five miles in the distance, we saw the lights of Gibraltar. Once inside the Bay of Gibraltar, still under the dark of night, we worked our way through an obstacle course of anchored freighters and tankers and dodged the high-speed ferries that appeared out of nowhere.

We reached our destination, Queensway Quay Marina, just as the sun was rising over the iconic Rock of Gibraltar, and tied up in a basin lined with luxury condominiums and restaurants. As we connected a cable for shore power and a garden hose for water, I asked the dockmaster, who introduced himself as Ian, if the dock water was drinkable. He crossed his eyes, jerked his head in spasms and stammered, "I've been drinking the water for years. Seems fine to me." Having been raised on Monty Python and Benny Hill, I appreciated British humor, but the joke went right over Valerie's head.

The first item on our agenda was to run to the customs office with the ship's papers and clear the boat out of the VAT zone. With the stroke of a ballpoint pen we saved a king's ransom. Just a couple blocks past customs we stumbled onto Morrisons, the first real supermarket we had seen since leaving America. We shopped our way through aisle after air-conditioned aisle, basking in the cornucopia of goods that included 14 varieties of Wheetabix products alone. Most of the brands were from the UK, and I noticed Valerie reading a lot of labels with a grimace on her face. When bad French chefs die, I wondered, are they condemned to shop the aisles of a British supermarket for eternity?

October 4, 2015

On this bright Sunday morning, tied up by an upscale restaurant serving outdoor brunch, we christened *Sacre Bleu*. When we had splashed her back in July, christening was one of those checklist items that never found its way to the top during the mayhem of commissioning. We had defied a centuries-old seafaring tradition and sailed 85 days and 1,236 nautical miles without christening our vessel for good luck and safe voyages. I was determined to right this wrong before a bolt of lightning shot out of the sky and sank us at the dock.

For the first time on the voyage, my blue blazer and necktie came out of storage, Valerie put on a nice sundress, and we arm-twisted the kids into wearing something besides sweatpants and T-shirts. Even more fun than dressing up was dressing ship. The international maritime signal flags that we bought in La Rochelle, when strung together and hoisted to the top of the mast, made any boat look like, well, a flagship.

The four of us assembled on the deck, smartly dressed, and I began the ceremony. I soon realized I had an audience. A reverent silence had fallen over the restaurant as all the diners stopped their table talk and followed along. I popped open the bottle of champagne, filled our glasses, and read from my script:

A Tax Haven with Monkeys

> Dad
>
> For thousands of years, we have gone to sea. We have crafted vessels to carry us and we have called them by name. These ships will nurture and care for us through perilous seas. To these worthy vessels we toast, and for this good ship we celebrate.

All raised their glasses.

> Crew
>
> To the sea, to the sailors of old, to the good ship *Sacre Bleu*!

All took a sip of champagne.

> Dad
>
> The moods of the sea are many, from tranquil to violent. We ask that this ship be given the strength to carry on. The keel is strong and she keeps out the pressures of the sea.

> Crew
>
> To the sea, to the sailors of old, to the good ship *Sacre Bleu*!

All took another sip.

> Dad
>
> Today we come to name this vessel, and send her to sea to be cared for, and to care for the Toomey family. We ask the sailors of old and the mood of God that is the sea to accept *Sacre Bleu* as her name, to help her through her passages, and allow her to return with her crew safely.

> Crew
>
> To the sea, to the sailors of old, to the good ship *Sacre Bleu*!

We all took one last long sip of champagne. Madeleine winced at the taste, but William seemed to like it.

At the end of the ceremony, the brunch crowd applauded. I was a little choked up, but having Irish blood, I cry for a good Super Bowl commercial. I poured some champagne over the bow to bless the ship and some more in the water to appease Neptune, god of the sea. Then I was told by a higher authority than Neptune to stop wasting good French champagne. We placed a branch of green leaves on the deck to ensure safe returns, and that was that. The good ship *Sacre Bleu* finally had her proper name in the eyes of the deities, though her name had already been recognized by the U.S. Coast Guard several weeks prior.

The levanter continued its assault, giving us plenty of time to explore Gibraltar. By the Rock, viewing platforms were packed with tourists, tour guides, and Barbary macaques, and the interaction between the three primate groups was a never-ending sideshow. Unlike dogs, who get what they want with cuteness and subservience, macaques favor naked aggression. They rip sunglasses off heads, steal candy from children, pick pockets, and do it all with a cleverness and intelligence that makes them seem like obnoxious, hairy little humans. In the parking lot, I saw one cast a furtive glance left and right, then try the door handle of a locked car. A macaque climbed onto Madeleine's shoulder and grabbed a clump of her hair at the roots. From the animal's demeanor, it seemed that eviction was going to be a long and painful process. Then one of the tour guides whacked the monkey with a newspaper, and it scampered off. "You cannot be submissive," he warned us.

To an outsider, Gibraltar is very British. On its streets you'll find the iconic red phone booths, police in Bobby-style helmets, and pubs with names like the Red Lion. Though a hike on one of the many trails that wind around the Rock feels tropical, with flowering plants and the famous monkeys, a walk in town feels like suburban London. Much of its tourism, besides the Rock, revolves around its legacy as a British military outpost: siege tunnels, gun batteries and other fortifications. Because of its duty-free status, Gibraltar is a surprising bargain. A liter

A Tax Haven with Monkeys

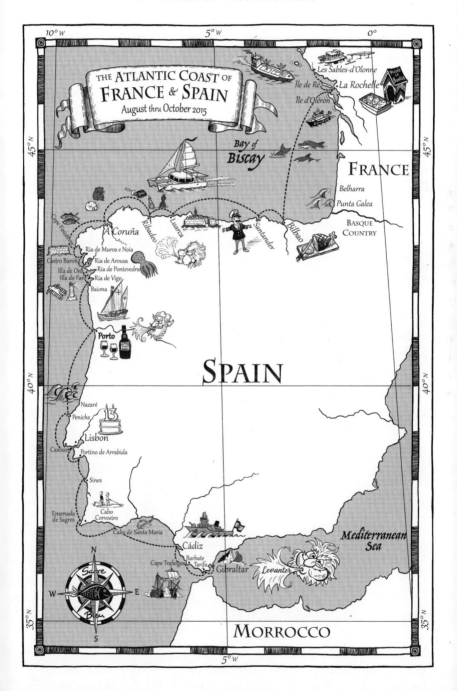

of diesel fuel was two-thirds the price we paid in neighboring Spain. For sailors like us who buy hundreds of gallons at a fill-up, it's a significant savings, which is why virtually every cruiser passing this way makes a stop in Gibraltar.

With our boat christened and 1,236 nautical miles under us, we thought we knew a thing or two about sailing. Next to us in the marina, a young couple and their two small children were just starting their adventure. They were a cruising family driven by one determined member, the dad, intent on fulfilling a lifelong dream before he turned into his father. They had just bought a traditional, two-masted Tahitian-style catamaran. On the platform between the hulls were a picnic table, a swing set, a few beanbag chairs, an inflatable palm tree, a kiddie pool and a variety of beach toys. They, too, were waiting for the levanter to pass before heading west into the Atlantic and up the coast. I recalled our entry into Cádiz and tried to imagine how they were going to manage two masts with two mainsails in heavy weather, not to mention two kids and a dog. Perhaps more easily once all the playground equipment had washed overboard. We gave them our cruising guides from the Atlantic and wished them luck.

7

The Mediterranean: In Poseidon's Realm

Spain
October 12, 2015

Motoring past the luxury condominiums and waterfront restaurants, through the busy harbor and into the Strait, we transitioned in less than half an hour from having a cozy home in a cosmopolitan tax haven on the Mediterranean to battling six-foot waves that hurled buckets of cold saltwater at us. On this sunny, blustery day, the North African coast was clearly visible ten miles to the south. As we crossed the invisible line between the Rock of Gibraltar and the mountains of Morocco, we passed through the Pillars of Hercules, the mythological gateway to the Mediterranean Sea. We were now in Poseidon's realm.

For bringing nightmares to sailors, Poseidon, god of sea and storms, and his brother, Zeus, god of sky, thunder and lightning, were full-service providers. The ancient Greeks were compelled to create mythology to explain the unpredictable Mediterranean weather. The sudden, violent bursts of wind (what sailors call white squalls because they occur in clear air with the only visible warning being white-capped seas) and the steep waves that form soon after could only be the work of deities who delighted in random acts of cruelty. Before we left for the cruise, a retired naval officer who had spent most of his career on ships confided in me that his Mediterranean deployment was his most frightening time at sea. He was on an aircraft carrier. When we crossed the Pillars of Hercules, we became novice sailors again.

Though the levanter had weakened, we were still fighting a headwind, so we stayed close to land, motoring our way along the Costa del Sol of Spain. Here, the coast is almost one continuous cliff, a legacy of the powerful waves that have been pounding the base of these coastal mountains for millions of years. Every few miles the cliffs fall away into a flat stretch of white sand, palm trees and high-rise hotels. After seven hours of sailing along this rugged coast, we anchored off Fuengirola, one of the resort towns, opting for civilization over solitude.

Anchored beside us was a 130-foot-long ketch with giant letters painted on the side reading Sailing for Jesus. Based out of Sweden, the *Elida V* carried a Christian youth camp, sailing and singing its way around the world. As we settled into our usual happy hour cocktails that evening—a gin and tonic for me and pastis on ice for Valerie—we were serenaded by twenty or thirty young voices singing gospel music.

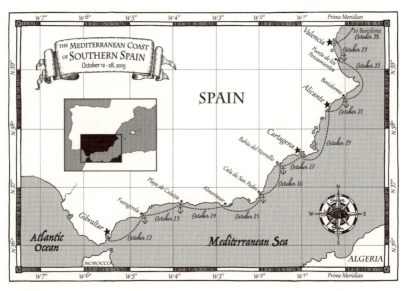

After a quick dinghy run to shore for fresh bread the next morning, we continued northeast along the Spanish coast, marking our passage by counting the stone towers that were once part of an elaborate medieval high-speed communication network. The towers rise from prominent points or hilltops at four- or five-mile intervals, where the signal sent by one could be seen by the next. A fire atop a tower announced an invasion or other threat, and word would quickly spread up and down the coast as towers passed their smoke signals up the line.

We kept up a steady pace of 40 or 50 miles a day, passing Playa de Calaiza, Almerimar, Cala de San Pedro, and Bahía del Hornillo, finding along the way exquisite beaches where we threw the anchor off the bow and the kids off the stern.

October 17, 2015

Today was William's eleventh birthday, and we had not found a gift or planned anything special for him. Madeleine made him a kirigami pirate ship, and Valerie baked a sheet cake with "11" written in M&Ms, but that looked to be the extent of the birthday celebration.

Then I saw a fin. We had seen many dolphins on our journey, but this fin was different, bigger and more curved, like a scimitar. We saw two more, and then five. A loud whoosh filled the air and clouds of mist appeared at the surface. That's when we realized we were being escorted by a pod of pilot whales. Fifteen whales altogether, mostly adults, with some youngsters in tow, were playing in our bow waves. I put the ship on autopilot and joined everyone forward, sitting on the forward cross beam with our feet dangling over these big animals, some directly under us swimming between the hulls. Then, as quickly as they appeared, they vanished. It's the same choreography with dolphins—they appear out of nowhere, perform their routine and abruptly exit stage right, as if they are an act on a variety show.

William and Madeleine both remained at the bow long after the whales had departed, hoping for a reappearance. They settled into their seats and, in one of the rare moments of the early cruise, seemed to be simply enjoying the boat ride. Fortune sent us a pod of whales on this lucky day, but the birthday present was greater than a mere spectacle of nature. Having gotten a tiny taste of what is hidden in the ocean's depths, they both seemed to have become more curious that day.

We reached the port of Cartagena by afternoon and found ourselves surrounded by Brits, Germans, Scandinavians, and other non-Spaniards who kept their boats at the marina, taking advantage of the reasonable fees and the short ride to the international airport. Because its clientele hailed from all over Europe, this marina had a different ambience. When cruisers settle into a particular location, a community and a daily rhythm quickly develop. These part-time Cartagenians held daily happy hours, movie nights and weekly potluck dinners, and have built up an impressive library of paperbacks at the book exchange. For a community in constant flux, they seem to have found just the right amount of self-governance.

As transients, we observed but did not join in. After securing and cleaning the boat, we strolled through town looking for a restaurant on the waterfront. Saturday night by the harbor was buzzing with locals and tourists biding their time before the traditional Spanish dinner hour. We were treated to an unexpected encore performance by Sailing for Jesus, which had arrived after us and been given a prominent spot on the city wharf. Working our way back to the marina, we found a restaurant where the birthday boy continued his tradition of ordering the oddest dish on the menu, oxtail stew. The wait staff brought cake with candles and sang a Spanish rendition of "Happy Birthday." What started off as a simple birthday celebration ended up being a memory for the ages: pilot whales, ox tails, and "Feliz Cumpleaños." Such is the cruising life.

October 19, 2015

We departed Cartagena early but did not reach Alicante until 9pm. Though I disliked night arrivals, driving into the port of Alicante under a dark sky was magical. The bustling, modern city lay in the foreground, its reflection sparkling in the serene harbor, as the sprawling, ancient Castillo de Santa Bárbara glowed on the hilltop beyond, its floodlit ramparts seemingly floating in the sky. Every new port brought the promise of a new adventure.

We began the next day as tourists, riding the elevator up to the castle, where a guide gave us the highlights of its thousand-year history, including a list of the usual invaders—Carthaginians, Romans, Visigoths and Moors—and violent episodes. We all agreed that life is hard, but Visigoths had it harder.

Early the next morning, we departed Alicante, running parallel to the Costa Blanca, sailing about 75 miles to Punta de los Pensamientos. We initially anchored close to the beach so the kids could easily paddle ashore. The waves were not breaking consistently, and it was difficult to tell where the surf line was. After about 15 minutes, we realized we were inside the break, so we anchored a second time farther out. As I studied the surf crashing around us, I got to thinking that maybe we were still not far enough out, so I floated the idea of anchoring a third time. Valerie replied that dinner was ready and there would be no further anchoring until after the cheese plate and dessert.

During our run to Valencia the next day, we encountered the temperamental breezes for which the Mediterranean is famous. Downslope winds called katabatic winds, from the Greek *katabasis*, meaning descending, are common along the coast of the Med. Sailors usually rely on mountains to provide shelter from the wind, but not here. These localized winds are completely independent of any weather forecast and can come on suddenly with no warning. The wind in this region of Spain typically comes from the Pyrenees and is called the *tramontane* by the locals, from the Latin *transmuntanus*, or over the mountain. The heavy, cold tramontane air rushes down the mountainside and across the water in powerful gusts, creating conditions that can change from picnic to panic in the time it takes to go below and get a beer.

Tramontane is only one of the many winds named by seafaring cultures surrounding the Mediterranean. The meteorological origins of these winds are complex, but for the ancient mariner, the direction from which they come speaks volumes.

Mistral comes from the north, funneling through the Rhone Valley of France into the Gulf of Lion and beyond. This legendary wind can reach hurricane strength and influences western Mediterranean climate, architecture, fertility rates, crime rates, and more.

Gregale, a cold wind, comes from the northeast, typically in winter, common especially in Greece.

Levanter, as we had experienced, comes from the east, most powerfully in the Strait of Gibraltar.

Sirocco comes from the south or southeast. Hot, dry, and dusty, it originates in the Sahara, and becomes humid as it picks up moisture over water. In Arabic, it is called the *ghibli* or *khamsin* wind.

Ostro comes from the south, hot and humid, mostly in the Adriatic Sea. In other parts of the Mediterranean, it is a sirocco.

Libeccio comes from the southwest, into the central Mediterranean, particularly the west coast of Corsica.

Ponente comes from the west, warm and dry, and in the Strait of Gibraltar, where it is strongest, blows opposite the levanter.

Tramontane comes from the northwest. Originating in the Atlantic Ocean, it blows across southern France into the Gulf of Lion as a dry, cold wind.

Besides these eight winds for each point of the compass, Med sailors encounter a few place-specific winds:

Bora – Affecting Croatia and the Adriatic Sea, especially in winter, it is a cold wind originating far inland from the north or northeast that can reach hurricane strength.

Jugo – Affecting Croatia and Adriatic Sea especially in summer, it is a hot wind from the south or southeast that originates in the Sahara and can reach hurricane strength. Jugo is the Adriatic version of the sirocco.

Meltemi – Affecting Greece, Turkey, and the Aegean Sea, it is a cold, dry wind from the north, common in summer. Also known as *etesian* wind.

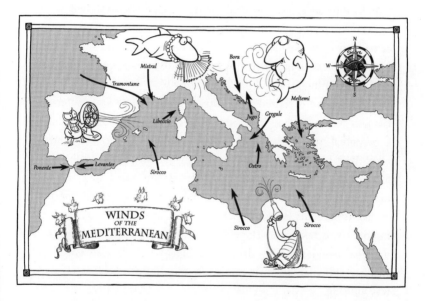

When navigating in the fickle Mediterranean breezes, crew must be ready to shorten sail at a moment's notice, which can lead to urgent and terse requests from the captain. With ordinary crew, the captain's status is never in dispute. With family crew, the captain's status is never secure, and no command is executed without a please and a thank you. With ordinary crew when the captain barks "trim the mainsheet," crew responds with a hearty "aye-aye" and executes. When the Dad-captain barks "trim the mainsheet," he is likely to get one of three responses:

1) "Where's the mainsheet?"
2) "I'll trim the mainsheet after I finish this chapter/sandwich/puzzle," or the captain's all-time favorite:
3) "I don't think the mainsheet needs trimming. If you want to trim it, trim it yourself."

Docking is just as demanding, and family-crew is not much more responsive in this role. By the time we arrived in Valencia, almost three months into the cruise, we were still not well practiced at Med moor-style docking. However, in Valencia, our disastrous attempt at docking came with a gift: We met Cecile and Harry, the charming Swiss couple in the boat next to us, when they came out to investigate the source of all the screaming.

Harry was a retired aerospace engineer, and like a latter-day Captain Nemo, he had built what was, for all intents and purposes, a perpetual-motion seafaring machine with a carbon footprint of zero. That night over cocktails, Harry gave me a tour of his custom-made catamaran. It was about the size of *Sacre Bleu*, but half the weight and a hundred times the complexity. If its computer-cut Kevlar sails lacked sufficient breeze, its solar-powered electric motors could take over. The electronics were all state of the art, and the boat could not only drive itself but also could also check the weather and plan its own route. For me, the prospect of no crew was alluring.

Harry helped me get tantalizingly close to independence from my passively mutinous crew. He politely suggested that we take a different approach to Med mooring. Instead of keeping the anchor chain taut throughout the process, I should set the anchor, let the chain go slack, fasten the stern lines to the dock, then tighten the anchor chain at the very end. Harry's technique was very similar to mine, only the steps were done in a different order. With many things in life, a slight change in order can produce an entirely different result. Pants before underwear, or underwear before pants: same steps, different order, different consequences.

For the five days we spent in Valencia, we were regulars at the parks and beaches, feeling the dirt under our feet and the sand between our toes, reveling in a terrestrial habitat native to humans that included restaurants and boutiques. Valencia is a beach town with a Roman past. The beachfront has a Southern California vibe, with a wide stretch of white sand that hosts sandcastle contests, volleyball tournaments, and rows of bronzed bodies. For the history buff or the just plain buff, the town is appealing. It is relatively flat and full of parks, so it is a good place to be a pedestrian—or a family of four riding on folding bicycles with only one gear and wheels the size of bagels.

October 26, 2015

We celebrated Valerie's birthday by going to the zoo. No doubt, she would have preferred a day at a spa, but our time in Valencia was drawing to a close, and Madeleine and William were eager to see if captive African animals living in Spanish zoos were any different from the ones in zoos back home. The Valencia Bioparc uses less intrusive barriers, such as water and rocks, to keep people and animals apart. As we made our way through the park, we were constantly getting the feeling we had somehow wandered into the enclosures. Now that Madeleine and William owned hamsters, they had a new appreciation for the work that goes into caring for an elephant or a hippo. "That's a lot of poop," was a frequent observation from the kids.

On the boat for our nightly happy hour, Harry and Cecile joined us for plates of lavish, overpriced pata negra and Manchego cheese wrapped in anchovies lovingly prepared and immediately devoured by the children. Harry gave me a demonstration of his navigation software. He powered up his navigation system, complete with a live weather map, and his demonstration turned to real-life drama when he recognized the mistral. With a concerned look, he pointed to the high-pressure system in the Bay of Biscay and the low-pressure system to the east of us. "A mistral in the making," Harry said. In a few days a violent wind was going to scream across central France, stripping leaves off grapevines and laundry off clotheslines, compelling farmers to retreat indoors and copulate, eventually turning the Gulf of Lion into a wind-torn chaos of angry waves. Harry asked about our plans. I said that we were hoping to cross the Gulf in a few days, but between now and then we were planning to visit Barcelona. He answered me with a grimace. It was time to put down my cocktail and think hard about this situation.

October 28, 2015

Early the next morning, we decamped. Our next stop was Port Ginesta, a marina close to Barcelona. Feeling a sense of urgency, Valerie and I stayed up all night and made the 160-mile run in an exhausting 24 hours, that, like driving a car in traffic, is tedious and unengaging, yet requires your full attention. At any moment, another boat, a change in wind speed or direction, or another complication might arise.

By the time we arrived in Port Ginesta the wind had picked up considerably. After staying up all night, the prospect of docking in a tight marina full of expensive yachts under blustery conditions added a layer of stress to our fatigue. The wind would push the boat in directions we couldn't counteract with the engines or rudders, with forces too great to fend off with arms or legs, and all we could do was watch the collision. We needed a tugboat.

The dockmaster kept us waiting ten minutes while I struggled to idle the boat in the small patch of water in the strong wind. He finally emerged from his office (where the open door revealed he was watching a soccer match) and gestured down a long, narrow stretch of water lined with sparkling white yachts to a tiny opening that seemed not quite as wide as our boat. "Just put it in there," his body language said, as if I were returning a rental car. I was about to reply with body language of my own, but Valerie convinced him that this was a bad idea for everyone involved. Speaking beyond earshot, the two of them did a lot of shoulder shrugging and pointing at me as if to say, "he couldn't park a wagon on the prairie." In the end, the dockmaster gave us a space on the end of the dock.

After we secured the boat, we set up the folding bikes and caught the next train to Barcelona. Barcelona is about as bicycle friendly as New York, which is to say that only the young, the fearless, and the highly motivated, such as bike messengers, dared cycling its streets. Instead of weaving between cars, we adopted the strategy of staying in the middle of a lane as a cluster of four cyclists. We frantically pedaled the busy streets as an eight-wheeled, open-air sightseeing bus, without the benefit of having an actual bus wrapped around us for protection. After thirty minutes at a galloping pace, we gave up, locked the bikes to a picnic table in the Parc de la Ciutadella and had a lunch of baguette sandwiches from a nearby market.

When we returned, another cyclist had locked his bike to the table *and* our bikes. Pre-cruise, I would have lost my temper, but life on a sailboat had taught me to see any disruption in the schedule as the new schedule. Switching our land transportation, we marched off to Gaudi's famous church, La Sagrada Família Basilica, which, like many of my home-improvement projects, has been a work in progress for what seems like an eternity (construction began in 1882). Years ago, when I was a 21-year-old backpacker wandering through Europe on a Eurail Pass, I had first seen Gaudi's Unfinished Church. Now it seemed even less finished than before, leading me to wonder if they built it during daylight hours and took it apart at night.

When we got back to our bikes, we found them liberated. That was one small problem solved, but a bigger one loomed. In this small park in downtown Barcelona, we noticed the tree branches were swaying unnaturally. Valerie checked the weather forecast with her cell phone and confirmed that the mistral was arriving early. We ended our day as tourists, became sailors again and returned to the boat to prepare it for heavy weather.

A safe harbor is the place to be when bad weather hits. But riding a storm in a boat in a marina presents its own challenges. We had to use every inch of dock line to secure the boat in a way that kept it well away from docks, pilings, and other boats. This operation left us about a four-feet leap to get aboard *Sacre Bleu*—especially difficult with a bag of groceries in each arm.

The mistral arrived that night, buffeting us with 50-knot winds as 10-foot waves crashed over the nearby seawall, filling the air with spray. Our slip was close to the entrance, and storm waves worked their way into the port, rocking our boat all night long.

The next morning, we were mortified to discover that about half of our dock lines had been sawed through by chafing against the concrete dock. Early in the trip, I noticed that most of the boats in the Mediterranean use steel chains for dock lines, but until that frightful morning it seemed like overkill. That morning, overkill became the ship's new motto. Since every good motto should be in Latin, we enlisted William, our resident antiquities scholar, to compose a proper Latin dictum that captured the overkill ethos. He obliged me with *Non Est Factum Usque Est Superoccidere*, or roughly, "It ain't over till it's overkill."

With time on our hands and a reliable internet connection, the kids threw themselves into watching Bob Ross videos on Netflix, and soon the family was gathered in front of the laptop to witness another whimsical landscape take shape through Ross' masterstrokes of the palette knife and brush. We could have chosen virtually any video entertainment on the planet, but nothing kept us riveted to the settee like an episode of *The Joy of Painting*. His seascapes feature rolling, graceful waves backlit by a dramatic sunset, and in their vivid, splashy pulchritude they seem harmless, almost gentle. In heavy weather, I relaxed by imagining we were sailing on the Bob Ross Sea, where there are no mistakes, just happy accidents.

France
November 4, 2015
The mistral passed, leaving dead calm seas between Barcelona and our next destination, Port-Cros, an island off the southern coast of France. After sitting out gale-force winds for six days, we now had the task of transporting a 16-ton sailboat over 250 nautical miles without a

breath of wind. A mere 24 hours earlier, the Gulf of Lion had been a frothy, windswept liquid tundra. Now it looked like a waxed floor. The indiscernible horizon lay somewhere between the sky and the perfect reflection of the sky in the water below, giving us the sensation of flying. Typically, when we're underway, even the smallest surface waves will produce a white noise of gurgling water, creaking rigging, pots and pans rattling in the galley drawers and more. But the drone of the engine was the only sound we heard as *Sacre Bleu*'s twin hulls cut through the flat seas like scissors through satin.

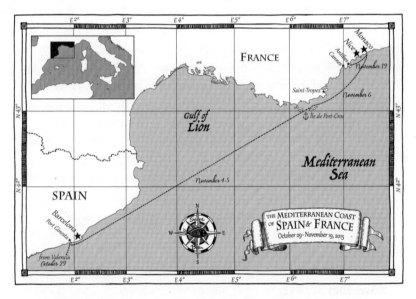

With a clear horizon and a boundless expanse of flat water to cover, we drove for hours with the autopilot engaged and nobody at the helm. Valerie was organizing art supplies, the kids were working on their homeschooling, and I was writing cartoons at my desk in our cabin when William broke from his schoolwork to remind me that these were the exact conditions on the *Titanic*—calm seas and a relaxed watch—when she hit the iceberg. I then worried that we had grown too reliant on technology, with the electronics acting as the fifth crewmember.

While we were running along at eight knots, me deep into writing and thinking that Valerie was keeping an eye forward, was she just as deep into organizing and thinking I was keeping an eye forward? I was keenly aware that even if the kids had their eyes open, they were not on watch. They would continue playing with their hamsters right up to when we smashed into the side of a container ship. I realized that I couldn't write cartoons while the boat was underway. The creative process demands a level of relaxation and daydreaming that is impossible when there's even the slightest chance of a sudden collision with a 30,000-ton moving object.

For safety's sake, we made other accommodations. We shunned firm commitments because they might force us to take risks to be at a certain place on a certain day. (We told friends who wanted to meet us that they could choose a location or a date, but not both.) We broke that rule rarely, yet one of those rare commitments was fast approaching. In four days, my short film *Two Miles Deep* was premiering at a film festival in Monaco. *Two Miles Deep* is a 12-minute documentary of my dive in the deep submersible vehicle *Alvin*, a mini-submarine that took me to the bottom of the Gulf of Mexico a year earlier. I had finished editing the film minutes before getting on the plane to France. In addition to showing the film, I was co-emceeing the film festival awards ceremony with Kelly Rutherford, from the television series *Melrose Place*. There would be no missing this party.

November 5, 2015

We arrived in Port-Cros at about two in the morning on a moonless, overcast night. As we inched our way around the island to the north, I studied the electronic chart for a suitable anchorage. Port-Cros is a national park, nearly undeveloped, and at two in the morning the island was completely black. With water indistinguishable from land and land indistinguishable from the sky, we were utterly dependent on our electronic navigation. The chart indicated that the best anchorage was in the Baie de Port Man, just off our starboard. In that direction, I saw nothing but black. Coming in blindly, I commenced a high-stakes video game on the electronic chart, keeping the little boat icon in the blue area and away from the tan area, all the while moving slowly ahead, keenly aware of the reality the screen represented.

Just as we were entering the bay, an audible ding broke my concentration. Then another ding, and another. I thought it was a safety warning and frantically scrolled through the navigation interface looking for the problem. Then I realized the sound was coming from my phone. A slew of text messages that had been queued up for me to get within range of a cell tower were all coming through at once. I looked at the screen and saw they were all from my sister. In a succession of four or five urgent texts, she asked me to call as soon as possible.

It was only nine o'clock in the evening in the U.S., so I had time to finish the task at hand before making that phone call. It was not a call I wanted to make because I was certain it was news about my father. Once we set the anchor, I called to hear my sister confirm my fears. Exhausted, I searched for the emotional energy to cry. In the black of night, I pondered the world without Dad.

The next morning, we were awakened by the rumble of a fishing boat passing by and its ensuing wake, which tapped the side of our hull just inches from my ear. I opened my eyes with the excitement of a new day in my heart, then remembered the dark reality of the night before. On deck, in the morning light I took in the natural beauty of Port-Cros. The island is completely forested in low, scrubby trees that have forced their roots into the rocky surface, somehow finding enough freshwater between the rock and the saltwater to survive the arid summers. The November air was clear and chilly, and for the first time since the start of the cruise I sensed a change in seasons. As the noise of the fishing boat faded, I heard songbirds in the trees and a passenger jet flying overhead. In the distance, on the French mainland, the morning traffic crawled along the coastal road as commuters made their way to work. This first day without John Toomey was business as usual for the rest of the world.

Dad passed suddenly, and chances are I would not have been at his side even if I had been living back home in Annapolis. My biggest frustration was that I could not be with my mother in the hours and days that immediately followed. Boat life is never spontaneous, even on occasions like this. The flight home was easy enough to arrange, but we had to secure *Sacre Bleu* in a suitable marina, and those arrangements were going to take time, research, negotiation, and some luck.

Since I would be flying home after the three-day film festival to stay for at least a week, we had to find a slip in a marina near Monaco where we could keep a 45-foot catamaran for a while. The more I thought about it, the more expensive it sounded. Monaco is home to the largest collection of mega-yachts in the world. Unlike us, their owners do not fret much about marina fees; they delegate the fretting to their captains. Furthermore, we were already into early November, and we still had no idea where we were going to shelter over the winter. Before us lay the French Riviera, a storied coastline awash in romance and glamor, but there was no time for indulging. As Valerie worked the telephone, I drove *Sacre Bleu* on a straight line to Monaco.

Monaco
November 8, 2015

Valerie secured a dock space in Port Hercules, the main port of Monaco, with an off-season rate that dropped my jaw only halfway to the floor. We arrived at sunset, sailing past the Oceanographic Museum and under the helicopters continuously coming and going. As we passed through the mouth of the harbor at dusk, all of Monaco opened wide before us, with the twinkling lights of hotels and casinos to the right and the majestic hillside mansions of the old town and the royal palace to the left.

I hailed Port Hercules on the VHF radio using my best French, and the harbormaster immediately dispatched a Zodiac with two dockhands to lead us to our dock. The location exceeded our wildest dreams: We were at the end of a long pier that extended well into the harbor, affording us a 360-degree view of the city. After a rough couple of days, our luck seemed to be turning around. That night, we watched

To Catch a Thief and immersed ourselves in movie trivia and the story of how Grace Kelly became a princess.

The next morning, we attended a reception for all the filmmakers at the Musée océanographique de Monaco. The featured speaker was His Serene Highness Prince Albert II, an ardent ocean conservationist. Prince Albert II is a graduate of Amherst College, speaks fluent American English and does not take himself too seriously. This provided some royal breathing space to the other speakers, mostly his friends, who poked fun at him for his mediocre fencing abilities and boring collection of ties, all of which he took with grace. The event showed Madeleine and William a prince up close so they could compare the real thing—a middle-aged man in a business suit—to the Disney version.

The reception was followed by the film program, which included my film. For a filmmaker, a film fest is work: I am expected to secure distribution and find a buyer for my film and negotiate a price. To this end, I had not set up a single meeting or made any attempt to publicize my film. Other filmmakers had printed up posters announcing the time and place of the showing of their films and plastered them all over the venue. They had built websites trumpeting the merits of their film and its appeal to audiences far and wide. I never liked that business approach to film festivals, preferring to watch films instead. That is one of many reasons I was showing my documentary in a fish museum and not a few miles down the coast at the Palais des Festivals in Cannes.

My film was reasonably well received and was nominated as a finalist in the short-film category. Since I was emceeing the prize ceremony the following evening, this presented a delightfully awkward situation. How might I present an award to myself? It would be an embarrassment of riches, the likes of which I had managed to avoid my entire life through carefully timed failures. There might even be a whiff of scandal in the air. The thought of being associated with a scandal in Monaco made me giddy.

The kids were not interested in or impressed by my nomination and just wanted pizza. We wandered out of the Oceanographic Museum and through the narrow streets of the old town until we found an Italian restaurant, which are common here, since Italy is almost jogging distance away.

We spent the rest of the day exploring Monaco, a country with a resident population of 38,000 people, a third of whom are millionaires. We strolled the waterfront admiring the mega-yachts and imagined how life might be different aboard their boats. No doubt, there was not a hamster in the lot. One yacht had a helicopter on deck that was meticulously wrapped in a hundred pieces of custom-made canvas that fit so perfectly that it made the helicopter look like a giant plush toy. With night falling, we could see the illuminated interiors of many of the yachts. The rooms were posh and immaculate, and most had enormous bouquets of fresh flowers. Uniformed crewmembers occasionally appeared and disappeared just as quickly, but owners or guests were nowhere to be seen.

At the top of the hill at the center of Monte Carlo (one of ten wards in the Principality of Monaco), surrounding a small park, are some of the most glamorous establishments on the planet: the Casino de Monte-Carlo, the Hôtel de Paris, and the Café de Paris. The front door of the casino was staffed by a dozen doormen and valets whose jobs are to assess the crowd and sort them into voyeurs and real clients. No children are allowed, and since we had Madeleine and William in tow, we were limited to gawking at the ornate lobby from outside the front door.

The film festival culminated in the awards gala. That afternoon, while Valerie and the kids stayed on *Sacre Bleu* to catch up on home schooling, I met with Kelly Rutherford to go over the script and the run of the show that evening. Emcee scripts can run the gamut from spelling out every syllable and timing every pause to minimal instructions, with lines like "MC to say something funny here." Our script was on the minimal side, but Kelly was a seasoned performer and saw opportunity in playing it straight. That turned out to be a good call, and the ceremony went well, even when we made mistakes like reading each other's lines.

Somewhere in the middle of the show, when I was not paying attention, Kelly threw the big announcement over to me. She handed me the envelope with the winner of the short film competition. I opened it, pulled out the card, and was at once relieved and disappointed. The winner was…not me.

A Quick Trip Home
November 10, 2015

On my first trip home, I would be dealing with the responsibilities associated with my father's death as well as visiting the renters of our house, checking in on the dog, making sure the car still started, opening mail, and a hundred other banal maintenance items that come with the glamorous ex-patriate lifestyle. A few days prior, we had loaded up on internet orders—homeschooling materials, cruising guides, oil and fuel filters for various engines, and kitchen items—sent to a neighbor's address. I was looking forward to being greeted with a chorus of smiles—on all the Amazon boxes.

I landed in Washington in the early evening. As an Uber shuttled me through the rush hour traffic, I got a strange feeling that the past four months had all been a dream. That night, at an impromptu neighborhood reunion, I regaled friends with sea stories, realizing that parts of our voyage seemed so much more glamorous as a yarn at a dinner party than they felt in reality.

The following day, Veteran's Day, I was at the funeral home viewing my father, Capt. John B. Toomey, USN (Ret). Dad was the quintessential engineer, a function-over-form kind of guy. In all his home improvement projects, like fixing the plumbing or hanging a shelf, he never worried much about what it looked like so long as it worked. He also had an engineer's obsession with efficiency. One Christmas, Mom surprised him with a Coach suitcase, an extravagance for this Depression-era couple. To make his suitcase easier to spot on the luggage carousel, he painted an orange "X" on the side. Mom was livid. "There're a lot of suitcases at the airport and they all look alike," he told her. When I showed up at the funeral home, I was expecting to see an orange "X" on painted his mahogany casket, as if to say, "There're a lot of caskets in this place and they all look alike. I'm in this one."

Dad could not be buried in Arlington National Cemetery until the following April because of the backlog of services there, a consequence of the Greatest Generation hitting its early 90s. The day after the viewing, we celebrated a funeral at the family parish, and I gave the eulogy. I had planned to talk about Dad's first day in Heaven: Though he could have indulged in any luxury imaginable, he would have requested Coca Cola and McDonald's cheeseburgers from room service because, for him, that *was* heaven. I imagined him confounding the angels in Heaven's procurement department because they would have to request those items be brought up from Hell.

At the pulpit, the floor seemed to move a little bit. I don't know if it was from nerves or from my spending the last two months at sea. I considered launching into my First Day in Heaven eulogy, but I took one look at the priest and lost my nerve. In the end, I kept it short. "My father was not an outwardly religious man, and even though Christian values came to him naturally, he did not manifest his religiosity in formal ways," I said. Dad always got antsy towards the end of a mass, and I could tell even through the closed casket that he was ready for this one to end.

Return to Monaco
November 18, 2015

I boarded a red-eye flight for Nice Côte d'Azur Airport and settled into my coach seat exhausted and a little overwhelmed by the mix of the deeply emotional and the banal that was my trip home. Landing the next morning, I found the only bus from Nice airport that services the entire Principality of Monaco.

November 19th is National Day in Monaco, and the ward of Monaco-Ville, home to the royal palace, was draped in red-and-white Monegasque flags, buntings, and rosettes, and all the yachts in Port Hercules were dressed in signal flags from stem to stern. As I approached our boat, my heart welled up with pride as I saw that Valerie and the kids, not to be outdone by our upscale neighbors, had dressed Sacre Bleu as well.

In the large courtyard in front of the palace, the military band of the palace guard performed its show as the prince and other royals watched from the balcony. Loads of red-and-white scarves must have been airdropped in the courtyard because virtually everyone in the streets, riding by on bicycles, eating at cafes, and gazing out of open windows was wearing one. As soon as we got near enough to the show, a kind woman, seeing that we were scarfless newcomers, presented us with one.

The palace guard band, a unit of the Compagnie des Carabiniers du Prince, is different from your average European military marching band. Although they wear the usual Nutcracker-style uniforms, this elite palace guard unit is just as likely to play funk or rock as a march. Accompanied by the Motorcycle Platoon, another performing unit of the military, they played Earth Wind and Fire's "September" while the motorcyclists performed tricks, zooming in circles and figure eights. The prince looked pleased as he and his bride watched from the balcony.

National Day was our last day in Monaco after an almost two-week stay. That afternoon, we cast off the lines and set a westward course for Antibes, France, a run of about 16 nautical miles. Antibes, we had decided, would be our base for the next five months as we took shelter from the winter storms, nestled safely behind a thirty-foot wall of boulders. Valerie had found a relatively bargain-basement rate on a 30-foot-wide slip in Port Vauban. As it happens, many Vauban tenants take their mega-yachts to the Caribbean for winter, which allows the Port to sublet a patch of water at monthly rates comparable to an apartment in town.

Antibes appeared on the horizon, with the town's trademark pair of tall, block-shaped stone towers in silhouette against a fiery sunset. The twilight was dead calm, and *Sacre Bleu*'s engines quietly growled as she cut through the flat water with a steady splash. The four of us sat on the bridge in silence, sizing up our new home as it drew closer. Once past the seawall, the harbor opened into a modern marina to the right and the original fishing port to the left, with a large basin of mega-yachts in the middle. We made our way to the old port, and just in front of the *capitainerie* (the harbormaster's office) our slip was waiting for us.

I backed *Sacre Bleu* into her new home for the winter, shut down the engines and poured a tall glass of scotch. November 18-19 had been a blur, starting in Annapolis, Maryland, passing through Paris, Nice, a National Day celebration in Monaco, and now, finally, ending on a dock in Antibes. Here, we would spend the next five months. It felt good to have a fixed address.

8

Winter in the French Riviera

Antibes, France
November 20, 2015

We woke up in Antibes to a new day and a new status as residents of the French Riviera. Still groggy and wearing my skivvies, I wandered into the cockpit to assess our surroundings in daylight and found myself in the background of a selfie being taken by a young couple strolling by on the dock. The American flag on our stern was a rarity in Port Vauban and carried some pop culture value. The unkempt, middle-aged man in his underwear brought the pop factor down a notch, and the couple quickly moved on.

Wintering over in Antibes represented not the midway point in our cruise so much as the end of the first act. It was early enough in the voyage that we were not yet longing to get off the boat. The fact that we stopped cruising before it became tiresome was completely inadvertent but strategically brilliant. We were looking forward to eventually getting back on the water, but for now we were happy to be docked next to solid ground.

From our boat slip, land was only a gangplank away. Looking aft, the capitainerie sat 50 feet away. Having the capitainerie and its bathrooms close by was an enormous relief, no pun intended. Since we were in a closed harbor, and could not release wastewater from the boat, we could not use the ship's showers or the heads without going through the hassle of driving the boat around to a pump-out station on a regular basis to empty the holding tanks. That was a hassle we were glad to trade for a short walk to the capitainerie for our morning shower and, otherwise, whenever nature called.

Looking starboard, we could see the city's ancient ramparts about 300 yards away, and through the portal, the bustling town of Antibes. To port, the view was dominated by Fort Carré, a 16th-century fortress guarding the harbor's entrance. Beyond the fort lay the French Alps, steep, jagged, snowcapped year-round, and easily visible on clear days. Looking forward, beyond a line of small fishing boats, was Billionaires' Row (formerly Millionaires' Row), a gated area of the harbor with a half dozen gargantuan private yachts ranging from 200 to over 350 feet in length, the size of a small cruise ship. The closest to us, the biggest in the port and one of the biggest in the world was the mega-yacht *Dilbar*, measuring 361 feet and owned by a Russian oligarch with a mysterious source of wealth. *Dilbar*'s displacement probably brought the level of the Mediterranean Sea up half an inch.

Dilbar was certainly well heated—with maybe even a few fireplaces—but our boat was damp and cold. This unfortunate fact reared its ugly head over breakfast on our first morning. I had been ignoring the issue since the planning stage of the cruise, but I was reminded with every cold surface I touched that we now had a problem that needed immediate attention. The boat had a built-in heater, but because it was designed for U.S. electrical service, which is different from the European service, we couldn't use it. After several marine contractors dropped by and suggested wildly elaborate modifications involving large transformers and thousands of euros, we bought four cheap space heaters at the hardware store.

Two boats down from us on our dock sat a bright orange rescue boat that belonged to the Société Nationale de Sauvetage en Mer (National Sea Rescue Society), or the SNSM. The boat, *Notre Dame de*

La Garoupe is 55 feet long, with orange topsides and a blue hull. Built like a battleship, she is typical of the Société's rescue boats at larger coastal stations, with a bulbous bow designed for moving fast through rough seas. I was especially impressed by the heavy sheet metal doors that slid over the exhaust outlets if the boat was in the upside-down position, preventing seawater from flooding the diesel engines should the boat capsize.

With stations all over France, SNSM is a volunteer organization that responds to distress calls from vessels at any hour in any weather. Most of its members are firefighters or paramedics, though it will train any motivated soul with the requisite amount of courage, stamina, and time.

Our second day in Antibes was a Saturday, a training day for our sea rescuers. Fifty feet from our boat, a dozen or so volunteers in their orange jumpsuits were practicing first aid. I made the mistake of saying to Valerie, "Maybe I'll volunteer. Wouldn't *that* be an adventure? And a good crash course in French to boot." Somehow those words found their way to the coxswain (ship's captain), and before long a man in an orange jumpsuit knocked at the door.

Wladimir was Croatian by birth but had been living in France since early childhood. Tall, square-jawed, and in his mid-forties, Wlad spoke flawless English and quickly won me over to going out in a small boat on freezing, dark, gale-swept nights to rescue distressed mariners who had no business being out there in the first place. After four months on a sailboat with two children, how hard could it be?

Wlad gave me a tour of the patrol boat and introduced me to the other volunteers. A good many of them were British (so much for that crash course in French). Jon was a retired professor in medieval literature; Phil was retired military; Charlie was in his twenties and crewed for one of the mega-yachts. The French side included Patrice, the boatswain; Alain, the president of the chapter; Nico, a paramedic; Remi, a retired local businessman, and a mix of young and old, men and women, about twenty-five in all. Wlad promised to have me wearing orange like the rest of them in no time.

November 22, 2015
Sunday marked the beginning of Thanksgiving week. I hoped to take in a few football games, but our mobile phone plan spit data out in dribs and drabs like a baby spitting out pureed carrots. Livestreaming the Lions vs. the Bears was not in the cards. A check of local programming revealed that the French were not willing to devote a single minute to NFL football or live coverage of a parade in New York City featuring giant inflatable advertisements. Dinner plans were uncertain, with the closest turkey being in a zoo.

Even back home, Thanksgiving had always been a challenge with a French wife who did not understand or appreciate why Americans took several hours to prepare a meal that was consumed in under 30 minutes. It was looking like Thanksgiving was going to be a bust. Then Corinne walked into our lives.

Corinne passed by our boat, paused, saw Valerie in the cockpit and introduced herself. She and her husband, Renaud, had a similar boat moored in Cannes. Soon, the rosé was flowing, and Valerie and Corinne were best friends. Not long after that, we had plans for Thanksgiving. "Does she know what she's getting herself into?" I asked Valerie. Turkey or chicken, canned cranberry sauce or fresh, I was just happy to have plans for the holiday.

When the big day arrived, we cabbed over to Corinne and Renaud's home. They had prepared a Thanksgiving lunch that could have graced a magazine cover. Unable to locate a turkey, Corrine tracked down the biggest chicken in southern Europe, seasoned it with herbs de Provence, and baked it to perfection. The stuffing featured prosciutto, walnuts and truffles, the vegetable was a fresh squash Carpaccio with olive oil and shaved parmesan, and the dessert was a plum tart with homemade vanilla ice cream. How different we Americans would be if the Pilgrims had been French instead of English Puritan.

The next day, we got out the folding bikes and embarked on our first foray into Antibes. Once through the gates of the city walls, we had to choose between several narrow streets. Valerie saw a farmer's market and headed towards it, down a one-way street the wrong way, and we followed. At the end of the block, a policeman materialized, wagging his finger at us with a stern expression on his face. In France this quaint finger-wagging custom is an accepted gesture between adults, as if to say "no, you don't." Wag your forefinger at the average American and you are likely to get another finger in response, or maybe the entire fist.

Valerie is a woman who does not reverse course easily, and being in her native France, and the daughter of a gendarme no less, she persevered. "We're halfway there," was Valerie's opening shot at the policeman, to which he countered, "and you're halfway back to where you came from." After some back and forth, lunge and parry, riposte and counterattack, we found ourselves taking the long way around to the market. Policeman 1, Valerie 0. A rare shutout.

As we cycled around the block, I said to Valerie, "Oh, well. Chances are we won't be seeing *that* guy again anytime soon." For the next five months, on our daily run to the market, we saw that same policeman at that same corner.

November 30, 2015

Before I could become an official volunteer for the Société, I had to pass a swim test at the municipal aquatic center just up the hill from the marina. The woman at the front desk pointed at my Hawaiian board shorts and declared that they were not suitable for the swimming pool, throwing in a finger wag to strengthen her position. Puzzled and a little offended, I explained that the garment I was wearing was clearly a bathing suit. "Regardez, monsieur," she said as she gestured through the lobby windows to the pool. All the men were wearing Speedos. Of course, they were; this was Europe. "Speedo?" I asked, and she said "Oui." I despaired. Where was I going find a Speedo bathing suit? "Monsieur," the woman said, reading my expression. "Là," she continued, pointing to the Speedo vending machine across the lobby, where skimpy bathing suits in clear plastic tubes were lined up on coils to be dispensed like candy bars. I had never worn a Speedo in my life, and I had been hoping to make it to the end without breaking that streak.

Emerging from the locker room wearing nothing but a Speedo—which felt like nothing—and a towel around my shoulders, I returned to the lobby. The woman handed me some paperwork on a clipboard and directed me to the outdoor pool, where a lifeguard was smoking a cigarette and looking very bored because nobody was swimming in his unheated pool on this chilly last day of November. I handed the lifeguard the clipboard and he asked me to swim a few laps and tread water. He scribbled a quick signature on the form, handed it back to me, said "Félicitations," and lit another cigarette. On my way out of the aquatic center, I bid au revoir to the woman at the desk and dropped my Speedo in the trashcan.

December 5, 2015

At the next weekly Société volunteer meeting, I was looking forward to my first day of drills and hoping to go out on the rescue boat. The winter swells just outside the breakwater were rolling in furiously, and I was curious to see how boat and crew negotiated the big surf. The previous Saturday, I had watched as the *Notre Dame de La Garoupe* smashed through the waves, kicking up an explosion of foam and green seawater as it labored its way out to deeper water. Whatever we were going to do today would be fun. Maybe we would learn some first aid from Nico, the paramedic, or try shooting the firehose.

Instead, Alain, the club president, produced several cardboard boxes, opened one and pulled out an official 2016 Société calendar. Amid approving nods, he handed out the calendars, produced a map of Antibes, paired us up, and assigned each of us a part of town. Today, we were not an elite team of brave, seagoing, orange-clad first responders. Today, my first official day as a volunteer, we were calendar salesmen. Luckily, I was partnered with Charlie, a young Englishman who spoke perfect French and delivered it with an effusive smile. I played the silent sidekick as he pitched the concept of displaying an official SNSM calendar in their shops and homes, showing them the dramatic photo from February, featuring the orange rescue boat with a French Navy helicopter hovering above. This, and eleven more equally impressive photos of an orange boat, all for only ten euros. Who could say *non*?

December 8, 2015
As the weeks passed, we settled into a routine in Antibes and soon felt like locals. The Société was a great gateway into the community, and we regularly socialized with Wlad, Phil, Jon, and the others. Wlad introduced us to one of his good friends, Séverine, and we became a frequent foursome in the restaurants, hiking trails and playing *pétanque*, the French version of bocce ball. The kids enrolled in art classes and brought home delicate ceramic creations that gradually filled every horizontal surface of the boat.

We were on a first-name basis with many of the chandlery owners, and they would drop by on a regular basis to see if the boat needed any repairs or modifications. We upgraded our dock lines to chains and installed a pulley system that allowed us to lift our passarelle like a castle gate. I accidentally left a circuit breaker on while the boat was connected to shore power, and the higher European voltage fried the US-built washer/dryer, so we had to replace it. Because the refrigerator-sized appliance was factory-installed and the walls were built around it, the entire cabin had to be disassembled, requiring a team of three men and a lot of cigarettes. The list of repairs always seemed to grow and shrink, but it never disappeared.

Because we were obligated to use the marina bathrooms instead of the bathrooms on *Sacre Bleu*, our lives resembled KOA-style camping even more than boat life usually did. Every morning, I packed a toiletry kit and a fresh change of clothes, walked to the marina bathroom, said "bonjour" to one of the attendants as I walked by her tip jar, got in the shower stall and closed the door, found a way to keep soap, shampoo and clothing off the floor—which was difficult since there were no shelves or hooks—took a shower and got dressed. Frequently, I would get to the marina bathroom only to realize I had left the shampoo in the boat or get back to the boat only to realize I had left my shampoo in the marina bathroom. Such is the glamorous life on a yacht in the French Riviera.

Truer to my imagination of life on the glamorous French Riviera were the bells of Antibes Cathedral, which ring every Sunday when mass lets out at nine, ten thirty, and noon, echoing through the narrow streets with overlapping arpeggio chimes that, for my ears, are the sonic portrait of Europe. With the peal of bells and the spectacle of an ancient stone church, it is easy to step back in time and imagine the narrow streets filled with the muted colors, coarse fabrics and somber faces of times long past.

The part of my daily routine that I looked forward to most was my run to the bakery every morning. I was supposed to return with two baguettes, but I routinely purchased a third because one would never survive the ten-minute walk home. Overwhelmed by its sweet fragrance and its warm touch, its golden flaky crust and its soft, cakey interior, seduced by this simple concoction of wheat flour, salt and yeast, executed to culinary perfection, I would stuff one of the baguettes into my gaping maw like a python devouring a rat, eating it in two or three enormous bites, leaving me unable to speak when I got back to the boat. "Did you remember the milk?" Valerie would ask, to which I would respond, "Mph."

December 13, 2015

The holiday season officially kicked off with the arrival of Valerie's parents, who made the six-hour drive from their hometown in Beaujolais. The kids helped them unload their one small suitcase, a half-dozen bottles of wine from M. Lefort's cellar, four bags of groceries, and a dozen Christmas presents. William was tapped to give up his cabin, which was never a problem because he hardly ever slept there. Whether he ended up on the couch in the salon, one of the exterior settees, or the exterior trampoline, like a dog, he lay down wherever his day ended, and from that same spot, he started his day again the next morning.

We spoke English on the boat, and most of my Société friends were English or spoke English when I was in their company. I was living in France, but I was inside an English bubble. When Valerie's parents visited, however, the conversation shifted to French. The kids were fluent, having grown up in a household where their father yells at them in English and their mother reasons with them in French. The first French-speaking day with Valerie's parents was the hardest. I would pretend to follow the conversation by simply matching everyone else's emotions. I laughed when they laughed; I rolled my eyes and exclaimed *Oh là là*! when they did. After two or three days of immersion, I began to understand what my in-laws were saying, but speaking French remained a challenge. In the time it took me to rehearse a sentence in my head, the conversation always moved on.

Gradually, however, French came to me. I recall one day when I began to understand what people were saying without having to translate it into English in my head first. With a few weeks' immersion, I'm convinced most anyone can become conversant in another language at any age. It's the immersion that becomes increasingly difficult as our lives get more complicated.

In the spirit of celebrating a Côte d'Azur Christmas, we brought home a lemon tree. We figured that when the holidays were over, we could plant it close by and have a member of the family in the French Riviera to visit for decades to come. Our lemon tree came in a terra cotta pot, measured about four feet high and was endowed with one large lemon that made the branch droop. I was reminded of the Christmas tree in the '60s animated classic *A Charlie Brown Christmas*. The kids had made porcelain ornaments in their pottery class, and with the addition of a modest string of lights, our lemon tree grew into a living, flashing, fruit-bearing tribute to the pagan and the Christian.

On Christmas Eve, Valerie and her mother got an early start buying groceries at the Marché Provençal for the big meal that night. Sheltered under an Art Deco-style, wrought-iron pavilion, the Marché Provençal is a quintessentially French experience. Regional producers transport their fresh produce directly from farm to *marché* every morning in tiny flatbed trucks loaded with crates of fruits and vegetables. Sometimes the meat products show up in a cage, still dressed like a live chicken or a rabbit. Farmers clad in denim coveralls and suspenders, wardrobe and wearer both showing the signs of a hard life, start at six in the morning and continue until one in the afternoon. Beneath many of the produce stands sits a bottle of red table wine, a couple of glasses, and a full ashtray. By seven a.m., the energy level is high as the market hits its crescendo of buying and selling, poking and squeezing, weighing and packaging.

Over our almost-daily runs to the market, we established our favorite vendors. Valerie liked a vegetable vendor because he had a broader selection and a bigger inventory from which to pick and choose. I liked him because, in his early seventies, a quintessential farmer with dirt under his fingernails, he was unfiltered and unapologetic. In a loud voice, coarse from years of chain smoking and hawking his produce, he would tell a customer to buy more fennel because it would improve her love life. Despite the carnival atmosphere, every vendor took his or her profession seriously and had a plausible argument why his or her radish or olive tapenade was superior. They were devoted to their craft and woke up every day wondering how to make a better baguette, not how to sell more of them.

On this Christmas Eve, the Marché Provençal was festive chaos with shoppers reaching over one another for goods, and merchants frantically weighing, bagging, taking euros, and returning change. The stalls that usually sold flowers were loaded with mistletoe, pine garlands, and holly branches. In the cafes and bistros that surround the market, patrons—mostly husbands watching their wives search for the perfect tomato—savored an espresso or a glass of wine.

By late morning, every appliance in *Sacre Bleu*'s little galley—the tiny oven, the three stove burners and the Vitamix—was stretching its capacity to produce Christmas Eve dinner for six. With the aroma of home cooking, the decorations that the kids had brought home from their art class, and presents accumulating under the lemon tree, it was beginning to look a lot like Christmas.

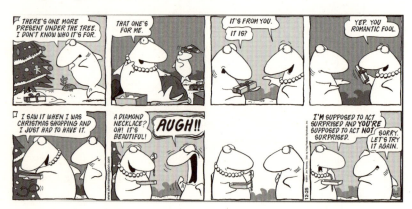

December 25, 2015

Christmas Day was overcast and chilly, and the town was silent and still except for the ringing of the cathedral bells as the Christmas masses let out. William was asleep on the settee in the dining area, where his day had ended the night before. The kids were no longer believers in Christmas magic, so there was no rush to have the presents under the lemon tree and the video camera ready. I wanted to brew some coffee, but I had forgotten to fill the teakettle the night before, and if I had tried to run water from the galley sink, the loud groan of the water pump would have woken the entire boat. So, I settled in the aft cockpit by the lemon tree and watched Christmas morning come to Antibes. Soon enough, everyone on *Sacre Bleu* was awake, the presents were unwrapped, and new toys with new noises entered our lives.

The day after Christmas is my birthday. It has always been an unpromising day for a birthday since nobody is ever in the mood for another party, which was fine with me. It was also a Saturday, and a small contingent of Société members who had had enough of Christmas were gathered by the clubhouse for a relaxed day of first aid training. The regulars were there—Wlad, Jon, Phil, Charlie, Alain, Nico, Patrice, and five or six others—standing in a circle around a mannequin lying on the ground. Nico was demonstrating CPR. When I saw my friends in orange, I decided the best birthday a guy could have would be to join them and help resuscitate that dummy.

It was looking like it was going to be a routine exercise day for the Société and a low-key birthday for me. That is, until Valerie sidled up next to me and informed me in a soft but emotional voice, "Mom's fallen down the stairs." A treacherous set of five steps leads from the upper salon to the lower cabins, and it is easy to forget they are there. "Is it bad?" I asked. "She hit her head pretty hard," Valerie said, with a crack in her voice. I looked around. There were a dozen first responders close enough to throw a shoe at. I turned to Valerie. "Do we want twelve rescuers in orange jumpsuits in our salon? I can make that happen." Better safe than sorry with a head injury, we concluded. Within seconds, twelve rescuers in orange jumpsuits were in our salon.

When Valerie described Mme Lefort's fall to Nico, "Oh là là" was his response. How serious did he think this injury was? The French always utter this expression with deadpan restraint regardless of the gravity of the circumstances. The meaning of the phrase can run the gambit from "Uh, oh" or "Wow," to "Holy shit! That plane is going to crash into the house!" The phrase can be lengthened to express a lingering woe, as in "Oh là là là là là là là," while changing a particularly messy diaper. In urgent or fast-moving situations, it can be shortened to "Oh là!" and sometimes delivered in quick succession. Put a French cowboy on a bucking bronco and you might hear "Oh là! Oh là! Oh là!"

This situation clearly fell on the high end of the oh là là spectrum. Mme. Lefort was lying on the sofa with M. Lefort sitting next to her holding her hand. Nico knelt by her with his paramedic kit and examined her pupils. He took her pulse and asked her a few simple questions. He tested the feeling in her fingers and toes. He checked her vision and memory. The others looked on in silence as the examination progressed. Finally, Nico declared that although Mme. Lefort appeared stable, she should go to the emergency room. A grumble of general agreement arose from everyone in the room.

Le Centre Hospitalier d'Antibes Juan-les-Pins was just a ten-minute drive, but Valerie's father, the retired policeman, made it in five. We brought Mme. Lefort, now in a wheelchair, into a large triage room with fifteen or twenty beds, all occupied by patients in varying degrees of urgency. Some were loud and emotional; others were resigned and stoic. A girl wearing equestrian wardrobe had clearly fallen off a horse. A young man in a soccer jersey limped on crutches. Newly arrived Christmas gifts were breaking limbs all over France. A doctor examined Mme. Lefort and wheeled her off to get an MRI. As we waited for the results, I listened in on the distraught conversions at other bedsides without making eye contact, trying to piece together the dramas that brought them there. Finally, the doctor reappeared and informed us that they were going to keep Mme. Lefort for at least another 24 hours. Downcast, the three of us drove back to the boat and had a quiet dinner.

The next morning, we brought Valerie's mother back to the boat. M. and Mme. Lefort packed their bag, pecked everyone on both cheeks, and set out across the marina parking lot dragging their lone rolling suitcase. We followed them to the car, where more cheeks were pecked, and where we talked for another twenty minutes while the car engine ran, trying to cover all remaining topics of conversation before they left and bring closure to the many open discussions.

January 6, 2016

Holiday celebrations in France do not end until the Feast of the Epiphany, twelve days after Christmas. It is also known as Three Kings Day, and the *galette des rois*, or kings' cake, is a delicious and ubiquitous part of the celebration. Hidden inside every kings' cake is a *fève*—a hard-as-a-rock porcelain figure about the size of a jellybean. Fèves can take many forms, from the sacred, like Baby Jesus, to the secular, like Shrek. One never eats a slice of galette des rois with gusto, but rather with careful, exploratory mastication, tongue poking through every layer of puff pastry before cautiously proceeding with a chew. Those lucky souls who bite into the slice with the fève hidden inside, assuming they do not need emergency oral surgery, become king or queen for a day and are entitled to wear the paper crown that a French bakery includes with every galette des rois.

During these two weeks, we attended a dozen Epiphany celebrations—at the Société clubhouse, the marina office, and the community center—where galette des rois and sparkling wine turned a room full of restrained Antibois (residents of Antibes) into best friends for an afternoon.

February 16, 2016

We always purchased our baguettes at the same bakery just off the Marché Provençal. Valerie got to know the proprietor the way she got to know so many other locals, by doing a little bit of business and having long conversations in the process. It was over one of these exchanges that she asked the owners, Nathalie and Didier, if they would give the kids a behind-the-scenes tour of the operation. They said they would be delighted.

We arrived at seven o'clock the next morning, late in their workday, and walked past the line of customers and straight to the sales counter. Nathalie lifted a hinged part of the counter to let us through, and her baker, a young man covered in flour dust, escorted us down to the basement. The bakery occupied a roughly twenty-by-twenty-foot square, which did not seem small on the open ground floor, but in the basement the walls closed in. The space was chilly and bright with fluorescent light, and the aroma of fermenting yeast filled the room. One wall was lined with large stainless steel refrigerators, and on the opposite wall stood a long stainless steel table. Against a third wall, a mixing machine labored away, producing a racket that required the conversation to be loud and brief.

Madeleine and William took turns measuring out a handful of dough, weighing it, adding or pinching some off to get the exact portion, and placing the blobs on a rack to rest and rise. The rested dough was removed from another rack, flattened, folded, and then rolled into oblong sausages. The baguette blanks were then placed on trays lined with floured linen and given a couple more hours to rise. The baker opened the large oven, releasing a sweltering blast of aromatic air, and with pincers, deftly removed trays of golden, baked-to-perfection baguettes, put them on a rack to cool, and placed the trays of dough in the oven. In the end, the kids were not so much inspired to become bakers but rather impressed with how much manual labor could be bought for a euro and twenty cents. Perhaps they were destined to become management.

March 6, 2016

Besides selling calendars during the holidays, the Société's major source of income is burials at sea—not bodies but urns of ashes. These ceremonies typically entail hosting a small group of mourners on the patrol boat, venturing to a certain location offshore and ceremoniously committing the urn to the deep. After years of the same ceremony in the same spot, surely the urns were piling up.

Today's burial would mark my first appearance before the public as an orange-clad member of the Société. The ceremony started at the dock with the crew welcoming the family onboard and explaining the safety procedures. After the boat reached the spot, one of the crew read a passage from the Bible. The urn was then dropped in the water, where it sank. Sometimes it didn't. During one memorable ceremony, the urn disappeared for a moment then floated back up, spooking some of the mourners. After we were certain that the urn had been dispatched to the inky depths, we tossed white rose petals in the water and drove the boat slowly in circles, honking the ship's horn. The rose petals were sometimes set upon by ravenous seagulls who mistook them for food, stealing some gravitas from the occasion. Despite these occasional departures from the script, the mourners disembarked content that their loved one was resting in peace, undoubtedly in the company of friends and neighbors.

During my five months in Antibes, the only rescue I participated in was my own mother-in-law's.

Another Trip Home
March 30, 2016

I had one more burial to attend. After several months' wait, Arlington National Cemetery was ready to provide full military honors for my father. The four of us boarded a plane at Nice Côte d'Azur Airport to fly home for the services, marking our first time back in the USA as a family.

We experienced some culture shock as we made the one-hour trip from Dulles Airport to Annapolis. We had forgotten how big American cars were and how much space Americans devote to parking them. Fast food and retail chains featured large in the landscape, and the sidewalks were bereft of dog poop. It is strange what one notices after being away so long.

Our house was still being rented, so we stayed with neighbors. On a card table in their basement, I set up a remote office, with laptop, internet, a checkbook, and five months of mail in a plastic bin. I had become a skilled itinerant and could work anywhere. William installed himself in front of the X-Box, his thumbs falling right back into place without missing a beat, blast or shot. Madeleine continued her habit of reclining in bed and sending Snapchats and Instagrams to her friends, despite the fact that they were now less than a five-minute drive away and she had not seen them in six months. Valerie threw herself into shopping for clothing, electronics, and home-schooling materials at big box stores, a uniquely American experience.

April 1, 2016

On this warm, early spring day, the trees were just starting to bud in Arlington Cemetery, and birdsong filled the air. A black caisson bearing Dad's flag-draped casket idled in front of Arlington House, drawn by six horses, three with riders in Army dress. Behind the caisson stood a marching platoon of Navy sailors in Service Dress Blues bearing rifles on their shoulders, followed by a band platoon in similar dress, followed by a Navy chaplain and a Naval officer of equal rank to the deceased—in this case, a captain.

The procession followed the roughly quarter-mile path to the gravesite, over grassy hills neatly lined with white marble gravestones in all directions, past the final resting places of presidents and generals, heroes and unknowns, and a gauntlet of tourists snapping pictures with their iPhones. The casket was placed graveside, and as the band played "America the Beautiful," the flag was meticulously folded by the six pallbearers. Seven riflemen fired three volleys over the grave, a bugler played taps, verse was recited by the chaplain, and the Navy captain, in tears, presented the flag, now folded into a triangle, to my mother sitting in the front row. From a nineteen-year-old lieutenant in 1944 to being laid to rest by two platoons at Arlington Cemetery, dad had traveled a long and remarkable journey set in motion by a world war and sustained by an undying optimism and love of family, work and golf.

At that same moment, up in heaven, an angel picked up the phone and ordered a Coke and a McDonald's cheeseburger to go.

April 8, 2016

We woke at sunrise after a late arrival from Washington to prepare for taking *Sacre Bleu* back out to sea. After five months, we were bidding farewell to Antibes and all our friends. Spring had arrived in the Mediterranean, the mistral had weakened, seas had laid down, and the rest of our journey beckoned.

Over the months, *Sacre Bleu* had been a floating apartment, stationary and peaceful, so when I started the diesel engines, the faint roar beneath the deck seemed alien. It was a Monday, but we had a strong contingent of Société members—Jon, Phil, Patrice, Remi, and Wlad—helping us with the dock lines. In a matter of minutes, the shore power cable was unplugged, the passerelle was stowed, and our transition from apartment to ship was complete. We cast off, and I eased Sacre Blue out of its tight fit between two neighboring boats and into the marina fairway, where I throttled up to gain steerage. The horns on *Notre Dame de La Garoupe* sounded, and we honked our shrill reply. We made our way past Billionaires' Row, past the long-silent cannons of Fort Carré and into the open sea. Clearing the breakwater, we immediately encountered large rolling swells that warned us we were once again a vessel underway.

9

Back on the Blue

Italy
April 12, 2016

A cool spring breeze blowing in from the Maritime Alps carried us east along the now-familiar coastline and past the many places we had visited during our five-month stopover. On a distant hilltop lies the village of St. Paul de Vence, where we played pétanque against local retirees and lost by a wide margin. Farther along, the sprawling city of Nice came into view, and memories of our day at its magical Christmas market came to mind. The flavor of crêpes will always bring us back to that day in Nice. Passing Monaco reminded us of our many excursions there by train to bask in its glamorous ambience. A little farther along came the town of Menton, where we attended the dazzling Fête du Citron, with its enormous sculptures rendered in locally grown oranges and lemons.

By late afternoon, we had crossed into Italian waters and were docked in the harbor town of Imperia with a new courtesy flag flying in our rigging. That evening, at a trattoria near the port, we savored real Italian pizza: simple, thin, crispy, garlicy perfection. The waiter spoke to us in a string of unbroken Italian, but with his effusive manner and remarkable inventory of body language, we somehow understood every word he said. In the cacophony of the tiny restaurant, filled to capacity, the four of us silently sized up our surroundings. Everyone seemed to be talking and nobody seemed to be listening. A recorded opera filled the occasional quiet moments. Tired as we were, we were all excited to be in Italy. Ahead of us lay 4,700 miles of Italian coastline. A year was not going to be enough.

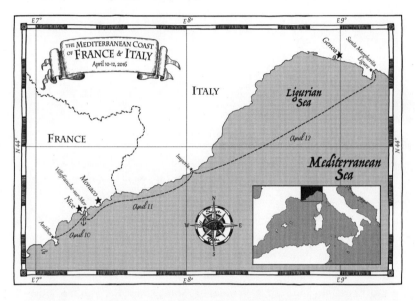

On the second day, now 40 miles into our trip, we ceased following the coast and sailed another 60 miles directly to Santa Margherita Ligure, cutting straight across the Ligurian Sea (Named for the Italian region of Liguria, it is one of many smaller seas within the Mediterranean). From the port of Santa Margherita Ligure, we planned to explore the Cinque Terre. Italian for five lands, Cinque Terre encompasses five villages farther south that are so singularly beautiful that they and the coastal area between them have been declared a UNESCO World Heritage Site. Each village is a cluster of pastel-colored, tall, narrow stucco buildings that seem to cascade over the cliff and into the ocean like a spilled load of bricks.

The five towns of Monterosso al Mare, Vernazza, Corniglia, Manarola, and Riomaggiore are connected by a six-mile footpath chiseled into the side of the cliff, running up and down steep stairways, across ravines and through the towns, providing a fine hike with spectacular views, not to mention ample opportunities for an espresso or a Campari along the way. As was our experience all over Europe, we found a train station within walking distance of the boat, and from there we caught a morning train and rode it 30 miles to Riomaggiore, the southernmost of the five towns, where we started our hike.

From the Riomaggiore train station, perched high atop the town, we descended the bustling main street, a steep incline lined with cafes and giftshops where the sidewalk turns to steps at times. At the waterfront, the main street becomes a boat ramp, and beyond, in the rocky cove, a few dozen fishing skiffs lie moored to buoys. From the water, the town looks like an immense cubist painting filling the sky with oranges, yellows, reds and pinks. Farther back up main street we found the footpath leading north and started our journey.

Over our three-hour hike we passed farmers tilling their tiny steps of land, vendors selling artisanal drinks, local commuters and fellow

The villages of Cinque Terre, Italy

hikers. As we made our way north, we passed through Manarola, Corniglia, Vernazza, finally reaching Monterosso al Mare, the northernmost of the towns, in time for a late lunch. After six miles of hiking, putting pasta into the kids' mouths was the most effective way to stop the complaining. From Monterosso al Mare, we rode the train back to Santa Margherita Ligure, where we fell back into the boat exhausted.

The following morning, we drove the dinghy a short mile in the opposite direction of the Cinque Terre to one of the most photographed villages on the planet, Portofino. As if this small stretch of coast isn't endowed with enough breathtaking, travel poster beauty, this town provides the dot on the exclamation point. In its sorbet-hued perfection, Portofino looks more like the Italian Pavilion at Epcot Center than a real town. Even the locals look like actors who have been hired to look like locals. With its upscale cafes and boutiques, Portofino is the richer, more refined cousin of the five sisters of the Cinque Terre. Its relatively large natural harbor has given the town strategic significance through the centuries, and today, that same harbor welcomes mega-yachts and the well-to-do who spill out of them into Portofino's quaint streets.

While docked in Santa Margherita Ligure—a beautiful town in its own right but too big to be part of the village circuit—I performed my first real mechanical repair on *Sacre Bleu*. Despite being a fourth-generation mechanical engineer, I never dirtied my hands tinkering with machines. Car engines, lawn mowers, even leaf blowers—with their hundreds of components, none of which seem to have any clear purpose—looked impossibly complex to me. When my car didn't start, I called AAA. Now that I was living on a sailboat, surrounded by thousands of machines each patiently waiting to break down at the possible worst time, I had to find my engineering gene.

The problem first appeared when the generator refused to start. The control panel flashed a cryptic warning, and luckily the owner's manual had the answer. The impeller, a small rubber paddlewheel inside the pump that draws in seawater and pushes it through the generator's cooling system, had worn out. Reaching the impeller inside the generator compartment turned out to be a job for a contortionist. For the 45 minutes I spent performing the repair, I lived in two contrasting worlds. Inside the compartment, lying on my back, head upside down, with most of my weight on one elbow, I was in a dark hell where bolts did not thread and tools vanished. When I pulled myself out of the compartment to let blood flow out of my head and back into my limbs, I was on a sailboat anchored off a charming village on the glamorous Italian Riviera.

After much trial and error, I installed the new impeller, seated the gasket, replaced the pump cover, tightened the bolts, crossed my fingers and started the generator. It ran. "Fixed it," I declared to Valerie, chest pumped appropriately, posturing myself for the shower of praise that did not come because she was deep into a Vitamix recipe. "Fixed it," I said to the kids. The hamsters were out and the kids were too preoccupied to respond.

On the fourth day, ready to move on, we motored into a rainy, blustery morning that, two months prior, might have intimidated us into staying in safe harbor. Now, Valerie and I were now confident enough in our abilities and familiar enough with the boat to carry on. Strong winds no longer deterred us. Strong tailwinds carry you through unpleasantness more quickly. Strong headwinds, and the steep head seas they create, on the other hand, extend the misery. Today, we faced a strong headwind, and the 30-mile run to Porto Venere that should have taken five hours took eight, providing three more hours for mishaps in conditions where mishaps were more likely. With each safe arrival I wondered, were we getting better at this, or did we just get lucky again?

By late afternoon we had reached Porto Venere, a coastal village that, similar to Portofino, is another earth-toned cluster of tall, narrow rowhouses with a natural harbor. Whereas Portofino is crowned by the elegant, peach-colored, baroque-style church, Chiesa di San Giorgio, the austere 13th-century Chiesa di San Pietro, hewn from raw stone, presides from a hilltop above Porto Venere. Approaching the stone church perched on a high stone promontory on a blustery, gray day gave the moment a timeless aura.

Time, however, was marching on. Madeleine and William were not only growing up, they were growing into sailors. Now that we had resumed our family adventure, Valerie and I decided we should give them more responsibilities on the boat. In port, we let them drive the dinghy, and soon we became comfortable sending them on errands to shore by themselves, though the sight of such young children driving a powerboat always turned a few local heads.

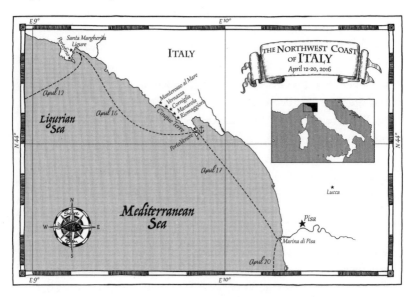

We included them more in the sail raising and lowering operation, which required many hands, sometimes asking them to steer the boat or work the lines, but never a task that might risk their falling overboard. They had also become our anchoring team. Anchoring was safe for kids because we were typically stopped, so there was no urgency if they were to fall overboard. Another advantage to delegating this responsibility is that when Valerie and I anchored, we almost always got into an argument over where to anchor, how much chain to let out, and whether the anchor was properly set. With one of us at the wheel and the other on the bow, the operation required us to shout to be heard over the din of the engines. Inevitably, shouting to be heard degenerated into just plain shouting, and when the engines went silent, the shouting would usually continue. We were happy to delegate this responsibility to our children in hopes it would be done with more maturity.

After choosing a location in Port Venere's natural harbor, the kids anchored the boat like a well-practiced team. We were tired from the long day, but the kids were ready for more, so they drove us ashore in the dinghy to see the dramatic church up close.

April 16, 2016

We woke the next morning to ideal sailing conditions. We were all looking forward to the day's journey, or rather, what lay at its end: Pisa and the famous Leaning Tower. Five hours of sailing on a beam reach and flat seas took us to Porto di Pisa, a recently renovated mega-yacht basin that, on this early spring day, was nearly empty. We were given a slip big enough for six *Sacre Bleu*s, providing stress-free docking for captain and crew.

William was particularly eager to see the famous Leaning Tower, so we wasted no time assembling the folding bikes to make the six-mile ride. We followed the Arno River into town and finally reached the piazza where the famous tower leans, seemingly on the verge of giving up right before your eyes. I had always assumed the tower developed its tilt sometime after it was completed in 1372. Not so. Because of a sorely inadequate foundation, it began to lean soon after builders finished the second floor, so construction was halted. A hundred years and a few wars later, somebody thought it was a good idea to add five more floors *in the leaning position*. Today, countless tourists come from all over the world to see how an engineering failure and a harebrained management decision came together to create an architectural wonder.

After we had seen the Leaning Tower and the adjacent cathedral, we pressed on to another regional curiosity. The nearby town of Lucca has no less than fifty churches within its ancient walls. A train station is never far away in Europe, so we continued our journey by rail, taking our bikes with us. For the first ten churches, we dismounted, locked the bikes and went inside to have a look at its mosaics, statues, dioramas, crypts, intricately carved altars and frescoed walls. Churches eleven through twenty warranted stopping the bikes and taking a well-composed selfie out front. Churches twenty-one through thirty were drive-by's. We trusted that churches thirty-one through fifty were beautiful, and instead we found a pastry shop.

The pastry shop changed our lives in a way that twenty more churches never would have. Here, in Lucca, we tasted our first Italian hot chocolate. A sunny, warm afternoon in April is not exactly a hot chocolate weather, but in Italy, it is a beverage for all seasons. "Beverage" is a misnomer because Italian hot chocolate is closer to pudding. The confection is gooey and rich, dark as coffee, and sets off a chocolate explosion with every spoonful. We had just discovered a new food group.

April 20, 2016

Content that we had explored the area, the next morning, we started the 55-mile run to the island of Elba, where Napoleon was exiled in 1814 after making a lot of powerful enemies and ultimately losing to one of them. As we were entering Portoferraio Harbor, picturesque yet busy, we crossed paths with a Carabinieri boat. The Carabinieri are Italy's national police, and like the gendarmes of France, they have a maritime unit. The boat was approaching us from the left, and according to the International Regulations for Preventing Collisions at Sea, or the so-called Rules of the Road, we had the right of way. But they were Carabinieri, so I slowed down to let them pass. When driving on American roads, I do the same. I let police cars pass even if I have the right of way. It probably annoys them, but I would rather have them in front of me than behind me.

I suspect that the Carabinieri approached me from my port side to test my knowledge as a captain, because as soon as I yielded right of way they turned on the blue lights. As they approached, one of the officers appeared at the rail holding the familiar long-handled net. Knowing this drill well by now, Valerie had the ship's papers in hand and dropped them in. They disappeared inside the ship to examine our documents, leaving two of their young officers on deck to stare at us silently. After twenty minutes, they returned the papers and shoved off. So much for yielding to the police.

On Elba, we toured Napoleon's house, photographed ourselves by his statue striking his signature hand-in-vest pose, browsed the Napoleon gift shop with its Napoleon statuettes and refrigerator magnets, and had our now-daily hot chocolate. I could understand how Elba, an island 11 by 18 miles, consisting of hilltops and rugged coast, might get boring for an overachiever like Napoleon. Nice place to visit, but I wouldn't want to be exiled there.

Back on *Sacre Bleu*, I checked the weather forecast:

DEVELOPING STORM 40°42'49" N, 13°04'53" E MOVING N at 15 KTS. WINDS INCREASING TO 35 KTS, SEAS BUILDING TO 5M.

Seas building to five meters! The forecast called for a system with strong winds and heavy rain in the Tyrrhenian Sea, moving north to Rome in three days. To beat the storm to Rome, we accelerated our plans and continued south to Isola del Giglio early the next morning. After the kids anchored us in the port, we reviewed the weather forecast, got a second opinion from another website, and dinghy'd ashore to get a third opinion from the Italian Coast Guard office. The

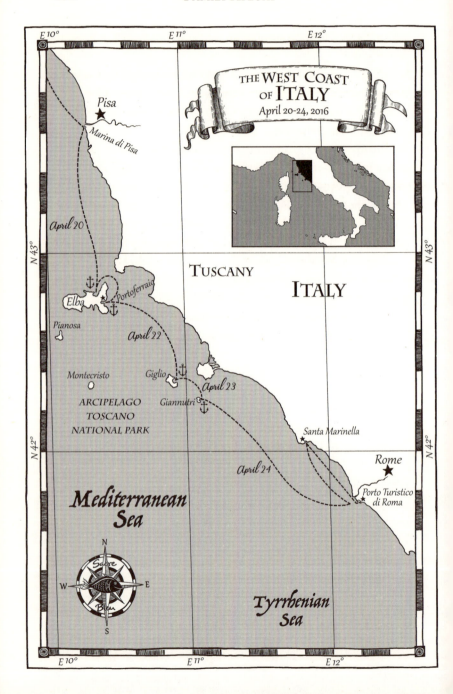

storm seemed to be weakening, so we relaxed and had a look around the island.

Giglio Porto is similar to the many towns we had already passed through with tall, narrow rowhouses painted in every color of the sunset. The port boasted a large fleet of fishing boats with crews busily preparing the vessels for a day's work, or perhaps the approaching storm. We hiked to the center of the island, where on a hilltop sits Giglio Castello, a near-perfect walled medieval town, its hundred or so block homes, large and small, built completely from brownish gray stone and terracotta roof tiles. Back in the port we bought locally caught fish and vegetables that, like us, had probably also ridden to the island by boat.

Hoping to stay ahead of the storm, we departed Giglio that afternoon for Isola di Giannutri, another island about ten miles to the southeast. Giannutri has traded hands between pirates, princes and popes over its two-thousand-year history, and over that time it has remained an undeveloped hideaway. It is the southernmost island in the offshore Arcipelago Toscano National Park, which includes the islands of Giglio, Elba, the equally famous Montecristo, and three other major islands. In Roman mythology, these seven islands off Tuscany are gems from Venus' necklace that have fallen into the sea. Giannutri is more of a diamond in the rough with pristine shorelines and long hiking trails.

April 23, 2016
On our way to Giannutri, the wind shifted onto our nose and the seas built to six feet. Our twin diesel engines were no match for the heavy walls of water crashing into *Sacre Bleu*'s twin bows, and we didn't arrive until midnight. Much like our experience in Port-Cros, the night I received word of my father's death, arriving in Giannutri, another undeveloped island, was like walking into a closet and closing the door. On this cloudless night, water, land and sky were all indistinguishable. Since this was going to be a difficult anchoring job, Valerie and I took over for the kids. With the unyielding southeasterly wind,

the only sheltered area was a patch of water in the southwest corner of the anchorage, an area big enough for one boat.

Unfortunately, that one boat was already there. We wanted to respect their space and anchor as far away as possible, but as we put distance between us and them the water quickly deepened. We found ourselves anchoring in 75 feet of water, a first for us. We would need to let out five times that amount of chain, or 375 feet, to set the anchor properly. I was not sure we had that much chain, but we were about to find out. Three hundred seventy-five feet of chain weighs more than the anchor, so confirming a proper set would be impossible. The good news was that with all that steel in the water, we weren't going anywhere.

Morning came, and the skies were noticeably darker. The unstable weather was an increasing concern for us, but with no mobile phone signal in Giannutri, we had no way of updating the forecast. To make matters worse, the electric capstan abruptly stopped while we were hauling up the anchor. I had visions of putting on scuba gear and sinking 75 feet through cold, dark water to unravel 300 feet of chain wrapped around boulders on the bottom while fending off a giant squid. We discovered that the capstan motor was overheated, so I pulled the remaining chain onto the deck hand over hand. This exercise was better than any workout I paid good money for at a health club. My arms ached for days. Despite the late start, we still anticipated having plenty of time to make Rome before dark.

But as we sailed southeast along the Italian coast, the sky grew more overcast, the headwinds stronger, the waves taller and the water shallower. This last trend, the shallowing water, was the most worrisome. If water is shallow enough and waves are big enough, waves roll over and break. Sailing in breaking waves is an entirely different exercise from sailing in sea swells. When swells roll across the open sea, their energy is oriented up and down. Steering a sailboat through big swells can be like slalom skiing. It can even be fun. However, when a wave breaks, its energy is redirected into a lateral force that pushes boats around like toys. The ski slope turns into a minefield. In daylight, it's stressful; at night, it's terrifying.

By midday, our progress had slowed to a crawl. We turned on the second engine in hopes that we could still make Rome before sunset. The wind was now 20 knots in our face, the seas were ten feet, the skies were completely overcast, and the water had shallowed up to 30 feet. We instructed the kids to stay in their beds to minimize chances of their getting hurt, or worse, falling overboard. Madeleine simply transported the project—kirigami, drawing, homeschooling—to her cabin. William, on the other hand, was immobilized by rough seas and would lie on his bed with a bowl by his side. Staying inside maximized both their chances of getting seasick, but we preferred cleaning up that mess to setting a broken arm. In the stress of managing a sailboat in a storm, the last thing we needed was an injury. Catastrophes are frequently the end result of a series of cascading problems: the weather deteriorates, the ship is not battened down, a crewmember gets hurt, another crewmember assists—leaving less crew for boat management—the skipper is multitasking, and suddenly the boat runs aground. In heavy weather sailing, it's critical to recognize the start of a cascade and shut it down.

I peeked at the cruising guide for Italy and saw that sunset was at 8:06 p.m. It was four in the afternoon; we had four hours to cover 18 nautical miles before darkness set in. We were progressing at about four knots. At that pace, we would get to Rome with a little light left in the sky, on a low tide, making the shallower water at the harbor entrance more likely to produce large, possibly breaking waves. This entry promised to be worse than Porto.

Rome's ancient port off the Tiber River, Ostia Antica, where her mighty navy took shelter from the same kind of Mediterranean storms we faced tonight, was silted in centuries ago. The modern Porto Turistico di Roma was built in 2001 next to the mouth of the Tiber. Consisting of a semicircle of boulders enclosing a basin with room for 800 boats, the new marina was dropped directly on the beach, just an arrow shot from the ancient port. Arriving vessels enter through a 100-foot-wide opening in the breakwater.

At about six o'clock, the harbor entrance appeared off our port bow. The depth sounder read just 25 feet, and the swells around us were collapsing into piles of white foam. We worried that the water was already too shallow and dared not get any closer. The winds had now backed around to the west, blowing straight onto shore and hurling big waves onto the breakwater. Hovering directly west of the harbor mouth, we considered making a straight run into the harbor with the following seas. We hailed the harbormaster on the radio and heard nothing but static, so we inched closer for better reception. Three miles out, I grabbed the binoculars, drew a bead on the entrance of the port, and saw something that made my stomach sink. All around the semi-circular breakwater, white explosions shot 30 feet into the sky before being carried away by the wind.

After a few more tries on the radio, the harbormaster finally answered our call. In broken English, he told us the port was closed and gave us peremptory instructions to stay away from the harbor entrance. Once again, we were caught in a decaying situation—sun setting, wind strengthening, seas building—with no Plan B. We had only one direction to run, north, away from the storm, so we frantically studied the chart, hoping to see an alternate port somewhere, anywhere. Five, ten, fifteen miles, and still the chart revealed nothing. Then we saw Santa Marinella, our only alternative, 26 miles away. At five knots, it would take us five hours if all went well, and things were not going well.

We turned north again, putting the wind and waves directly on our beam. The waves smashed into our port side as if we were a seawall, rolling us and pushing us sideways. From the flybridge, behind the protection of clear plastic and the canvas, I scanned the darkness and worried about rogue waves lurking out there. How far would we roll over if one hit us? With capsizing on my mind, I called the kids out of their cabins and up onto the bridge deck. I was breaking our golden rule about keeping them inside during night passages, but I was more concerned about how we might reach them in their cabins if a large wave were to flip the boat. We intentionally did not clip our safety har-

nesses into the jack lines because being clipped onto the deck is also a problem if the boat turns turtle and the top becomes the bottom.

With the right combination of sail, wind, and waves, nearly any sailboat can get knocked down. As a boy sailing a Hobie Cat on the Chesapeake Bay, I capsized routinely. Before we settled on buying a catamaran, I read everything I could about their chances of capsizing. With high performance catamarans like those in the America's Cup, or even some high-end recreational catamarans, capsizing is possible if the helmsman is not careful. With recreational cats like ours, the rig is not strong enough to flip the boat over on its side. The boat is too heavy, and the mast and rigging would simply break. Large side waves generally will not capsize a recreational cat because the keels are shallow, and the boat will slip sideways rather than dig into the water and flip over the way a high-performance catamaran with deep keels might. That night off Rome, riding bare-pole (with no sails up), we knew the chances of capsizing were remote, but with every wave that slammed into our hull, the possibility seemed more real.

In the dark, raging seascape I could make out much larger waves rising up and breaking into avalanches of white foam. I said to Valerie, "If one of those waves breaks over us, we're screwed." With that, Valerie, looking beyond me, said "Oh, shit," as a mountain of water emerged from the darkness and crashed over the boat, burying the forward deck in white foam and green water. *Sacre Bleu* rolled slightly to starboard and slipped sideways with a shudder. It was at that moment, oddly enough, that I stopped worrying. Neptune had given us everything he had, and all he got from us was a little roll. Although we were going to be spending another damp, windy, cold night at the helm, I took comfort in knowing that we were going to make it.

The rest of the rollercoaster ride up the coast was stressful but manageable. All through the storm, up on the flybridge, the kids were quiet as a picture. They had not seen mom and dad quite so anxious before, and they were feeling it themselves.

We reached the shelter of the port of Santa Marinella in the shadow of imposing Castello Odescalchi di Santa Marinella at midnight and tucked in among a mix of small fishing and recreational boats. Unlike most of our ports of call, Santa Marinella had no mega-yachts, or any yachts to speak of. A cruising sailboat like ours is an oddity. Designed to accommodate workboats coming and going in all weather conditions, it was a haven on this night because its breakwater was oriented in such a way that entering vessels could find protection behind a large seawall before the trickier part of negotiating the port's entry.

Wet, cold and exhausted, we were too worked up to go to sleep right away. Feeling like we had just walked away from a train wreck, Valerie and I stayed up a while longer talking about what we had just experienced. Too tired to take her raincoat off, hair in a tangle, Valerie settled into the settee and admitted that there were moments when she was scared. If she was, she didn't show it. Despite the fear and frustrations of our long day, we retired that night better sailors, and, in a strange way, that made it one of the best days of the cruise. We had been tested by conditions that were far more challenging than any we had encountered before, but our five months of cruising had prepared us. We were on a learning curve that was steep enough to be challenging, but not so steep that we were going to fall off.

In Jules Verne's novel, *Twenty Thousand Leagues Under the Seas*, Captain Nemo's futuristic submarine, the *Nautilus*, displayed on its name plate the Latin motto *Mobilis in mobili*, roughly translated as "moving within the moving element" or "changing in the changes." That morning in Santa Marinella, we had finally achieved mobilis in mobili. Here we were in a town that was not part of the plan, and a town that was not known for anything in particular, at least not in the guidebooks. Santa Marinella gave us a delightfully refreshing peek into untouristed Italy, and Valerie and I decided we needed more unplanned stops like this. That was the gift the storm brought us.

I checked the weather forecast that afternoon and confirmed that the storm was passing, but another storm was looming, leaving us a weather window of only a few hours. This second system was larger and could potentially keep us in Santa Marinella for several more days. We were forced to choose between leaving for Rome at midnight or staying in Santa Marinella until the second storm blew through. We contacted Rome and confirmed that the port would indeed be letting vessels in, at least until the second storm arrived. How big was the window, how strong was the storm, and when would the port close again? A weather forecast is only an educated guess, and we had to make an educated guess based on an educated guess.

At 11:30 p.m., in the quiet of night, we departed Santa Marinella. The seas were flat, the winds were but a puff, and the boiling fury from the evening before was now placid darkness. At four in the morning, anticlimactically, we motored into Porto Turistico di Roma, tied up in front of the completely dark harbormaster's office and slept until the harbormaster woke us up with a loud knock on the side of the hull. He did not speak English, and our Italian was rudimentary, so the discussion we wanted to have about the previous night's storm and our near-arrival and subsequent detour was reduced to a simple, inadequate "Ciao." He boarded an inflatable boat and signaled for us to follow him to our slip.

Rome was a city we had all dreamed of seeing. For me, Rome is an immersive history lesson. I looked forward to standing in the footsteps of emperors, touching the walls that gladiators touched, walking where chariots raced. Valerie loved what modern Rome represents: food, fashion, and living in the moment. Madeleine was looking forward to seeing some of the famous works of art, and William had Julius Caesar's grave on the top of his list.

Despite our late night and early morning, we boarded one of Italy's ridiculously convenient trains that afternoon for Vatican City. Approaching St. Peter's Square, we saw a large gathering and stepped off to see what was up. Today happened to be Wedding Wednesday, or Sposi Novelli, the weekly event where the Pope blesses newlyweds, with hundreds of brides in flowing white gowns. Standing on a dais in his distinctive white robe and zucchetto skull cap was the supreme pontiff himself, Pope Francis. After the blessing, he mingled with the brides and grooms, setting off a small stampede. In our first five minutes in Rome, we managed to get a papal viewing. The children had now seen a prince and a pope. We were checking a lot of boxes.

Over the next morning's coffee, while I was savoring my internet connection and catching up on news, a story about a sailor's death at sea caught my eye. Manfred Fritz Bajorat was a German in his late fifties sailing solo in a 40-foot sloop off the Philippines. Fishermen discovered his boat drifting in the open ocean, and when they boarded it, to their horror, they found the captain in a mummified state. The article included a photo of Bajorat, hair still perfectly combed, slumped over at his desk as if he had given up the ghost while paying his bills. The forensics experts estimated that he had been drifting for many weeks, though how many could not be determined because the dry salty air had done such an effective job at preserving him. I showed Valerie the article and said, "How hard could ocean sailing be? This guy managed to do it for weeks, weathering storms and avoiding collisions, and he was *dead*."

The next day, we toured ancient Rome, starting with the Colosseum. When it comes to history, I have an affinity for banal details that might provide insight into what the past was really like. Waiting in line to enter the Colosseum, I saw Roman numerals chiseled into the stone over each of the entrances. Our tour guide informed us that, like modern stadiums, each seat and sector of the Colosseum had a number, and though the show was free, a ticket was required to get in. I pictured scalpers, tailgate parties and overpriced concessions.

Walking the timeworn paths of the Forum, it was easy to imagine Rome's ancient citizens treading on these very stones for the same reasons that still put us on a city sidewalk: a quick lunch, a business meeting or a run to the market.

We visited the Pantheon, high on William's list because it is an engineering marvel; the Spanish Steps, where Valerie wanted to take a family portrait; and the Trevi Fountain, where we indulged in the tradition of throwing coins into the water—always with the right hand over the left shoulder—and making a wish. William declared that he wanted to live in Rome later in life once we released him into the wild. He was awed by the scale of the structures that could be created with simple blocks of stone. For him, Rome was a giant Lego installment. For Madeleine, the sheer volume of human creativity on display in Rome broadened her perspective of her own art. More than any place we had been so far Rome opened up the world for her.

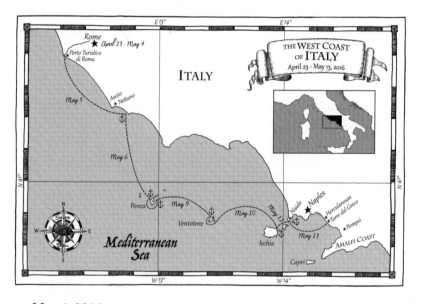

May 4, 2016

We departed Porto Turistico di Roma after a week being tourists in a glamorous, world-class city. It was time to become sailors again. With near-perfect sailing conditions in flat seas and 15-knot breezes, our enormous, bulging code zero sail pulled *Sacre Bleu* through the water like a team of horses, leaving a wake that vanished almost instantly, erasing any trace of our journey as quickly as the present was becoming the past. I noted today's sailing conditions in the ship's log, a journal of discrete daily snapshots of our trip, so that the past would not vanish completely. We sailed by Anzio, the site of the ill-fated Allied invasion during World War II, and I was reminded that not all history in the Mediterranean is ancient.

That evening, we anchored off the town of Nettuno, far away from the city lights, hoping to get a good night's sleep, but it was not to be. At two in the morning, we woke to an intense light shining onto the aft cockpit, lighting up the salon. My initial thought was that we were being abducted by aliens, so I chose a shirt and shorts suitable for presenting a friendly demeanor to visitors from another planet, and I went out to investigate. Twenty feet from our stern a large gray patrol boat hovered, with black letters on its hull that read "GUARDIA di FINANZA." We had met the Carabinieri, and now it was time to meet Italian customs.

Valerie joined me on deck. When we saw that the patrol boat about twice the size of *Sacre Bleu* was preparing to tie up next to us, we both frantically broke out all the fenders from the storage lockers and positioned them before the boat slammed into us. Maritime law enforcement may be good at law enforcement, but they are notoriously bad at seamanship. Once we were rafted up, two officers dressed in navy blue coveralls jumped onto our boat. Through the beam of their flashlights they inspected the mess in the galley sink, the improvised Lego structures on the dining table, the two hamsters—spinning away on their wheels oblivious to the drama—and concluded that *Sacre Bleu* was not a threat to the financial security of the European Union. As I was rifling through the nav station looking for the ship's papers, they disappeared as quickly as they had arrived.

Under way again the next morning, we continued our island-hopping itinerary and set a course for Isola di Ponza. William, our resident scholar of classical antiquities, pointed out that Isola di Ponza might well be the mythical island of Aeaea from Homer's *Odyssey*. The pinkish-yellow cliffs that ring most of the island are riddled with caves and grottos, any one of which might have concealed Circe the sorceress, who reputedly turned Odysseus' crew into pigs. As we were learning with every glance in the mirror at our knotted hair and slept-in shirts, this transformation is not necessarily a supernatural phenomenon and could befall anyone who spends too much time on a boat.

We anchored off Ponza—another fine job by our young anchoring team—and rode the dinghy in to get a closer look at the island's arches, natural bridges, caves, and grottos. On this run, we let the kids take turns driving, and we all had fun zooming along the coast in big waves, getting soaked and bruised but enjoying every bump and splash. Until now we had been using the dinghy mostly for grocery runs and other errands, frequently with the kids driving. They enjoyed these utilitarian missions, but only when dinghy driving had no purpose did it truly become fun.

May 9, 2016

At Isola d'Ischia, an island farther down the coast, our collective anchoring skills finally betrayed us. As we approached, a picture-perfect medieval castle perched atop a rocky islet came into view. With its imposing walls, towers, windowed banquet rooms, and chapel, all seemingly chiseled out of the rocky island, Castello Aragonese looks more like a fantasy than a real fortress. We just *had* to spend the night there. The kids dropped the anchor, I backed the boat down, and we felt the familiar tug. The boat was safely settled in for the night, so we prepared to go ashore.

After setting the anchor, I confirm it's not dragging by scanning the shoreline for two reference points, one behind the other. If you can stand on your deck and line up the closer tree with the farther hilltop, then your boat must sit on the extended line defined by those two points. In navigation, this is called a transit. After we drop the anchor and let some time pass, if that tree and hilltop are still lined up, then we are still sitting on that transit line, so I relax.

That day, as we went through our usual departure drill before going ashore to visit the castle, I saw that the boat had moved off its transit; we were dragging anchor. On recent stops, as we pulled the anchor off the bottom, we were bringing up more and more seagrass with it. Seagrass, especially the shag carpet-thick seagrass in the Med, aptly named Neptune grass, provides just enough resistance to give sailors that anchored feeling, but it won't let anchors dig in. Luckily, we happened to be on the boat, awake, in the middle of the day for our first anchor dragging. Most anchors pick a supremely inconvenient time to try this trick on you. Maybe we didn't have a playful anchor.

Hoping our second try would be better, we dinghy'd off. But I was not at ease. Castello Aragonese afforded a sweeping view of the anchorage, and with every embrasure I passed, I peeked through to check on the boat. Truth be told, I never trusted the concept of anchoring. Use an 80-pound hook and a length of chain to keep your multi-ton boat from floating away, possibly forever. Blindly drop it over the side and tug on it. If it tugs back, you're good. Somehow it's been working for centuries—most of the time.

The walled fortress was a small village in its day, housing a convent, an abbey, a bishop, a prince, his court, a garrison of soldiers, and the usual contingent of knights, jesters, ladies-in-waiting and lords a-leaping. With a torture chamber and a decomposition room where the dead were kept until their bones were fit to be relocated to an ossuary, Castello Aragonese delivered medieval weirdness in spades, appealing to the entire family's morbid curiosities.

William, of course, became obsessed with the topic of human decomposition. Over lunch at a restaurant in the nearby town, he peppered me with questions about the bodies on the *Titanic*: what they looked like and whether they were still wearing clothing. As I dismembered a chicken with my knife and fork, I tried not to imagine a dark, foreboding space with free floating bodies dressed in 1912 clothing, some wearing their formal attire from that evening's dinner, others in their White Star Line uniforms, the band members still clutching their musical instruments, the tuba player wearing wire-rim glasses. I failed and gave up on the chicken.

May 12, 2016

We departed Isola d'Ischia and motor-sailed south through the Gulf of Naples under light breezes and flat seas, passing the city of Naples on our port side, while off to starboard, the island of Capri loomed behind a shroud of haze. We were approaching the storied Amalfi Coast, with its enchanting hillside towns and their designer boutiques and five-star restaurants. The marina prices on this stretch of glamorous real estate are also five star, ranging from two- to three-hundred euros a night, so we stopped short and scanned the chart for alternatives. Valerie found a marina closer to Naples that was a relative bargain, in the fishing village of Torre del Greco.

The kids dropped the anchor, I gently backed *Sacre Bleu* into a tight space between two fishing trawlers, the kids joined Valerie to help fasten the stern lines to the dock, and we all assessed our new home. Just behind us was a chain-link fence keeping a diverse array of locals at bay, from children kicking soccer balls to teenagers smoking cigarettes to older men fishing. The security camera actually made me feel less safe because I wondered why they needed it, whether it was working and if someone was watching on the other end.

The local yacht club, Circolo Nautico Torre Del Greco, lay fifty feet away at the end of our dock. That night, they literally opened the yacht club for us. We walked through the front door, held open by the manager on duty, and found ourselves in a spacious but empty lobby. The manager gestured for us to ascend the elegant staircase to the dining room, where we had our pick of thirty empty tables. The maître d' ushered us to a table overlooking the water, allowing me to keep a stray eye on the boat the entire dinner. We were seated only a moment before a waiter appeared to take our drink orders, with another server close on his heels with glasses of water. They allowed twenty seconds to go by before sending the sommelier with the wine menu. Soon, the waiter reappeared to take our dinner orders, and the rest of the evening progressed at a similar tempo. At the end of the evening, we had made a dozen new friends, and said *grazie* and *buona notte* to each one individually on our way out.

The next day, we caught a train to the modern city of Pompeii, which is adjacent to the ancient archeological site. From there we took a bus to the foot of Mt. Vesuvius and climbed up to the rim. With the steaming caldera behind us and the long slope leading down to ancient Pompeii in front of us, we imagined that cataclysmic morning in AD 79.

The famous eruption that killed most of Pompeii's residents buried the Roman city in ash and small pellets of pumice. This not only protected Pompeii from weather and looters through the centuries, it also protected the city from progress, the force most responsible for erasing the physical evidence of the ancient world. Unlike virtually every other site of antiquity that has been abandoned and left to decay or be dismantled and scavenged and ultimately buried under centuries of development, life in Pompeii stopped in time one morning, entombed in lightweight pumice pellets that acted like packing peanuts. Its preserved state cannot be truly appreciated without physically walking its streets and appreciating details: the wheel ruts left in the paving stones by decades of wagon and cart traffic, or the open kitchens with tiled countertops that served hot street food to passersby.

The following day, we visited Herculaneum, Pompeii's less-famous sister city that suffered the same fate. Ancient Herculaneum is embedded in and surrounded by the modern city of Ercolano. The constant tension between preservation and progress is far more evident in this modern beach town, where real estate is at a premium. In many ways, it is better preserved than Pompeii because the volcanic ash, having cooled some by the time it reached Herculaneum, carbonized rather than incinerated wooden doors, beams, furniture, and even loaves of bread, all of which are on display. Some of my attempts at bread have come out of the oven looking much worse.

The magical island of Capri was the last must-see item on our list in the Gulf of Naples. We considered sailing to Capri instead of taking the ferry, but the ocean swells were formidable that day, and the Capri marina was charging €350 a night for a patch of water. Now that we were an experienced sailing family, we were not intimidated by the big waves, but we were still cheap. We had heard that a train strike was imminent, so we woke early and rushed to catch the last train to Naples, where the Capri ferry departed. The question of how we would get back to Torre del Greco did not concern us much after navigating a violent storm in a small boat. The passage off Rome was a watershed experience for us as a family, and we had become much more intrepid and confident as travelers. Our adventure now had a clean break: before Rome and after Rome. William's one-word answer about his worst day on the boat: "Rome."

The ferry ride started off well enough. The 150-foot, three-decked ship was packed with about a hundred passengers, most of them seated in rows in the forward part of the ship. As the ferry departed and cleared the breakwater, it immediately began pitching in the heavy seas. The ship climbed over the first wave and dipped into the trough, and all the passengers gave out an "ooh!" and an "ah!" as if they were on a giant amusement park ride. Children screamed and parents feigned wide-eyed fear, drinks were spilled and toys were dropped, giggles erupted, and a spirit of fun and adventure filled the air. The next swell was bigger, and the "ooh's" and "ah's" were louder and even more joyous in response. As we got farther out to sea, the swells got progressively larger and the sea spray was hitting the windows three decks up with startling force. The chorus of "ooh's" and "ah's" gradually went silent as everyone realized it was not an amusement park ride. It was a ship in heavy seas, and we were on it.

For the Toomeys, this white-knuckle ride through frighteningly violent open sea was just another day in the life of a family afloat, and a relatively carefree one because somebody else was driving the boat. William, who was gradually becoming inured to seasickness, never looked up from his book. Madeleine stayed focused on navigating Mario safely through his Nintendo world, collecting coins and stomping on enemies, while the ship's captain wrestled his 3,000-ton ferryboat through mountainous waves. With every stomach-churning dip, more and more passengers became seasick. After a while, it seemed we were the only four souls on the manifest not heaving our breakfast. In desperate situations where cool heads are scarce, Valerie loves to step in and fill the void. I admire this quality in her, except when she drags me into her heroics. Soon enough, the Toomeys were walking the aisles like nurses in a battlefield hospital, calmly handing vomit bags to all interested parties. Some passengers assumed we were on the ship's payroll and handed full vomit bags back to us, with not the least bit of embarrassment. We answered their appeals with a "keep your vomit" look and kept moving.

At Marina Grande, on the northeast coast of Capri, the ferryboat discharged a hundred green-faced passengers into the streets. A funicular transported the new arrivals up about 500 feet in elevation to Capri town in less than five minutes. It was a remarkable piece of 110-year-old infrastructure that ran like a ride at Disney World. A bargain at two euros, the funicular so delighted the kids that I was tempted to take them down and up again. Then Valerie saw the designer boutiques lining the streets of Capri town.

We inevitably made it into the Louis Vuitton boutique, and after seeing the breathtaking prices I wondered, who would buy a Louis Vuitton purse on a visit to Capri? "Price be damned, I need a fancy purse now!" These were not people who remotely resembled my wife. Valerie loves her luxuries, but only after carefully considering her options and contemplating the role this new item would play in her life, a process that can take hours and drive store clerks to tears.

After considering more extravagances that we had no intention of indulging in, we boarded a bus to Anacapri, a smaller town a couple miles to the west. Ahead of us lay the highlight of our trip to this island of romance and intrigue, both fictional and real. In Anacapri we caught a chairlift to the top of Monte Solaro, where we could take in the entire south coast with its sheer cliff faces, natural arches, and rocky outcrops shooting vertically out of the water like breaching whales that had turned to stone. At the foot of the cliffs is the aptly named Marina Piccola (Italian for "small marina"), where I had considered mooring *Sacre Bleu* before we opted to take the ferry. Fortunately, that really bad idea was never executed. The marina was tiny, and even if there had been space for us, docking there would have left us at the base of a towering cliff with nowhere to go but straight up. I was maturing as a captain, developing an inner voice that alerted me to bad ideas before my wife's voice did the same.

The ferry ride back to Naples was far calmer, and the train strike was over, so getting back to Torre del Greco and the boat was delightfully boring. It was an exhausting day, but an efficient one. We had thoroughly explored Capri, a destination that Valerie and I had put near the top of our list when we were planning the cruise. Though Capri did not disappoint, seeing it the way we did, as another stop along the Italian coast, we found it far more crowded with tourists. Apparently, Capri is near the top of a lot of lists.

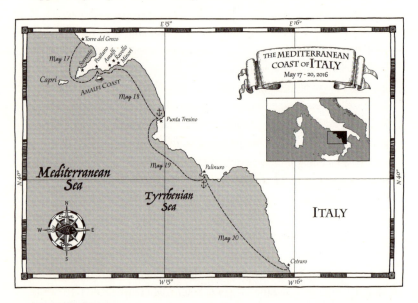

May 17, 2016

We got an early start for the Amalfi Coast, which, like Cinque Terre to the north, is a UNESCO World Heritage Site that not only includes the villages but the entire stretch of coast between them. Today's destination was Positano, the first of a dozen towns that cling to the cliffs along this picturesque coastline, a collection that includes Sorrento, Amalfi, Ravello and Minori.

We planned to anchor off Positano, but we did not know what to expect when we got to this glamorous playground of the rich and famous. How feasible was anchoring? The chart indicated that the bottom was rock and the water was deep. As we were getting good at improvising, we simply shoved off. Just two weeks earlier, in the chaos of the storm off Rome, I had resolved to always have a Plan B, but lately we did not seem to even have a Plan A.

As we cast off the lines, the lonely staff at the yacht club assembled on the balcony and waved goodbye. We answered with a few honks from our shrill air horn, which gave our stately yacht a falsetto voice, like a great Dane with the yelp of a terrier. It was wrong and distinctly unnautical. On occasions like this, I wished we had a cannon.

Our four hours of motoring included a stop to put on dive gear and untangle a plastic bag from the propeller. I saw that white plastic grocery bag coming a mile away, but I did not bother to steer around it, thinking that it could not possibly pose a problem. When a severe wobble developed on one side of the boat, I knew I had somehow beat the odds. I should not have been surprised. I have traveled to some of the remotest corners of the planet, including the bottom of the ocean in a submarine, and everywhere I have gone I have found that white plastic grocery bags have gotten there before me.

On our early afternoon arrival, we discovered that anchoring off Positano was restricted to mega-yachts with reservations. Commoners were required to use the mooring balls closer to shore. That simplified the plan. For this primate, it was nice to have just one branch on the decision tree to swing on. The exorbitant mooring fee included a "free" water taxi, so we jumped in and rode to the town dock. Positano wafted glamor and charm out of its manhole covers, and walking its enchanting streets made Valerie and me feel like two characters in a romance novel, albeit two characters followed around by their two children. Madeleine and William tended to evaluate our ports of call based on the quality of the pizza, but even they were smitten by Positano's beauty. As the weeks went by, as we passed through one captivating place after another, the kids were spending less time in their own world and more time appreciating the world around them.

The following morning, we climbed aboard a bus that carried us through many of the villages on the Amalfi Coast. It ran along a harrowing catwalk of a coastal road carved out of the rocky cliff, barely wide enough for one vehicle. Looking out the cliffside windows, we could see neither the road nor the cliff, creating the illusion that we were flying. Because the road theoretically ran both ways, the bus had to occasionally stop and back up to let oncoming traffic pass, a maneuver that brought the terror to an entirely new level. We rode the bus as far as Amalfi town, kissed blessed Mother Earth, and then found hot chocolate.

Like many other villages on this stretch, Amalfi is a town of stairs. The bus stop was near the waterfront, roughly at sea level, and all paths led straight uphill. The highlight was the cathedral, Cattedrale di Sant'Andrea, an ornate Byzantine structure sitting atop another 150 steps, perched on high like heaven itself. Even the promise of seeing the relics of St. Andrew himself was not enough to motivate William to make the ascent. "I'm not going up all those stairs to see another church," proclaimed William stubbornly planting his feet. His sentiment was echoed resoundingly by his sister. So we sat on the first step and watched other families approach, stop, contemplate the stairway much like we did and have conversations much like ours.

The next morning, we cast off the mooring lines and drove south along the Amalfi coast. With *Sacre Bleu* on autopilot, the four of us sat on the port side watching the towns go by in what was one of the most memorable sailing legs of the entire voyage. We had explored these towns ashore, where we appreciated their details up close—a farmer's market, the inscription in a monument, the façade of a church. Sailing offshore gave us a perspective that few visitors enjoy—a village clinging to a cliff, a strategically placed watch tower, a secluded beach. In the days that followed, we worked our way farther south, anchoring off Punta Tresino and Palinuro. Fives weeks in, Italy was feeling familiar, downright comfortable. We had learned some Italian (including hand gestures), broadened the range of our culinary skills (Madeleine became a pizza chef), and found that wines made with Nebbiolo grapes were our favorite. Navigation in Italy also required some acculturation. Restrictions posted on the nautical chart, such as speed limits or the boundaries of marine reserves, were largely ignored even by the commercial boats.

At Cetraro, we eased into a small harbor in to buy fuel and ended up staying the night, sharing an otherwise empty fueling dock with a wooden sloop. Valerie, being the ship's extrovert, walked over to say hello, and on her return she declared that a nice German family was coming over for drinks. That evening, a young couple and their three children, ages two, five, and nine, appeared at our passerelle, dad with a guitar, mom with a violin, and the oldest child with a melodica. They were the Grateful Dead meets The Partridge Family. They regaled us with folk music in vocal harmonies and rhythmic precision. Even the two- and five-year-old joined in, clapping their tiny hands. An unexpected benefit of living on a boat was these continuous encounters with others living on their boats, many of whom were unapologetic outliers. I wondered if we looked that way to our friends back home, and whether I cared.

From Cetraro, we continued along the west coast of Italy another 50 nautical miles to Tropea, whose stunning beaches seem to be lounged on strictly by Italians. The mouth of the harbor is close to the shoreline, and vessels must drive along the beach, parallel to the surf, in the run-up to the entrance. The waves were near breaking, and *Sacre Bleu* rolled as each one passed under her keels. As we made for the entrance, I noticed another catamaran approaching from our starboard side. Although the other boat technically had the right of way—because it was approaching from the right—I was confident we were going to enter the harbor first with room to spare. Then the other catamaran caught a wave and surfed right in front of us, forcing me to throw our boat into reverse. In surfer slang, this is known as dropping in, and it's considered bad form. But we were not surfing, we were driving multi-ton sailboats, and the Italians tend to drive them like Vespas.

On the boot that represents the Italian peninsula, we were sailing along the instep, approaching the toe. Between the toe and the island of Sicily to the west lies a two-mile-wide stretch of water called the Strait

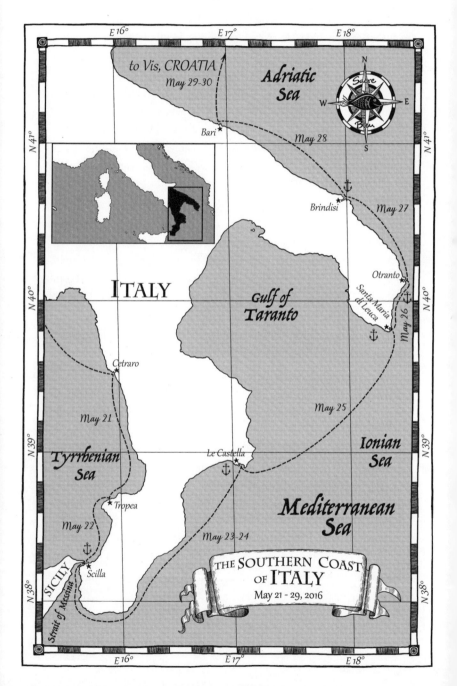

of Messina, which connects the Tyrrhenian Sea to the north with the Ionian Sea to the south. For the ancient Greeks, navigating this stretch of water meant keeping their distance between two sea monsters: the voracious six-headed Scylla and the whirlpool-inducing Charybdis. According to legend, Charybdis swallowed copious volumes of water three times a day, as well as any ships that happened to be nearby. Scylla, on the other hand, rose from the water without warning and devoured crew right off the deck of a ship. It's no wonder the Greeks were never big recreational boaters. Odysseus, in his attempted passage through the Strait, took care not to get too close to Charybdis only to end up too close to Scylla, and he lost six of his crew to her six gaping mouths. The cruising guide did not mention Scylla or Charybdis, but it did provide a warning about whirlpools and currents, with some technical jargon about semidiurnal tides and vortices. Maybe its editors did not want to alarm us.

Just to tease the gods, the night before our transit through the Strait, we anchored under the Rock of Scilla, in the very backyard of the mythical six-headed sea monster herself. "Dad, this is quite possibly your worst idea yet," warned William, after consulting his *Percy Jackson—The Sea of Monsters* edition. Madeleine rolled her eyes. I was more concerned with the tide and the current it produced through this two-mile bottleneck. To catch the tide at the right time to push us south, we had to be underway by 5:30 am. Why isn't it ever 8:30, just after breakfast?

As glimmers of morning sunlight broke over the Rock of Scilla and the ramparts of Castello Ruffo di Calabria, a fortress built by the Dukes of Calabria to maintain control of this strategic point of land. I scanned my surroundings for signs of the supernatural and concluded the sea monsters were still asleep. We drove south under both engines, anticipating a sudden encounter with strong currents or whirlpools lurking beneath the deceptively calm sea. Eddies and whirlpools not much bigger than what we witness in our own bathrooms appeared and disappeared on the surface of the water, having no effect on the boat. We were in the company of several huge oil tankers and container ships, also riding the southbound current.

Flush with the confidence of sailing these many months, we were now improvising our float plan, not thinking much about where we would spend that night until we were underway. The weather was our only concern, and the forecast looked good. Now, studying the chart, we realized the first suitable anchorage was too close, and the next was over 120 miles away. We girded ourselves to sail another 20 hours.

We passed through the Strait of Messina and rounded the toe of Italy early that afternoon, working our way northeast along the sole of the boot. We were now in the Ionian Sea, with the rugged southern coast of Italy on our port side, making great time in a stiff breeze. As the sun set, the wind climbed beyond 20 knots, so we reefed the mainsail.

I took the first watch because Valerie doesn't mind being up late, but she hates waking up early. That meant I got the eight-to-midnight slot, and then again at four in the morning. At midnight, Valerie appeared on the flybridge to take the watch, but the weather was decaying, so I stayed with her in case she needed a second set of hands. We sat on the bridge, taking comfort in each other's company on a lonely, starless night, five miles off the coast of southern Italy, as heavy seas, 25-knot winds and driving rain pummeled the canvas over our heads. Suddenly, the cave-like darkness turned to blinding white daylight. A spotlight originating not one hundred feet off our port side was sizing us up, piercing the sheets of rain as its intense beam quickly scanned every part of the boat, starting at the bow, up the mast, and finally to the stern, where it lit up our U.S. flag. Just as suddenly, the spotlight vanished into the darkness. It was obviously a patrol boat.

At that moment, we both realized that when we rounded the toe of Italy, with clear water between us and North Africa, we had entered the refugee zone, and, consequently, a heavily patrolled area both day and night, regardless of weather conditions. I recalled other cruisers warning us about sailing in these waters. Human traffickers do not use navigation lights, of course, so night encounters are impossible to avoid. Bad weather like tonight's provided the best cover for traffickers, but it made the crossing that much more dangerous, and they were known to rush boats to rid themselves of their human cargo at sea rather than risk making landfall. According to the United Nations Convention of the Law of the Sea, in an encounter such as this, we would be obliged to take the refugees onboard. With every breaking wave off our bow looking like a refugee boat, our night watch suddenly became very quiet and tense.

May 24, 2016
After a long night of reefing and unreefing the sails, and, thankfully, no confrontations with human smugglers, the storm finally passed leaving us a calm sea to complete our transit. In the morning light, we dropped anchor off Le Castella, a small town on Italy's southern coast with a storybook-perfect castle, set on an island just offshore, built in the 15th century to protect the village from Turkish pirates. We did not take the dinghy to land and explore, as was usually our custom in a new place; we simply went to bed. We stayed on anchor for another 24 hours, napping frequently, hoping to find the night of sleep we had lost in the Ionian Sea.

Getting a late start the next day, we made the 77-mile run across the Gulf of Taranto, sailing from the ball of the foot, cutting across the very high arch to the tip of the heel, arriving in the town of Santa Maria di Leuca that evening. The town has a distinctly North African look to it, with low, flat-roofed buildings hewn from yellowish-pink stone and a line of royal palms running along its waterfront. That evening, Valerie and I rode the dinghy into town, leaving the kids on anchor to make a pasta dinner and watch a movie. Pasta and a movie were the standard bribe when we wanted an adult night out, and it was an offer they always eagerly accepted. While the children watched *Guardians of the Galaxy*, the adults savored their dinner ashore.

The next morning, we rounded the heel of Italy, and made our way up the east coast, crossing an imaginary line into the Adriatic Sea, on a course for Brindisi, a city on Italy's east coast. Valerie and I studied the chart and the calendar; the time was passing much more quickly than the miles. We decided that after six weeks in Italy, it was time to make the hop to Croatia.

10

Young Countries, Ancient Histories

Croatia
May 30, 2016

We sailed into Italy knowing what we were getting into. Italian food, fashion, cars and other aspects of the culture are part of life in America. In varying degrees, France, Spain and Portugal were all familiar as well. Croatia is different. Croatia is Eastern European. Croatia has a Socialist past, a recent war, and was complicated geopolitically. Until we dropped into a chandlery to buy a Croatian courtesy flag, we didn't even know it looked like. Somewhere in the middle of the Adriatic Sea, we sailed out of our comfort zone.

The 150-mile crossing of the Adriatic Sea took a full day. We made landfall at the town of Komiža, on the island of Vis, the first Croatian territory with customs facilities on our route north. Immediately, we got to know Croatia's distinctness. Komiža is more architecturally homogenous than Italian towns, and more orderly, and Croatians dressed more casually. This former member of the Eastern Bloc is now part of the European Union but, unlike most E.U. nations, Croatia uses its own currency, the kuna, not the euro. It is not part of the Schengen Agreement, a treaty that eliminated border controls, so we were required to contact customs and immigration on entry.

This was our first time crossing a secure border since Gibraltar. We were used to how formalities were done in laid-back Gibraltar, and the even-more-laid-back Caribbean, our only other border-crossing experience, where entering boats have an unofficial grace period of a few hours before notifying customs. What we were not used to, because it had never happened to us before, was being electronically tracked by border security as soon as we entered territorial waters and having a customs agent waiting for us at the dock the moment we arrived (Like most newer boats, *Sacre Bleu* was equipped with an automatic identification system, or AIS, that made our identity and location known to anyone with a receiver). We were blissfully unaware of all of this when we dropped anchor in Komiža harbor at six in the morning and crawled into bed after the all-night transit. Little did we know that a customs agent was standing on the dock, tapping his nightstick against the palm of his hand, scowling at *Sacre Bleu* anchored in the distance. Truth be told, that image was wildly inaccurate. We later learned that there were *three* customs agents waiting for us on the dock.

Valerie and I finally woke at ten in the morning and found the kids already awake, deep into activities not even remotely related to homeschooling. We tied the dinghy to the city dock and stepped ashore smiling in anticipation of spending the next few weeks in Croatia. Since Komiža is a seasonal port of entry for cruising boats, a customs office is not a permanent fixture on the island. Our three friends had decided to turn the tables on us and force us to find them. We asked a passing a pedestrian in pantomime where the customs office might be, showing him our passports and pretending to stamp them, and he directed us down the waterfront.

We studied the classical stone exterior of the government building for a moment, then opened the enormous wooden doors that led into a cavernous lobby full of stale air. The doors slammed behind us, and the bang echoed down the quiet hallways. We looked around hoping, oblivious to the irony, that our arrival might have been noticed. As the echoes faded, a young woman rushed into the lobby. She brought us up a stairway to an office where she handed us off to three uniformed customs agents. This is when we met our friends for the first time.

The senior agent sitting at the desk was a man in his fifties. He projected the uncompromising demeanor of a bureaucrat who had begun his career in a socialist republic. His sidekick, a young man wearing a much simpler uniform, stood in the corner and listened. It was the thirty-something woman in the Sam Browne belt who had something to prove, and she was threatening us with a five thousand-kuna fine, or about $800, for not reporting to customs immediately on arrival.

The senior agent waved off her suggestion with a slight movement of his left hand, then reached into his desk drawer, pulled out some forms, and handed them to us. "Welcome to Croatia," he said as he stamped our passports, returned them to us and gestured us out the door.

In a few days, Wlad and Séverine, our friends from Antibes, were meeting us in Zadar, about 60 miles north. The next morning, we cast off the mooring lines and set a course for the Dalmatian coast. Wlad was born and raised in Croatia, and his family had a summerhouse on Ist, an island farther north. He had offered to give us a tour of his island and his country, and we enthusiastically accepted.

On our way to Zadar, we stopped in a tiny, clear-blue lagoon surrounded by low, scrubby trees. It was the perfect anchorage to attempt our first Med mooring in the wild, so to speak, with an anchor off the bow and our stern secured to a sturdy object on shore. We had Med moored enough times to be confident with the procedure, but always in a marina, where fastening lines to a dock cleat is easy. I dropped the anchor and backed down towards the trees while William and Madeleine set out on the stand-up paddleboard with the stern lines and paddled toward the shore. Somewhere along the way, William dropped the stern line in the water, where it sank and wrapped around one of the turning propellers, disabling the boat. I had to quickly put on a dive mask, jump in the water and unwrap it. Then the anchor came loose and had to be re-set. Then the kids were unable to find a suitable tree and tie a knot. In half an hour, we turned this peaceful little blue lagoon into a picture of family dysfunction, the air filled with profanities and verbal skirmishes among all parties. Our neighbors stared in disbelief—the Loud Family had arrived. In the end, the boat was a spiderweb of rope, but we finally declared ourselves Med moored and opened a bottle of wine, while the kids, still on the paddleboard, went ashore to explore the island.

We arrived in Zadar the next afternoon and met with Wlad and Sévre, who had made the twelve-hour trip from Antibes by car. One of the remarkable benefits of living in Europe is the ability to drive in a car to a completely different country, culture, language and history in half a day. By contrast, a twelve-hour drive from Annapolis, Maryland, gets us to Orlando, St. Louis, Chicago or Quebec, which wins the prize as the most exotic in the group.

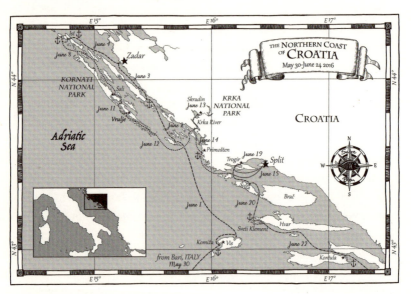

June 4, 2016

After five months in Antibes with Wlad in command of the sea rescue boat, I felt odd being the captain, but Wlad was happy to play tour guide. We made a slow, meandering run from Zadar to the butterfly-shaped island of Ist, population 182. The moment we stepped out of the dinghy, we realized that Wlad had 182 close friends and family. At the foot of the dock, the owner of the waterfront restaurant appeared in a Croatian soccer jersey holding a bottle of rakija and four shot glasses. We were his guests for our first hour on Ist, slugging several ounces of the clear, flammable brandy before continuing fifty feet into the welcoming arms of the next long-lost relative holding a plate of grilled sardines and four bottles of beer. Bottles of soda pop came out for Madeleine and William. They had been soda deprived for much of the voyage, so they took a quick liking to Ist. In this fashion, we made our way up the main street, finally reaching Wlad's summerhouse, a charming cottage built of fieldstone.

I tried to get a sense of what life was like on an island with barely enough residents to put on a production of *West Side Story*. There were three bars, two restaurants, one church, and no secrets. With no hotels or guesthouses, tourism was restricted to boaters like us who brought their homes with them. As we cruised, I joked that we could have reached most of our destinations in a rental car, driving the coast and staying in hotels along the way; we didn't need the boat. Here in Croatia, our self-contained mobility was paying off; we were reaching places no car could take us.

June 9, 2016

We hoisted our anchor off the sandy bottom of Ist harbor and set a southerly course for the Kornati National Park, a chain of 89 rocky, scrub-covered islands that are mostly uninhabited except for the occasional village or restaurant. Having Wlad and Sévre on board as guests created a new boat dynamic that put the Toomey family on good behavior. Open fights ceased, hygiene improved, and mealtime brought civilized discussions about mature topics. As a party of six, we did not have to seek out the company of strangers in restaurants. We stayed in the remote parts of the Kornati, anchored in quiet coves, going ashore by day to hike the undeveloped islands and enjoying dinners together back on the boat.

Our week with Wlad and Sévre went by quickly. We dropped them at the ferry terminal in Sali, on the north end of Kornati National Park, and then set a course for the tiny village of Vrulje, about 15 miles to the south. As we approached, I hovered in the small port to evaluate the docking possibilities. The few slips had already been taken, with no room for another sailboat, much less a catamaran the size of ours. Just then, four very enthusiastic young men in red shirts appeared at the water's edge waving their arms. They gestured towards a tiny slip with walls built of jagged rock. It seemed impossible to shoehorn our boat into this space without damaging the fiberglass hull. I idled close, put the engines in neutral, and let the red-shirted acrobatic team take care of the rest. They positioned themselves with dock lines on each corner of the boat and gently coaxed *Sacre Bleu* into the slip without so much as a scratch. The team quickly morphed into three waiters and a bartender in the nearby restaurant, so not only did we have a slip, we had dinner reservations as well.

Croatian cuisine was yet another part of the culture that was unknown to us when we arrived. Croatia has many regional cuisines, but where we sailed, the most common menu item was meat or fish grilled on a spit. A restaurant experience is typically outdoors and casual, and a major feature of the dining room is the wood-fired grill. Wine-making in Croatia goes back at least 2,500 years, and their wine selection is as complex and varied as any in Europe. Dining out in Croatia is like attending a friend's barbecue party: the aroma of wood fire fills the air, the ambience is relaxed, the earthy red wine complements the grilled duck perfectly, and you wish the moment could last forever.

In our first three weeks in Croatia we had spent most of our time in the offshore islands. Now we turned our attention to the mainland. Valerie was reading up on sights deeper in Croatia and became intrigued with the idea of an inland passage. Less than ten miles to the east lay the mouth of the Krka River, which cuts through the heart of Dalmatia, ending in a maze of pristine waterfalls and clear pools in the Krka National Park. The chart assured us that the river was deep enough and wide enough, and the bridges were tall enough. We couldn't think of a good reason why we couldn't drive our catamaran on the Krka River, so off we sailed.

Our journey into the heartland of Croatia began at the Canal of St. Anthony, which connects the Adriatic Sea to the large inland Bay of Šibenik. On the north end of the Bay, the Krka River meanders inland through deep valleys and under sweeping suspension bridges until it spills into Prokljansko Lake. On the other side of the lake, the river continues for another few miles until it reaches the charming mountain village of Skradin, after which the water is no longer navigable.

We dropped our anchor off Skradin and planted ourselves for several days. With a gentle current keeping the anchor firmly set in the muddy river bottom, I forgot I was a boat captain for a while. We explored hiking trails flanked by crystal-clear streams, roaring waterfalls, and calm, clear pools teeming with trout. We sampled Skradin's pizza and strolled its streets. The gentle pace of life on this river provided a welcome change from the ocean and all things aggressive and salty. At the end of each day back on *Sacre Bleu* we basked in the summer sun while Madeleine and William fed breadcrumbs to the swans—the swans gliding elegantly towards their floating treat like figure skaters. Feeding seagulls, by contrast, is like hockey, with a brawl for possession of every loose crumb. This tranquil life on the river suited us just fine.

For all its primordial beauty, the Krka National Park also has a place in industrial history. Just a little farther up the river lay one of the first hydroelectric power plants ever built, designed by one of Croatia's most famous native sons, Nikola Tesla. Tesla went on to greater fame in America, where he went head to head with Thomas Edison over whose electricity standard would prevail. Though Tesla won, most American school children would tell you that Edison is the Father of Electricity while Tesla is a car.

June 14, 2016

Two days felt like enough time anchored on the Krka River and exploring the national park, and with no place to go but downstream, we ended our freshwater adventure and made the four-hour run back to the Adriatic Sea. By evening, we were anchored off Primošten, a quintessentially Dalmatian town consisting of a cluster of limestone buildings with terra cotta roofs, crowned by a 15th century church.

Our time in Croatia had thus far been smooth sailing in every sense of the phrase, but the tranquility ended when the weather forecast called for a jugo, a strong weather system from the south, bringing with it hot, moist air, strong winds, and rain. Sometimes jugos can reach hurricane strength, so we needed a hurricane hole—shelter that offered protection from all sides—not just another anchorage. The storm was arriving in 48 hours, forcing us to act fast since dozens of other boats would also be looking for safe harbor. Instead of scanning the nautical charts, Valerie worked the phones and found a Lagoon catamaran dealer in the city of Split, just a little farther down the coast. So, early the next morning, we weighed anchor and set a course for Split.

After a 10-mile run south through the still air and flat seas that were the calm before the jugo, we arrived at the Marina Nava, securing a slip safely situated deep into the port of Split. The jugo might bring high winds, but the swell would not reach us, and wave action tends to do more damage than wind.

Split is Croatia's second largest city after its inland capital, Zagreb. We had a day to kill before the jugo arrived, so we toured this ancient Roman outpost, where Emperor Diocletian, Croatian by birth, built his retirement home in AD 305. Only one part of his palace, the peristyle (courtyard), with its perimeter of archways and Corinthian columns, remains, and now serves as a gathering place for tourists and vendors. There, we took selfies with two local drama students dressed as Roman centurions. Valerie asked if they were there to do a show. They replied that this was the show, and then they produced a donation cup.

That evening, we dined on lamb peka, a hearty stew this is the signature dish of Dalmatia, in one of the many outdoor restaurants installed in the foundations of the old palace. The European Football Championship happened to be taking place, and all eyes in the restaurant were fixed on one of the six flatscreen televisions showing the match between Croatia and the Czech Republic. The crowd erupted with each Croatian shot on goal. With a hurricane-force storm approaching, didn't anyone want to watch the Weather Channel?

Late that night, the jugo arrived. By two in the morning, the hot, sand-filled Sahara winds were whistling through the rigging at over 50 knots. Sleep was impossible. With the violence outside—shackles banging and canvas flogging and debris flying—I feared that something would come crashing down on us at any moment. Storms bring two sounds that frighten me to my core: the roar of big water and the howl of wind in the rigging. The big water roar was safely distant, on the breakwater of the port, but the howl was all around us. On an ordinary, blustery day on the water, the rigging whistles when the wind climbs above 30 knots. Familiar to all sailors, that sound is a warning to reef the sails and batten down the hatches. At 50 knots, the wind in the rigging has a completely different voice. It is spooky and alien. It is the chorus of generations of lost sailors crying their warnings from the deep. Even with the boat safely in port, it unnerved me.

At the first sign of light, I surveyed the ship. The wind had died down some, and the storm was less frightening in daylight. As soon as I slid the salon door open, hot air rushed in and papers went flying. I quickly slid the door closed and glanced around expecting the worst. What caught my attention first was the destruction on shore: downed trees, signs, and power lines, and debris littering the streets. I looked up at the mast and was relieved to see that the rigging was not damaged. I examined the canvas, then walked the perimeter to make sure the fenders and dock lines were still in place. *Sacre Bleu* had made it through the night unscathed.

Over our morning coffee, I thanked Valerie for arranging the safe harbor for us. Then the four of us dressed in our trademark Maine lobsterman's foul weather gear for a walk through town. The waters of the port seemed to be boiling as swells slammed into and over the seawalls, flooding the waterfront paths. Despite the continuing storm, the ferry was still operating, plowing through waves, rolling steeply as it fought its way out of the harbor. Along the shoreline, several small boats had been hurled up onto the sidewalk, looking as if they had been dropped from the sky. *Sacre Bleu*, I told myself, is a lucky boat. I was growing superstitious, like so many before me who took to the sea and needed to rationalize its random destructiveness.

By the next morning, the seas were flat, a gentle breeze filled the air, and boats, big and small, were once again plying the waters of the port. The jugo had departed as abruptly as it had arrived. In those next few days, we stopped in Trogir, then island-hopped down the Dalmatian coast, visiting Šolta, Brač, Sveti Klement, Hvar and Korčula. These islands typically consist of scrubby interior hills descending to a rocky shoreline, with a walled village at a salient point of land or a fishing port in a protected cove. The villages appear almost monolithic, with all buildings constructed from the same parchment-colored stone and terra cotta roof tiles. A church steeple crowns the high point in the center of each town.

Despite their outward homogeneity, Dalmatian towns are full of surprises. Korčula, for example, is the birthplace of Marco Polo. The large row house where he was born is now an elaborate museum with dioramas and costumed mannequins reproducing the stops in his journeys along the Silk Road to Asia. Our history lesson was upstaged by an encounter immediately after we exited the museum, when a British woman approached us as if she knew us and declared "Britain has just voted to leave the European Union." She just had to tell somebody. "History never stops happening," I said to the kids.

The next morning, we set a course for the Mljet National Park, where we anchored off the town of Polače, in a cove overlooked by the ruins of a third-century Roman palace. The three-story stone structure must have been impressive in its day. What was life like two thousand years ago in a large palace on a small island in a remote corner of the Empire? If ever there was imperial excess, it had to have been here. We caught a bus inland that dropped us by a lake, where we hopped on a boat that took us to an island, where we found a monastery. By the twelfth century, the party was long over and Benedictine monks had taken charge of the island. The ultimate in monkish isolation, they had installed themselves on an island in a lake on an island in the sea.

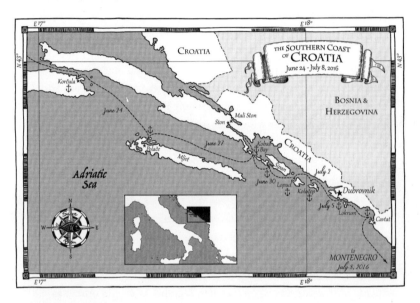

June 27, 2016

We left the islands and turned *Sacre Bleu* towards the mainland, anchoring in Kobaš Bay, where William drove the four of us in the dinghy to the village of Ston. Ston is famous for its three-mile-long stone rampart, a wall second in size only to the Great Wall of China. It was built in the 14th century to protect salt ponds, a key part of Dubrovnik's commerce at the time, from its unruly neighbors. The wall began at the village of Ston, wound its way up a steep hill, and descended into the village of Mali Ston. For a small fee, tourists can walk along the wall, up the steep hill and down the other side, and then turn around and do it all over again. For an additional fee, tourists can ride the bus back. After a one-way hike, even the kids were winded. We all agreed that half the hike at twice the price was the better deal.

At the island of Koločep, we found a beautiful cove to drop anchor. That night, June 28, was our wedding anniversary, so we let the kids have their usual movie night with pasta while we treated ourselves to dinner out. Valerie noticed a very swanky restaurant with its own private dinghy dock perched on a cliff overlooking the cove. It seemed suitably glamorous for the occasion.

When we arrived, we had the restaurant to ourselves. Since Spain, we had grown accustomed to opening restaurants. As we barged into a restaurant at the stroke of 8pm, invariably the startled maître d' would give us a look that said, "You're not here for dinner, are you?" The waiter seated us at a table overlooking the water, our boat and our children. Not long after we sat down, a colossal mega-yacht eased into the cove and anchored close to *Sacre Bleu*. The sun had set, the cove was dark, and the mega-yacht was lit up like a Christmas tree, with blue underwater lights surrounding its waterline. The name of the yacht, *Quantum Blue*, emblazoned in big letters on its top deck, was backlit by more blue lights. "Nice boat," I said to Valerie. "I wonder where his money came from." We both had our cell phones, and Google had the answer.

The 341-foot, $250-million yacht was owned by Sergey Galitsky, the founder of Russia's largest retailer, Magnit. As we did our research, we noticed that the yacht's tender was coming straight towards the restaurant's dinghy dock. As we read his Wikipedia page, Sergey himself walked into the restaurant, looking a little older than his picture. The restaurant owner greeted him enthusiastically and quickly shuffled him and his entourage into a private dining room. Instead of celebrating our anniversary reminiscing on our years of wedded bliss, we both dug deeper and deeper into Sergey Galitsky's life. "Which boat would you rather go back to?" Valerie asked at the end of dinner, "*Quantum Blue* or *Sacre Bleu*?" At that moment I pictured our two children eating spaghetti while watching a *Die Hard* movie. It was a tough call.

The next day, we dropped our anchor just off the ramparts of Dubrovnik. The pristine condition of this walled, medieval jewel belies the centuries of conflict it has endured, the latest being the Croatian War of Independence that finally ended in 1995. I studied the sandy bottom through the clear water and imagined the sailors through the ages who had dropped their anchors on that very same seafloor. Noticing my ragged shorts and unmanicured toenails, I concluded that I had finally achieved the look of an ancient mariner.

As we walked along the city ramparts, we happened on a television crew filming the HBO series *Game of Thrones*. We could not get close enough to watch an actual shoot, but from our elevated positions on the wall, we did get a spectacular view of the craft services table. It was appropriately long, like a medieval feast, but covered with sandwiches, wraps, salads, and energy drinks. Waiting in line with paper plates in hand were peasants, foot soldiers, a knight covered in blood, a princess, two noblemen, and an electrician. At the end of the day, the streets outside the old city walls filled with similarly medieval-looking characters waiting for the bus or calling an Uber, smart phone in hand, hair in a tussle, a rivulet of blood running down the forehead.

At sundown, our bar of choice most days was the flybridge on *Sacre Bleu*, but every now and then we did better. The best view in Dubrovnik could be found at one of the cafes built just outside of the city ramparts overlooking the sea. Customers pass through a narrow opening in the eight-foot-thick stone defensive wall to access a terrace that overlooks a 50-foot drop into the clear blue Adriatic. It was a nice place to savor a cool fresh-lime mojito and reflect on the poor souls through the centuries who had gasped their dying breath in pitched battle over the thin stretch of real estate our table occupied.

As soon as we sit down at a bar or restaurant, we reflexively reach for our phones and make use of the wi-fi connection that usually comes with being a patron. Valerie and I were both too engrossed in our emails to pay much attention when Madeleine and William asked, "Is it okay if we jump in the water?" "Fine," I said, without looking up. After a few minutes, the customer at the table next to us cast a side remark our way in English. "Your children don't scare easily." "Yeah, they've seen it all," I said, my thumbs ablaze as I responded to an email. I considered his statement further, then I turned my gaze up just in time to see Madeleine step off a 30-foot cliff and plunge into the water. A group of college-aged kids stood on the rock platform where she had just launched trying to summon the courage to take the same leap.

William politely got in line behind them, but when it became apparent they were not jumping, he casually walked around them and stepped off the cliff. We finally discovered the answer to that age-old question: "If your sister jumped off a cliff, would you jump off too?"

"Oh, shit!" I said to Valerie, "They're jumping off the cliff!"

"Maybe you should go down there and tell them to be careful," Valerie admonished.

"Be careful jumping off a cliff?" I asked, as I started down the stairway.

A couple of days later, we made the 12-mile run to Cavtat, a waterfront village that would be our last stop in Croatia. Before departing Croatia, we had to clear out at the customs office in town, leave the country once and for all and finally let those three customs agents in Komiža relax.

But we were destined to leave Croatia as awkwardly as we had entered. There were few places to drop anchor in the crowded Cavtat harbor, and the water was deeper than usual, so Valerie and I anchored the boat this time instead of the kids. We stood on the bow and studied the inky black depths, but it was impossible to determine the bottom conditions, and the chart provided no seabed symbols. After Valerie let out the required amount of chain, which was over two hundred feet, I backed the boat down until the chain was tight, and then backed a little more until I felt that familiar tug that told us the anchor was set. At this point in our cruise, our anchor had reassured us over and over with its firm grip, as if to tell us, "I got this. Go make yourself a cocktail."

Later that night, we dozed off, looking forward to a new day and a new country. When Valerie woke me in the middle of the night screaming, I thought maybe she had had another dream where I was being an insensitive jerk. Then I heard the two sounds that make my stomach sink: wind whistling through the rigging and the roar of breaking waves. But this time, the roar was just outside our cabin window.

A squall had come up suddenly in the middle of the night and *Sacre Bleu* was dragging anchor. Once we were out on deck, our worst fears were confirmed. We were about 20 feet from a rocky shore in unknown depth and possibly already aground. It was an overcast night, dark as a lockbox, the wind was roughly 40 knots, and the seas were in a fury. I could just barely make out other boats pulling angrily at their anchor chains, weaving back and forth as the gusts pushed them to one side and then the other.

I started the engines and powered up the electronics, nervously eyeing the depth sounder as it booted up. It came to life, and to my horror, it displayed "4.1 ft." (We had never properly calibrated our depth sounder because we never thought inches would matter.) Since *Sacre Bleu*'s draft is 4.5 feet, I thought we were surely aground, and we probably had some propeller and rudder damage as well. But we did not seem aground. The boat was bobbing like it was still afloat.

I crossed my fingers and put the engine in gear. Fully expecting to hear a propeller grinding against rock—a sound I had never heard and could only imagine—I eased the throttle forward. The engines were not powered up enough to counteract the headwind, but the fact that the propellers were even spinning was a major turning point in the night, and, in retrospect, the entire cruise. With a blend of urgency and caution, I continued nudging the throttles forward until the boat made headway against the wind and the anchor chain sagged as the force of the boat lifted off. As we inched forward, we slowly gathered up the chain until the anchor was up and *Sacre Bleu* was free. I felt a combination of relief and panic. Our boat was safe, so far, but we were now underway in a crowded anchorage on a pitch-black night in a violent squall.

Valerie stood on the bow with a powerful flashlight scanning the water ahead as we continued into the dark, rainy night until we found a clearing big enough to attempt another anchor drop. Our second try at anchoring did not feel much different from the first, but since we were going to stay up the remainder of the night anyway, we took our chances and kept a close eye on our position, as displayed on the electronic chart. By morning, the wind had subsided and the other boat owners were relaxing on their decks greeting the new day, oblivious to the chaos of the night before.

We pulled our anchor off the Croatian bottom for the last time and drove *Sacre Bleu* around to the western side of Cavtat to complete the customs procedures. Valerie and I moored the boat and took the dinghy to the customs office, where we presented the ship's papers to an agent. The woman stamped our exit papers and informed us that we had to depart Croatian waters immediately. "Could we buy groceries on the way out," Valerie asked. The response was a perfunctory "no." I wondered if she had a sister in Komiža.

As we were about to cast off from the mooring ball, we realized we had forgotten to mail a pile of postcards with Croatian stamps. Our next stop was Montenegro, so we had to decide: let $4.50 of Croatian postage stamps go to waste or flout the law and risk prosecution and jail by going ashore and mailing the postcards. Valerie and I had the same thought at the same moment: "Let's get William to do it." It occurred to us that although customs knew us and possibly our dinghy, they did not know our children. So, we sent William ashore on the stand-up paddleboard, postcards tucked into his bathing suit, with instructions to drop them in the first mailbox and run. For his part, William relished the opportunity to embark on a mission that got him off the boat and away from us. With Operation Mail-and-Run successfully executed, we humbly withdrew from Croatian waters and set a course for Montenegro, where we hoped the customs officers had better dispositions.

Montenegro
July 8, 2016

A cold wind off the mountains carried us 35 miles along the coast from Cavtat, Croatia, into the Bay of Hercegnovski Zaliv, and eventually to the town of Zelenika, where vessels entering Montenegro clear customs.

Along with Croatia, Montenegro is one of six independent republics that emerged from the protracted and bloody dissolution of Yugoslavia that played out in the 1990s. Although we were entering one of Europe's newest countries (it achieved independence in 2006), its rich and tumultuous history dates to the Roman Empire. Like Croatia, Montenegro has a socialist past, yet Croatia is now fiercely democratic and free market oriented. Would Montenegro be the same? During our five weeks in Croatia, we learned the recent hostilities were still simmering. A casual conversation with a waiter in Dubrovnik about visiting neighboring Bosnia and Herzegovina was politely truncated. No comment. We experienced similar short conversations whenever the topic wandered towards neighboring countries.

The politics in this part of the world are complex, for sure, and we were encountering some of that complexity at a practical level. While Croatia is a member of the E.U., it is not part of the Eurozone; it uses its own currency, the kuna. Montenegro, on the other hand, is *not* a member of the E.U. but *is* a member of the Eurozone. Here, we faced volumes of paperwork to bring our boat into the country, but we could pay the fees in euros. Neither nation is a signatory to the Schengen Agreement, so in Montenegro, as in Croatia, we had to clear customs.

The customs officer at Zelenika asked for my skipper's license, which, of course, I didn't have. I explained that the U.S. does not require a license to operate a boat. He looked at me politely, as if to say, "That's interesting but not relevant to this conversation." I went on to explain that I had been skippering our boat through European waters for well on a year and this was the first time anyone had ever asked for a skipper's license. He pondered this last piece of irrelevant information, then politely told us to continue to Kotor and clear customs there, where we would be somebody else's problem.

We had not planned to sail as far as Kotor. The town is very far inland, and to reach it from the Adriatic Sea we had to pass through three separate bodies of water. From the Bay of Hercegnovski Zaliv, we proceeded through a narrow strait into the Bay of Kotor, which is two separate bodies of water. From the western part of the Bay, we passed through an even narrower strait into the eastern Bay of Kotor.

Entering the eastern part of the bay, we all stood on deck, mouths agape at the stunning beauty we had accidentally discovered. I was convinced we had passed through a magic portal that had transported us into Shangri-La. The bay is walled in by towering mountains of raw granite veiled in mist, and the shore is dotted with red-roofed villages crowned by church steeples that seem lifted right out of a fairytale. In the middle of the bay are two tiny islands, only a stone's throw apart, one covered shore-to-shore by a church and the other by a monastery. At first glance, the structures appear to be floating rather than set on land. Most of the villages feature community swim areas with diving boards and floating platforms, and on this summer day, the waterfronts were teeming with children playing in the water and adults keeping watch. At the extreme end of the eastern Bay lies the town of Kotor, flanked by soaring cliffs stretching into the clouds. We had come all this way to do paperwork, but we had stumbled into paradise.

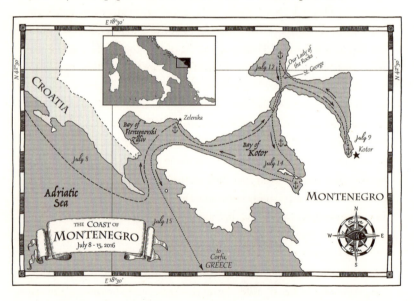

Shangri-La ended at the customs office in Kotor, where Agent Two read from the same script as Agent One and asked for my captain's license. Since Agent Two had no Agent Three to punt to, she relented, stamped our passports, charged us €100, and sent us on our way. All four of us were excited to see this storybook town up close, so we made quick work of departing the customs dock, anchoring nearby and riding the dinghy to shore.

We stumbled onto an English-language walking tour of the town, where we learned that Kotor acquired its unique charm from the most tasteful of its oppressors, the Venetians, who built in the Gothic, Romanesque, and Baroque styles. They called their outpost "black mountain," or *monte negro*, and the name stuck. The Venetian-style churches, palatial homes, city walls, and clock tower give this small town of thirteen thousand people an embarrassment of rich architecture. The tour ended in the market square, where a folk dance troupe was performing. That was the clincher for me; I wanted to move there.

After a couple of days, we drove to the other end of the Bay of Kotor to be better situated for the dinghy run to the two small islands, Gospa od Škrpjela (the Church of Our Lady of the Rocks) and Sveti Đorđe (the monastery of St. George). According to legend, in the 16th century two fishermen found a painting of the Virgin Mary and Baby Jesus on a rock in the middle of the bay, so they enlarged the rock into an island and built a church on it. Finding a painting does not logically lead to building an island and a church, but legends do not have to answer to logic. After touring the church island, with the famous painting on display at the altar, we returned to the dinghy and motored over to the monastery island. We discovered no visitors were allowed, but we got close enough to see women sunbathing in bikinis, prompting us to wonder if the monks in this monastery play by different rules.

The next day, we reluctantly departed the Bay of Kotor and made our way back through the narrow straits to Zelenika, where we cleared out of customs. By this point, they had given up on seeing my skipper's license and just wanted us out of their country.

Albania lies between Montenegro and Greece, but we had heard and read too many stories of bad experiences with Albanian customs and confrontations with smugglers off the coast. Valerie was more in favor of stopping in Albania than I was. I did not know if it was the father in me that didn't want to endanger the kids, or the chicken in me that didn't want to endanger myself. The chicken-dad won, so we made the 140-mile overnight run directly to Corfu, Greece. Not stopping in Albania is one of the few regrets of our cruise for two reasons. Firstly, we did not know what to expect in Montenegro and it took our breath away. Coming directly from that experience, we should have been more open minded about Albania. Secondly, we were almost a year into our lives as cruisers, and I should have had more confidence in my abilities to handle a potentially difficult situation. At this point in our journey, storms and breakdowns did not worry me, but human encounters still did. Captaining a boat was helping me grow beyond those fears, but not in time for taking a chance on Albania.

Family Photos

The view from our bathroom window as the drama unfolded.

Sacre Bleu *touches water for the first time.*

Family Afloat

The first day of the cruise, setting out from Les Sables-d'Olonne, France, into the big ocean.

Sailing along the breathtakingly beautiful coast of Spain, seeing the world from a perspective only a boat can provide.

Family Photos

Crossing the Bay of Biscay, we picked up our first of many dolphin escorts.

Heavy seas and 55-knot winds near Ribadeo, off the northern coast of Spain.

Family Afloat

In A Coruña, Spain, two new additions to the manifest: Snowball and Squirt, dwarf hamsters.

Castro de Baroña, an Iron Age settlement near Ría de Muros, Spain.

Family Photos

The entrance to Porto the day after our arrival. Arriving vessels make their approach between the red lighthouse to the left and the green one on the right.

Homeschooling was complemented by a USB microscope, lab experiments, books, Legos and other toys, and other items that we found along the way.

Family Afloat

Anchored off the spectacular southern coast of Portugal.

Dressing ship for the christening in Gibraltar.

Family Photos

Madeleine guides Sacre Bleu *past the Musée océanographique de Monaco on our way to our winter home in Antibes, France.*

Wintering over in Antibes, France. Family drawing class met Tuesdays and Thursdays.

Family Afloat

Watching our neighbor Dilbar *depart was like watching a city block grow legs and walk away.*

The SNSM crew embarking on a training session.
Waving from the aft cockpit, I have yet to earn my orange jumpsuit.

Family Photos

Farm-fresh products, from flowers to live rabbits, could be procured at the Marché Provençal. On the right, Valerie moves in for a purchase.

Christmas morning under the lemon tree.

Family Afloat

Willim tries his hand at making a baguette in a local bakery.

Manarola is one of five towns of the Cinque Terre, Italy, one of the most beautiful coasts in all of Europe.

Family Photos

William trying with all his might to straighten the Leaning Tower of Pisa.

Getting stopped by the Carabinieri near the island of Elba, off the Italian coast.

Family Afloat

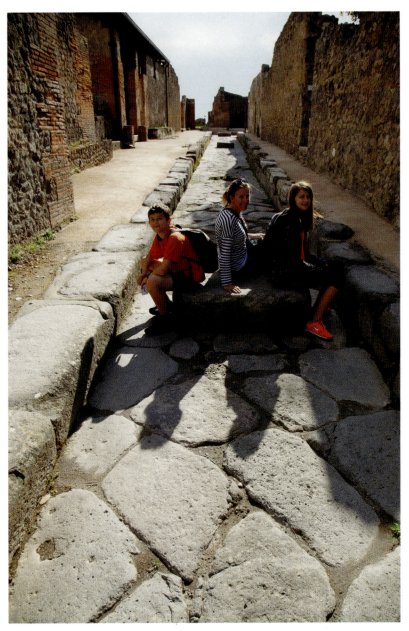

On a pedestrian crosswalk in Pompeii, Italy.

Family Photos

Moored off the magical town of Positano, on the Amalfi Coast, Italy.

The view from the bus window as we traveled the road that runs along the Amalfi Coast.

Family Afloat

In Cetraro, Italy, a German family put on a show for us.

Tropea, Italy: the fresh markets come in all shapes and sizes.

Family Photos

*Looking from atop a hill on the island of Ist, Croatia,
Sacre Bleu is a tiny speck.*

Sacre Bleu *was shoehorned into her slip in the village of Vrulje, Croatia.*

Family Afloat

Driving up the Krka River on an inland river excursion in Croatia.

The jugo in Split, Croatia, brought hurricane-force winds.

Family Photos

The Great Wall of Moli Ston proved to be too much for our children.

In Croatia, tiny villages and colossal yachts.

Family Afloat

Madeleine takes a leap just outside the ramparts of Dubrovnik, Croatia.

FAMILY PHOTOS

Stunningly beautiful mountains and storybook villages in Montenegro.

Madeleine snorkeling off a remote beach on the island of Paxos, Greece.

Family Afloat

The four-mile-long Corinth Canal provided a shortcut to the Aegean Sea.

We had the entire island of Delos, Greece, and its ancient ruins to ourselves.

Family Photos

We hoisted Madeleine 75 feet up the mast to fix an antenna in Messolonghi, Greece.

Family Afloat

Baking projects on the boat rarely came out right. Fortunately, a bakery was never too far away.

Both Madeleine and William benefitted from having long stretches of time that required them to find creative ways to stay busy.

Family Photos

Near Bonifacio, Corsica. In the background, Madeleine prepares to dive off the cliff.

Halloween in Gibraltar was all trick and no treat.

Family Afloat

A camel ride on a beach in Morocco.

Provisioning for a 2,600-mile transatlantic voyage was no ordinary grocery run.

Family Photos

During the Atlantic crossing, each day at noon, Madeleine took the positions of the other boats in the rally and plotted them on a chart.

In the middle of the Atlantic our wind died.

The hair salon in the middle of the ocean was always open, but some of the customers were not always pleased with the results.

Sacre Bleu and another transatlantic rally participant, JoJo 1, met up halfway between continents.

Family Photos

When we arrived in the Caribbean, we spent much more time off the grid and in the water.

Madeleine was happy to have Belle, the family dog, back with us. Note the pink claw caps on Belle to protect the deck.

Family Afloat

When the sun rose the next morning in Saint-Pierre, Martinique, we realized how lucky we were.

William swims with the local wildlife in Guadeloupe.

Family Photos

Humpback whales were a frequent sight in Guadeloupe, on the surface and just below.

A family snorkeling adventure off Cocoa Point, Barbuda.

Family Afloat

In the British Virgin Islands, getting a close-up of some passing wildlife with the GoPro camera.

Pigs in paradise: Big Major Cay, Bahamas.

Family Photos

The driftwood collaborative art project atop Boo Boo Hill, Bahamas. Note Sacre Bleu's contribution at center.

The Bahamas: knee-deep, crystal-clear, bathtub-warm water for miles around, with the occasional stingray.

Family Afloat

Madeleine and William are surrounded by Caribbean reef sharks in The Bahamas.

One of our last days of the cruise, on an empty beach with a happy dog, Hughlett Point Natural Area Preserve, Kilmarnock, Virginia.

11

Ouzo with a Side of Meltemi

Corfu, Greece
July 15, 2016

When we decided on a Mediterranean setting for the cruise, we imagined ourselves in Greek waters, anchored in an aquamarine cove by a whitewashed village with the ruins of an ancient temple presiding from the hills above. As the cruise unfolded, this was the dream that kept us sailing farther and farther east, day after day, month after month, going on a year now. Greece represented the ultimate Mediterranean experience, and it was now just a day's sail away.

After motoring most of the 140 nautical miles—a 22-hour journey—for lack of wind, we anchored off the Greek island of Corfu. With ship's papers in hand, we boarded the dinghy, looking forward to whatever surprises Greek customs was going to throw at us. The customs officials were very nice, but the paperwork was voluminous. After many rubber stamps, signatures, and a dozen different forms, all carefully handwritten by the agent, we were presented with a transit log, a booklet that we were supposed to have stamped entering and departing every port in Greece. Our transit log was good for 30 days, after which time it had to be renewed at any customs office along the way. When we got back to *Sacre Bleu*, the transit log went into a drawer and never came out again.

That evening, eager to experience Greece, we returned to Corfu town for dinner. I had come to Corfu as a young backpacker, and I was feeling nostalgic, so, over gyros, I proposed to the family that we see some of the places I had visited way back when Greece was slightly less ancient.

We started at the Achilleion, a palace built in 1890 for the Empress of Austria, and occupied by various European aristocrats through the years. What impressed us most was not its history or provenance, which included Kaiser Wilhelm, but its starring role as a casino in the James Bond film *For Your Eyes Only*. Next, we headed off to rediscover the village I had stayed in those many years ago: Pelekas. Framed on a wall back home, I had an artsy black-and-white photograph of a street scene in Pelekas I had snapped with my coal-burning Minolta XGM film camera. Now I was on a mission to find that same building on that same street. I succeeded, but it was all different. The building was no longer white but an ugly brown color marked with graffiti. Roof tiles were missing and trashcans were overflowing. Even little Greek villages change over the years, and my mental photo album of Pelekas was now defaced by these more recent images. Traveler's note: if you are nurturing a fond memory of a magical place from your youth, don't mess with it.

Heavy winds were in the weather forecast, so we took refuge in the yacht club marina and explored Corfu town the following day while the system passed. When calm returned a day later, we sailed to the island of Paxos. The west side of Paxos features a rugged shoreline of cliffs embedded with small coves and tiny beaches accessible only from the water. There were no suitable overnight anchorages on the west side of the island, and the most practical way to see it was to make the five-mile trip in our dinghy.

We packed our snorkeling gear and lunch, and William drove us all in the dinghy to Blue Caves beach, a cove about a hundred feet wide and walled in on three sides by tall cliffs. The beach is not made up of

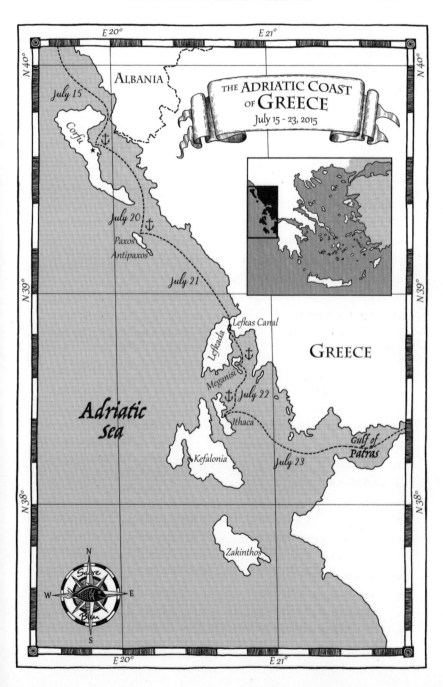

sand but white Carrera marble stones, oval and smooth, the size of potatoes. The shoreline also had more than its share of debris: plastic bottles and bags, buckets and straws, toys, ballpoint pens, a construction helmet, flip-flops and athletic shoes, fragments of Styrofoam coolers, mylar balloons and those ubiquitous grocery bags. William dressed up in the construction helmet and a fishnet toga, and we declared him Detritus, god of flotsam and jetsam.

The four of us pulled on our snorkeling gear and went for a swim along the cliffs by the cove. The pinkish-yellow wall dropped through the clear, cold water another 20 feet to a white sandy bottom. Sunlight dappled the rocks, coating them in shifting geometric patterns. Caves and swim-throughs near the bottom tempted us to dive deeper, but when we tried, the water got colder and finally too cold. Madeleine, undeterred, reached the bottom and peeked into caves and swam through arches. Occasionally, a fish passed through, but for the most part the cove was lifeless.

July 21, 2016
Compared to the west side of Paxos, where we had a cove to ourselves, the east side was crowded with cruising boats, so, at first light, we began our 60-mile run south to the island of Meganisi. The route included a transit through the Lefkas Canal, which opens a few times a day for a strict half hour window and then promptly closes like an elevator, leaving stragglers waiting for the next opening. When we arrived, about 30 boats, mostly cruising sailboats, had already formed a neat queue on the north side of the canal. Once the canal opened, the boats scattered like a litter of puppies at feeding time and raced for the opening. As I drove, Valerie assumed the role of tactician, coaching me to go here and there, drop in behind that one, in front of this one, cut him off, jump in there, slow down, stop, now full throttle, no, wait, now, go. We made it.

The next morning, anchored off Meganisi, Valerie and I walked five miles round trip to buy a loaf of bread, which I contended, was still easier than making bread. With our hard-earned loaf we set sail for the island of Ithaca, 20 miles south, encountering fierce tailwinds on the way that were a prelude to the fickle breezes that we would eventually associate with Greece. Ithaca, William informed us, is where Homer's Odysseus spent his final years as king after his fabled voyage. The principal town, Vathi, where we anchored, is loaded with souvenir stores selling *Odyssey* merchandise—T-shirts and snow globes with cultural resonance.

Like Odysseus, we kept an eye on the calendar but never tried to be on a schedule. His goal was to return home; ours was to sample a broad swath of Mediterranean culture, so we could not linger too long in any one country. We could have spent weeks touring the Greek mainland alone, not to mention the over 200 islands scattered across two seas. We had to be strategic. Rather than circumnavigate Greece, as we had done with every other country, we would cut through the middle. Starting on the west coast of mainland Greece, the Gulf of Patras and the Gulf of Corinth are connected end-to-end, running east-west. On the east coast lies the Saronic Gulf and eventually the Aegean Sea. These bodies of water line up in such a way that they nearly divide the mainland in two; the four-mile Corinth Canal finishes the job. This shortcut would allow us to sail from the Adriatic to the Aegean Sea, and ultimately to the Cyclades Islands, where those whitewashed Greek villages of our dreams lie.

We faced another 60-mile run, so we got another early start. We were making good time on our way to the Gulf of Patras when the argument broke out. Valerie had asked Madeleine to remove the laundry pinned on the lifelines. The clothes all belonged to Madeleine, so to me this seemed like a reasonable request. After the second petition received no response, Valerie commenced throwing the clothing overboard. This caused immediate anguish and a lot of screaming, but neither woman budged. Finally, Valerie grabbed the fuzzy brown blanket that Madeleine constantly had in her possession and threw it overboard as well. More screaming ensued. Madeleine went to her cabin, Valerie went to her cabin, and I lowered the sails, started the engines and circled around to rescue the laundry and blanket.

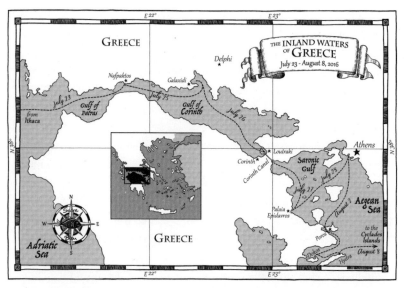

By sunset, everyone was calm. The jettisoned items had all been recovered, and we were anchored off Nafpaktos, a gem of a village with a tiny harbor enclosed by medieval walls. In Greece, one expects to see classical architecture—columned temples elegantly rendered in white marble. With its crenellated stone walls in brownish gray, Nafpaktos looks more like a Scottish castle. We considered nudging *Sacre Bleu* through the narrow harbor gate and into the walled harbor, but it didn't look much bigger than a duck pond, so we vetoed the idea.

That night we dinghy'd ashore and found ourselves the only tourists in a town full of Greeks. Travel by boat brings storms and night watches and customs hassles, but it also brings us to places like Nafpaktos, beyond the range of tour buses. That night, as we dined on lamb souvlaki at an outdoor table, we watched the nightly ritual of townspeople, young and old, gather around the waters of the port to socialize, play games and catch up on the latest gossip.

My weekly comic strip deadline approached, so I sent Valerie and the kids to town in the dinghy while I stayed on the boat to find my muse. These rare opportunities to sit at my desk all alone and work in peace and quiet were moments to savor. I scribbled a cartoon shark on my note pad and drew an empty speech bubble over it. Pausing, I thought about how to fill it. Suddenly, the silence was broken by the pitter-patter of little footsteps scurrying over my head. They were too big for a seagull and too small for a pirate. I went outside to investigate and found four children standing on the roof looking back at me in wide-eyed shock. They had been watching the boat from a distance and assumed that everyone had left in the dinghy. They shook off their initial surprise, let out squeals of laughter and plunged into the water. I stood on the deck until they swam away, then returned to my desk.

Soon, I heard more footsteps on the roof, followed by more squeals of joy and splashes. Back on deck, I found the same four children treading water nearby. I was pretty sure they did not speak a word of English, so I simply pointed to shore with a stern expression, hoping they would interpret this as "go away." They swam some distance from the boat but no farther. I grew tired of the standoff and returned to work. Moments later, the footsteps were back. The sound of their unbridled joy brought back a childhood memory of playing in a stream near my house. A grouchy old man owned the property, and he would sometimes open his backdoor and scream "Hey! You can't play there!" I was now that old man. I resolved to let them have their fun while I continued working.

The children leaped off the roof into the water, swam to the stern, climbed back onto the roof, and jumped into the water again and again and again. More of their friends joined, and eventually the queue grew into one continuous loop of kids as they vaulted themselves into the water again and again and again. Suddenly, a voice rang out: "Hey! You can't play there!" Valerie had returned in the dinghy. With the sound of her genuine fury and the promise of real consequences in its timbre, the little trespassers scattered like water bugs. My "what she said" look undoubtedly strengthened her position.

July 26, 2016
After a 35-mile stretch of sailing in ideal conditions, we stopped for the night off Galaxidi, another postcard-perfect town bereft of tourists.

While wandering its quiet streets, we discovered that a bus left every morning for Delphi, home of the famous Oracle. One of the most significant sites of antiquity was just a short bus ride away.

The next morning, we were standing between the columns of the Sanctuary of Pythian Apollo, where the Oracle herself stood 2700 years earlier, veiled in a cloud of ceremonial smoke, draped in a violet cloak of linen, gold bracelets dangling from her wrists, hair in a jumble, speaking gibberish, possibly a result of inhaling too much ceremonial smoke (The Oracle required an interpreter to translate her gibberish into prophecies for her audience). We continued to the stadium, an elongated circle of stone tiers that held 6,500 spectators when it hosted the Pythian Games every four years, an event similar to the more-famous games held at Olympia. We had the stadium completely to ourselves, so Valerie, Madeleine, and I sat in the stone bleachers and cheered on William as he performed the hundred-yard dash in the footsteps of the ancients. To honor the Greek goddess of victory, he wore Nikes.

We returned to *Sacre Bleu* at four in the afternoon and made a decision that went down in the ship's log as one of the worst of the entire cruise. We convinced ourselves that we had enough daylight to get as far as the mouth of the Corinth Canal, where we planned to anchor and spend the night so we could catch an early passage when the canal opened the next morning. It was a short run east—about 15 miles—and with any luck we would be anchored off the town of Loutraki with a cocktail in our hands by sunset. It was not to be our lucky day.

As we left Galaxidi, a powerful northwesterly filled our sails, forcing us to reef the mainsail and jib. Over the next hour, the wind and waves gradually built and veered west, straight into our face, so we struck the sails and motored. The seas grew very steep and choppy, forcing us to reduce our speed to keep the dishes from breaking inside the cabinets.

We continued towards the lights of Loutraki, expecting to find shallow water for anchoring, as the chart promised. When we arrived, the chart indicated that the water around us was 30 feet deep, but the depth sounder indicated 70 feet. For the first time on our journey, two electronic gadgets did not agree. We figured the chart must be wrong, so we inched closer to shore and worked our way along the coast hoping to find shallower water. By this time, the sun had set and a dark, moonless night had fallen over us. We sent the kids to their cabins and settled in for a difficult night ahead.

Midnight arrived and we were still blindly following a featureless black shoreline, keeping our eye on the depth sounder for a suitable place to drop anchor. We thought that if we edged up closer to the hills we would get more protection from the powerful wind, and we would eventually reach shallow water. Blindly trusting our electronic chart, which had just proven itself to be unreliable for the first time on the cruise, we probed deeper and deeper towards the dark hills and the indeterminate lights on shore. (Though *Sacre Bleu* was equipped with a radar, we never became confident operating it.) At about 30 feet of depth, we tried anchoring, but the anchor did not set, so we inched a little closer and tried again. After a second try, the anchor seemed to set, so Valerie and I shut down the engines and stretched out on the flybridge with a blanket to keep anchor watch the rest of the night.

The morning sun peeked over the hills, illuminating a very different, cloudless and calm day. I lifted my head to check our position, then stretched out again, relieved that we had not moved from the night before. As I lay there trying to get a moment's more rest, I heard splashing at the front of the boat. I dismissed it as large fish. Hearing more splashing, I lifted my head higher, hoping that the mystery would reveal itself without my having to get up. I vaguely recalled from the chaos of the previous night that we had anchored near an array of lights on shore, which daylight revealed to be a five-story apartment building.

I noticed a woman in her seventies swimming by, wearing a bathing cap, doing the breaststroke. Another similarly mature swimmer passed. I looked around the boat and noticed small buoys with yellow cord running between them, and larger yellow floats defining the corners of what amounted to an open-water swimming area. We were anchored in the middle of the community pool, and we were apparently in the way of the early birds and their morning swim. I quickly scanned the waterline for close-by swimmers, then we started the engines, hoisted the anchor, and slinked away, taking our 45-foot catamaran with us.

The mouth of the Corinth Canal was a short trip, so while Valerie drove the boat I studied the cruising guide to determine the procedure for transiting the Canal. After stopping at the toll station and paying our €240 toll (in cost per mile, the most expensive canal in the world), we heaved to and waited for a voice on the VHF radio to tell us that the canal was open to eastbound traffic. We eventually got the green light and instructions to proceed at four knots, no faster, no slower, to maintain our distance with the other eastbound vessels.

The separation between the Gulf of Corinth and the Aegean Sea is a mere four miles, but this storied stretch of dirt has proven to be a formidable obstacle over time. For Caesar to deploy his mighty navy from the Adriatic to the Aegean Sea, he had to divert it 375 miles around the stormy Peloponnesus. This vexed the great and powerful emperor, who was keenly aware the land route could be traversed by a three-legged donkey in less than an hour. But, alas, Caesar failed to build a canal. Over the centuries, that inconvenient four-mile land barrier frustrated many an emperor's ambitions. In the 7th century BC, the pragmatic Periander simply built a portage road to transport goods over the distance, charging a healthy tariff for his trouble. In 67 AD, emperor Nero officiated at the ground-breaking ceremony for his ambitious Corinth Canal infrastructure project, filling the first basket of soil himself and leaving 6,000 slaves to finish the job, which they didn't. Through epochs and empires, this four-mile stretch was not breached until 1893, when the Corinth Canal was finally completed by Greek contractors who had taken over for the bankrupt French contractors who were working for the Ottomans.

The rough-hewn rock walls of the canal soar up both sides, over 150 feet at places, creating a calm inside that belies the blustery conditions common at both ends. As we exited the east side of the canal and entered the Saronic Gulf, we were hit with a mighty wind, a warning from Poseidon himself that modern sailboats are still no match for his power to humble any mariner who dares ply his waters.

Our first hour in the gulf was a white-knuckle sleigh ride through strong winds and choppy seas. "I wonder if this is a bad day or a normal day in the Aegean," I said to Valerie. "We better reef the sail," she replied, and we did. As the boat lurched to port under a gust, William rushed below to rescue his Lego structures that were in danger of falling off the table. Everyone had their priorities. We found a peaceful anchorage off the town of Palaia Epidavros. There, we went for a walk and stumbled onto a team of archeologists restoring an ancient amphitheater. We were the only visitors, and I got the impression that around these parts ancient amphitheaters and archeologists are as common as the dirt they dig in.

July 28, 2016

We departed for Athens at noon, arriving at the Marina Zeas on the outskirts of town that afternoon. The harbormaster insisted on seeing our original U.S. Coast Guard registration, another first for us. This was a problem because we carried only a photocopy. I made a quick call to a neighbor back in Annapolis and asked him to overnight it to us in Athens. We had not been in this ancient city more than five minutes and we had a desperate need for modern conveyance. The Greek police, who happened to drop by while we were registering, confirmed that they would not let us leave the marina without seeing the original document. I suppose there are worse places than Athens to be stuck.

We spent the next two days touring Athens. The Acropolis, of course, was the highlight, but we discovered other treasures as well. The Presidential Guard, dressed in khaki tunics, white cotton tights and a long-tasseled fez, with pompons on the tips of their shoes, and 9mm rifles on their shoulder, puts on a high-stepping display at the Tomb of the Unknown Soldier. These ceremonial guards allow tourists to stand next to them shoulder to shoulder and pose for photographs, all the while maintaining their serious demeanor, making the moment that much more photogenic.

At the open-air market we bought a ukulele. We happened to have an entire series of ukulele instruction videos on our hard disk, so the purchase was not completely irrational. I never thought it would see much use, but soon William was strumming "Take Me Out to the Ball Game" and other classics. From that day on, ukulele music, played slowly and tentatively, abruptly stopping at random moments, and lacking in any musical expression or rhythm, became a regular part of life on *Sacre Bleu*.

August 1, 2016

According to the Athens FedEx office, our "overnight" package with the original Coast Guard registration was still somewhere in transit, but where, exactly, nobody knew. I dropped by the marina office to give the manager a status update, but it was closed. We had hoped to leave that day for the Saronic Islands, a group of islands just south of Athens, but the weather forecast called for 35-knot winds and six-foot seas, so even if we had received the FedEx, we likely would have stayed put.

In the early afternoon I returned to the marina office, but it was still closed. On the stroll back to the boat, I noticed that the actual weather did not match the forecast, so I continued strolling to the nearby beach to get a closer look at the ocean. Heavy swells were rolling in, and powerful gusts were pulverizing the wavetops, sending spray high into the air. To my captain's eye, it was a 25-knot wind and four-foot seas. In other words, it was just another day in the Mediterranean. I walked back to the boat and suggested to Valerie that we depart—despite the strong winds, rough seas, and possibly becoming wanted criminals.

In minutes, we had started the engines and were on our way out of the marina, striving to be as inconspicuous as possible in our 45-foot-long, 75-foot-high catamaran. As we entered the choppy Saronic Gulf, I imagined what we might have seen if we could have dialed the time machine back to September, 480 BC, when, in this very place, a Persian fleet of over 1,200 rowing galleys attacked a vastly outnumbered Greek fleet and ultimately lost to them in the Battle of Salamis. I watched the depth gage drop through 200 feet and wondered what treasures and lost souls lay in that dark realm below, sent to the bottom 2,500 years ago.

After three hours of sailing, we arrived at the island of Poros, where we found a suitable cove to spend the night. By this time, the Med mooring drill had evolved from chaos into a proper maneuver, with Madeleine and William going to shore on the stand-up paddleboard, tying a line to a tree or rock, and waiting with line in hand while we set the anchor. Of course, as soon as we got settled in Poros, we received a call from the Athens FedEx office telling us that our parcel was ready for pick-up. Valerie managed to wrangle the person on the other end of the line into putting it on a ferryboat to Poros town, which was a short dinghy ride from our mooring.

After picking up our Coast Guard registration at the FedEx office, we strolled through the streets of Poros town, shopping and not buying. Much to the frustration of many a shopkeeper, shopping was a form of sightseeing for us. Then we set a course for the small, sparsely populated island of Dokos. We were the only cruising boat in the anchorage, and the solitude was a welcome change after a week of big-city Athens. (After a dozen Greek ports of call, nobody had asked for our transit log, and by this point I was sure the harbormaster in Athens had forgotten about our Coast Guard registration.) We settled in for a couple of days while Valerie and the kids explored the island and I got caught up on work.

Soon after I sat down at my desk to draw the comic strip, I heard a motorboat putter up. I came out on deck and was greeted by a local fisherman in a wooden skiff. In broken English he asked if I wanted to try catching sea urchins. "Why?" I asked. "So you can eat them," was his reply. In my mind, urchin diving seemed close enough related to drawing an undersea comic strip to still be considered work, so I grabbed my snorkeling gear and joined him in his boat.

He motored to a nearby patch of water, dropped his anchor—which consisted of a rock—and we put on our dive gear and dove in.

After we harvested two-dozen blackish-purple urchins, he showed me how they are eaten. He cracked the outer shell with a knife, revealing an almost-completely hollow interior that contains about a teaspoon of ochre-colored slime. This is a delicacy, he insisted, as we both ate a spoonful of urchin guts. It was a fine day and I had a mouthful of urchin guts. This is the gift of travel.

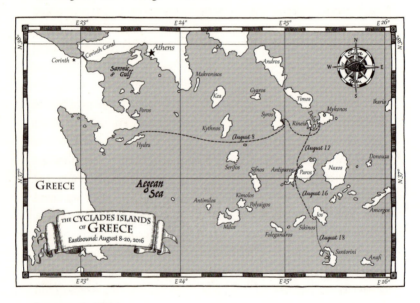

August 6, 2016

We departed Dokos and made our way east along the jagged shoreline of the island of Hydra. Med-moored in a cove, we spent the next two days exploring Hydra's hiking trails and getting to know the staff at the beachfront taverna. It should have been a relaxing time, but I was worried about one of the more challenging passages of our cruise: the 80-mile eastward run out to the Cyclades Islands, a group of over two hundred islands, large and small, that occupy a broad swath of the southern Aegean Sea. We would need a perfect weather window for this stretch of notoriously rough water that necessitated the creation of temperamental deities to rationalize its unpredictably violent nature.

After sailing twelve hours under reefed sails in howling wind, we finally reached the island of Syros. We needed to perform routine maintenance on our diesel engines, and I had arranged to a meet a mechanic there. When we arrived, two mechanics in blue coveralls were waiting for us at the dock, with toolboxes in hand and a grocery cart full of oil and filters. The father and son team were meticulous, humble, and courteous, not to mention a fifth of the price we had paid for the same work in Rome. For the first time in my life, I tipped a mechanic.

August 7, 2016
One year ago today, we left the safe confines of Les Sables-d'Olonne, France. Our original plan was to sail the Mediterranean for a year, but in the weeks leading up to this anniversary, we slowly conceded to the reality that a year was not going to be enough time. Three hundred sixty-five days was an arbitrary number in the cruise plan anyway. The cruise was never about how much we could see or how far we could go in a year. It was about exploring the Mediterranean—a once-in-a-lifetime adventure—over however much time we thought necessary. Our pace was not too fast and not too slow. We still had most of Greece ahead of us, and so much more of the Mediterranean: Sicily, Sardinia, Malta, Corsica, and the Balearic Islands. Even a year in, we didn't feel compelled to make a more detailed itinerary, but we did need an exit strategy. Once we decided that we had had enough of the adventure, then what? Sell the boat and fly home? If so, where?

We left that bigger question for another day. The decision we made on this day was where we would turn around and start heading west, back to France, or wherever we ended up. Every mile we traveled added a mile to our return trip. At some point, we had to stop getting farther away. If we cruised beyond the Greek Islands into Turkish waters, we would want to spend another six weeks there. We decided that we would go as far as the Cyclades Islands of Greece; then we would start the return trip westward, destination unknown.

We left for Mykonos at 4:30 pm, sailing on a beam reach in strong winds and moderate seas, going as fast as we've ever gotten *Sacre Bleu* to go—a whopping 12 knots. A beam reach, with the wind blowing over the side of the boat, or the beam, is the optimal point of sail for a catamaran, and with a stiff breeze and flat seas, a cat can find its groove like a galloping horse.

That night, we found a charming cove with crystal clear indigo water on the south side of the uninhabited island of Rineia.

August 11, 2016

The neighboring island of Delos was just a short dinghy ride from our cove. It looked like just another scrubby hunk of rock when we initially sailed by it. We only realized its significance after we wandered close enough in the dinghy to get a better look. We landed just as a ferryboat full of visitors was leaving the island and stood on the dock transfixed. Before us lay a sea of carved white marble, complete with columned temples, an amphitheater, paved streets lined with large homes and public buildings, marketplaces, mosaics, statues, and fountains. The ruins and structures went as far as the eye could see, and the only other human being on the island, besides us, was the man who sold us our tickets.

The ancient Greeks considered Delos the most sacred of all islands. It is the mythical birthplace of Apollo, god of daylight, and Artemis, goddess of night, and was a thriving crossroads of ancient civilization with its roots in the Bronze Age. It is also one of the best preserved and most significant sites in all of antiquity. We walked its streets, explored its buildings, took a front-row seat in its theater and imagined the show, stood at the altar in the Temple of Isis, and did it all as an intimate family adventure on a self-guided tour of an archeological wonder we had all to ourselves. It was an experience that could have been possible only through self-determined travel on a boat.

Back on our floating home, I checked the weather forecast. My go-to weather website, featuring color-coded wind forecasts any idiot could interpret, had become a regular source of entertainment for me. But tonight, much to my dismay, I had tuned in to a drama. Displayed on the computer screen was a red and purple mass just north of us, and like an anomaly on an X-ray, its presence was worrisome. I quickly cross-referenced another weather website and confirmed that there was a powerful meltemi headed our way. This is the dark side of self-determined travel.

The nautical chart revealed the perfect refuge 20 miles south of us: a cove on the island of Paros that was protected to the north by a line of hills. Knowing that a hundred other sailors had the same idea, we left immediately. When we arrived, the cove was already crowded. One of the advantages of a catamaran is that it draws very little water for its size since it does not need the deep keel of a monohulled sailboat. This allowed us to motor right through the anchorage and drop our hook in the shallow water close to the beach. Then we all dove in the water and swam ashore to make the most of the fair weather while it lasted.

As predicted, the next morning brought a complete change in the physical environment. The brilliant light and sparkling water were gone. The whitewashed buildings of the town of Parikia, gleaming in the previous day's sun, took on a gray pall. The azure waters of our cove turned a slate gray, and the air became angry and cold. A meltemi is a north wind that brings cool breezes and overcast skies but little rain. *Sacre Bleu* was tucked up close to the hills to the north, and the wind and the swells, though harassing boats in the anchorage downwind, did not have much effect on us. I strapped on a dive mask and dove to the anchor so I could have a closer look at how it was set. The seafloor was a muddy sand—perfect for our kind of anchor. As the meltemi winds exerted more and more force on the boat, the anchor would only dig in deeper.

We each claimed our space on the boat and settled in for the duration of the storm, which was forecast to last three days. Each of us had projects: reading books, building Lego structures, and drawing cartoons. Undaunted by the whitecaps in the harbor, Valerie got in the dinghy to go grocery shopping, and after a couple of hours on shore, she returned with favorable reports of the town and its stores. Even better, one of the most important holidays on the Greek Orthodox calendar, the Assumption of the Blessed Virgin Mary and Dormition of the Theotokos, was going to be celebrated the next day with a religious procession and other festivities.

August 15, 2016
The streets of Parikia were filled with those participating in the ritual of the Assumption and those watching, the watchers outnumbering the worshipers by a wide margin. As we passed the 4th century Byzantine church, The Holy Monastery of Panagia Ekatontapiliani, dozens of Orthodox priests, bearded, garbed in black robes and cylindrical black hats, chanting a Greek hymn in unison, spilled out of the church, followed by the white-bearded bishop wearing a gold brocade robe and a gold miter in the shape of an onion dome. They carried a large painting of the Virgin Mary, its gold frame covered with fresh-picked flowers. The procession made its way towards the market square, flanked on both sides by Hellenic Navy sailors bearing rifles, forming a corridor to keep the watchers at bay. After seeing Pope Francis in Rome, we had now ventured into a different realm of Christendom, crossing an invisible line that was drawn in 1054 during the Great Schism, when the Orthodox Church broke with Rome and cast its loyalties to Constantinople.

That evening, with the meltemi winds still blowing, we installed ourselves atop the ancient city walls with our feet dangling as crowds of people ebbed and flowed below us. Fireworks filled the sky, and folk dancers performed on the waterfront. A procession of local fishing boats filled the harbor, with crews setting off flares and Roman candles. For Orthodox Christians, the two-week fast from meat, poultry, fish, dairy, and wine was over, and they could now indulge.

On our third day in Paros, the meltemi winds continued to scour the deck. In town, the festival crowds had dissipated, so we took the dinghy to shore to have a more relaxed look around. There was no space for our dinghy at the city dock, so the captain of a fishing boat gestured for us to raft up to his trawler. We had to climb through his boat to get to shore, so the fisherman, who spoke not a word of English, helped us aboard. This man, who was very friendly and courteous, happened to be wearing a T-shirt that said "FUCK this shit" in big letters. He probably had no idea what the words meant, since the Latin alphabet was likely foreign to him; "It's Greek to me" works in reverse too. As he returned to cleaning his fish, Valerie saw an opportunity to buy directly from the producer at discount rates. She struck up a friendly conversation that quickly transitioned into haggling over a fish. A price was struck, and he eagerly cleaned and wrapped the fish in paper, and we went on our way. Moments later, passing by another fish market on the waterfront, we saw the exact same kind of fish at a better price.

"Looks like 'FUCK this shit' didn't give you such a good deal after all," I said to Valerie.

"'FUCK this shit' sold us a higher quality fish," she replied.

"Even if you knew what kind of fish it was, would you really know a good one from a bad one?"

"It's good to support the locals. You know, the workers, like 'FUCK this shit' who actually catch the fish," she said, deftly shifting the argument to the plight of the working class.

When Valerie shifts arguments, it's a warning to her victims, much like a rattlesnake or a poisonous tree frog, that this fight is already lost. The argument will shift as many times as necessary until the victim, in exhaustion, capitulates. Through our years of marriage, I have come to respect this warning sign and acquiesce early.

The meltemi passed and the wind abated to a mere 25 knots, so we left for Ios, an island about 26 miles south. The route from Paros to Ios can be long or short, depending on how brave the captain is. The short way requires passage through the Andíparos Strait, a shallow ribbon of water between Paros and Antiparos, its sister island a stone's throw to the west. I was of the opinion that sailing a boat that draws four and a half feet in water that was six feet deep, through three-foot swells, throwing in a tide of a foot or so, and seafloor anomalies like rocks and whatever else might be on that bottom after five thousand years of boat traffic, would be foolhardy. Valerie had a different opinion, and unlike her arguments, her opinion did not shift. I reluctantly turned *Sacre Bleu* into the Strait of Antiparos and hoped for the best. We sailed the three miles with a few inches of water under our keels and consumed copious amounts of dumb luck in the process.

As we entered the harbor at Ios, a departing high-speed ferry passed a little too closely and its wake washed over us, burying the deck in ankle-deep water. The hatches were open, and a torrent of saltwater entered our cabin right onto my desk where my laptop computer was sitting. I rushed below and saw my Apple MacBook, my Rosebud, in a puddle of water. I turned it upside down and saltwater drained out of the keyboard. I slid my fingertip over the wet touchpad to try to turn it off, but the computer froze up. The consensus of online advice suggested putting the computer in a bag of uncooked rice and letting it sit two or three days. Good thing we had plenty of time and rice.

With the boat settled into the city dock, I sulked over an ouzo and used Valerie's computer to search for the closest Apple Computer repair center. The answer was none other than Santorini, the glamorous poster child of the Greek Islands. Better yet, it was a direct ferry ride from Ios, so we didn't have to leave the dock. The last ferry had already left (probably the same ferry that flooded our deck), so the trip would have to wait until morning. In the meantime, I poured another drink and watched my bag of rice.

I needed my laptop computer. There were cartoons to draw and bills to pay and weather forecasts to check. Sadly, after spending a full day in a bag of uncooked rice, my laptop did not respond to my entreaties. I held the keyboard upside down and a few more drops of saltwater dripped out. My beloved computer and I cried together for a while longer, then we made plans to spend the next day in Santorini.

While I grieved, a man appeared on the deck of the neighboring boat. I recognized him as a long-term cruiser by his unkempt appearance and the sleep-deprived look in his eyes. Since we had never Med moored to a city dock in Greece, I had a question for him.

"Hi there. Say, we haven't done this Med mooring thing here in the islands before. How's it work?"

"Just tie up, stay as long as you want," he replied. He was an Englishman in his fifties. His wife came up on deck as soon as she heard the conversation.

"No, I mean, how much is it?"

"I have no idea," he replied. "We've been here for a week and nobody's come around asking us for money."

"Some chap in a uniform passes by every now and then, but he doesn't ever say anything," his wife added.

I liked Greece more and more with each passing day, but I was beginning to understand why its economy was languishing.

August 18, 2016

As we walked up the gangplank for the 7:30 ferry to Santorini, I cradled my computer like a sick child, wondering how much of my life's work was lost. At the Apple Computer repair center, I assumed my place in line behind a crestfallen twenty-something with a water-damaged iPhone who, out of sheer muscle memory, continued to glance at her dead screen every idle moment.

The technician made quick work of my MacBook: "Flooded, huh? Oh, yeah. We see this a lot. Looks like the hard drive is fine. It'll take us a day to get the part. €110 to fix it." "Sold" was my one-word response.

The island of Santorini, known as Thira to the Greeks, represents one side of the rim of a colossal volcano that erupted 3,600 years ago, all but obliterating the Minoan civilization. Savoring a Greek salad and an ouzo in a restaurant overlooking this flooded caldera—a gulf of water that measures roughly four miles by six miles, containing a half dozen cruise ships—I was unable to wrap my mind around the scale of the cataclysm.

The foods we had sampled on the cruise up to this point were all part of a continuum of Western European cuisine. Though Spanish food and French food are very different, they share a lot of common ingredients and spices. As we traveled from France to Italy, and Italy on to Croatia, the cuisine evolved, but the ingredients remained familiar. Greek food represented the biggest departure from that continuum.

Mint, fennel, cinnamon, coriander, nutmeg were all new flavors to us. Ingredients like yogurt and honey reminded us that we were wandering ever closer to the Middle East. Olives became the new snack food on the boat—we bought them by the bag. The family's favorite discovery was tzatziki, a zesty, yogurt-based sauce that seemed to come with every meal. Over time, each of us found our favorite Greek dish. For Valerie and me, it was Greek salad; Madeleine's favorite was moussaka, and William nearly always ordered souvlaki when we sat down at a restaurant.

Full but undaunted, we followed a winding path down to the waterfront, where we boarded a square-rigger ship that was offering a tour of the neighboring islands. Our first stop was Nea Kameni, where we hiked across the barren, scorched landscape of this active volcano, then swam in the warm the waters that surround the island. By sunset, our ship was at anchor at the north end of Thira. Moments after the sun dropped below the horizon, a crescent moon rose in the east, and with the last rays of the setting sun casting on orange glow on the cubist fantasy of Fira, the island's capital, the moment took on the photogenic perfection of a corporate motivational poster. As touristy as the excursion was, the four of us were nothing short of ecstatic to be guests on somebody else's boat.

Back home on *Sacre Bleu*, we devoted the next day to utilitarian activities. Lacking a computer, I tried to compose my comic strip the old-fashioned way, with paper and pencil. After fifteen years of working on a computer screen, where I could do and un-do, write and un-write, draw and un-draw, not to mention check my email every five minutes, working with pencil and paper felt like cave painting. Like a roomful of chimpanzees at keyboards, given enough time, I might have produced something great, but that moment seemed very far off. To make matters worse, Valerie and the kids were cleaning the deck of the boat with hard-bristle brushes, so I spent an unproductive afternoon staring at a blank page and listening to scrubbing sounds overhead.

12

Turning West

Ios, Greece
August 20, 2016

My heart fluttered as the noon Santorini ferry docked in Ios. The ramp lowered and the first wave of eager passengers flocked off the boat, followed by crew member holding a carefully wrapped box with my laptop computer inside. The €110 repair fee included free door-to-door delivery from Santorini. I love Greece.

With my beloved Rosebud in my arms once again, I dashed off a week's worth of comic strips, slightly past deadline, and then we cast off the lines and set a course for the island of Milos, 35 miles to the west. The weather forecast called for 30 knots of wind and six-foot seas—nothing out of the ordinary.

Some moments in life can be subtle, seeming so routine that their significance is not appreciated until later. It did not occur to me until I was catching up on the ship's log that evening that we had turned west. We had decided that the Cyclades Islands was the farthest east we would sail, but we never settled on where that farthest point would be. It turned out to be Ios. After over a year of sailing east, ever deeper into the Mediterranean, we were now heading home.

All of us were now seasoned sailors, each playing a role in the operation of the boat. Valerie's greatest fear was docking, so in recent dockings, she took the helm. She soon realized that docking a big boat was no harder than docking a small one, and in some ways it is easier. Sixteen tons is not a fickle mass that reacts to wind shifts and currents like a smaller boat might.

Madeleine was becoming fearless on the deck, attending to flogging sails with a trim of the sheet, setting up the lines for a hoist, and even piloting the boat. William was particularly adept at the navigation software and assumed the role of ship's navigator. When we resumed cruising after our stayover in Antibes, we gave the kids the responsibility of anchoring, and they had grown into a coordinated team. We let them decide where to anchor and how much chain to put out. Valerie and I determined whether the anchor was properly set, until even that role fell to the kids. When we Med moored in a natural setting, we sent Madeleine and William to shore to fasten the stern lines to a tree or a rock. They had refined this maneuver into a well-choreographed routine. As we made our turn west, we had hit our stride as a crew and a family.

Because of the rough seas, we stopped short of Milos and Med moored against the steep, rocky southwest side of Polyaigos, where we found protection from the wind and waves. There were no trees on shore, so the kids secured the stern lines to a large rock. Polyaigos is a sparsely populated island, and, as beautiful as it is, what really sold us on the location was the presence of two mega-yachts also Med moored against the same stunningly beautiful cliff that rose out of the crystal-clear waters. We may not have known all the secret spots in the Greek islands, but the captains of the mega-yachts did, and we were never too proud to plop down next to them with our pool toys, set the kids free, and raise the cocktail flag.

We should have paid more attention when both the mega-yachts departed. The setting sun painted the calm water in streaks of gold, and the air was dead calm. Why were they not spending the night in such a beautiful place?

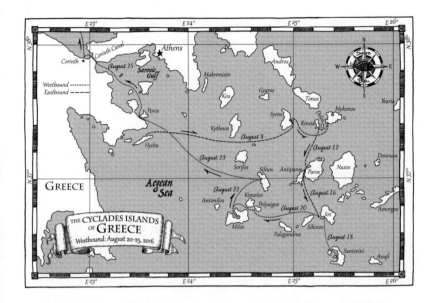

Early the next morning, alone in the anchorage, we woke to a sudden, violent wind that threatened to rip the cleats out of our deck. I strapped life preservers on Madeleine and William and sent them out on the paddleboard to unfasten the mooring lines while I started the engines. The kids understood the urgency of the situation and made quick work of collecting the lines and returning to the boat. With children, lines, and anchor safely stowed, we worked our way west to Milos, where we found calmer water moored to the seawall in the town of Adamantas. The kids had proven themselves to be reliable crew during our hasty departure. Their shift from dependent to dependable was making our lives easier every day.

In 1820, when a farmer on Milos who was looking for stones to build a wall uncovered a life-sized marble statue of an armless Aphrodite, the Greek goddess of love, he did not think much of it, so he sold it to a French naval officer for a modest sum. Under her Roman name, Venus of Milos, or *Venus de Milo*, it went on to become a gift to the King of France, an icon of classical art and a centerpiece at the Louvre. As we toured the scrubby interior of Milos in a cab, I wondered if Venus' missing arms were leaning against a wall in a barn or an attic, found later by that same farmer and kept out of spite.

That afternoon, we savored a lunch of tiropita—phyllo dough stuffed with feta cheese—at a taverna, and then we hiked back to the boat along a coastal trail. Though the trek is steep and cluttered with loose rocks, a reward awaits the brave few who choose this path of most resistance. Along the way, we happened onto a 3rd century BC Roman amphitheater, and once again, we had this ancient monument all to ourselves. Back in America, any building older than 200 years is turned into a museum. On Milos, a 2300-year-old amphitheater does not even merit a sign.

Mornings frequently bring a weather reset. A blustery afternoon the day before often gives way to a calm morning, and then all is right in our weather-dependent world. However, on this morning we woke to stronger winds from the day before that signaled the approach of a system. A check of the forecast confirmed another meltemi was bearing down on us. Rather than getting pinned down in the Cyclades Islands for what could be another week, we sailed west for Poros.

We ran an exhausting 20 hours with Valerie and I trading off the watches while the kids stayed indoors because of the heavy seas. We Med moored along the seawall of Poros town, where we had picked up our FedEx package a few weeks earlier.

Our visit this time would be short. After shopping for groceries we set off for the east entrance of the Corinth Canal. Since we were covering old ground, we continued to drive west at a steady clip. Our initial plan was to anchor before the canal and spend the night; however, in the meltemi winds we made excellent time. We arrived at the dock to pay the canal toll in the early afternoon, just as it was opening to westerly traffic, so we decided to keep going.

Our proximity to the Corinth Canal always seemed to bring out the worst judgment in us. We knew the winds were likely to be strong on the other side, and we knew that anchoring in the Gulf of Corinth was difficult. This was all seared in our recent memory. Yet, optimists that we were, we carried on.

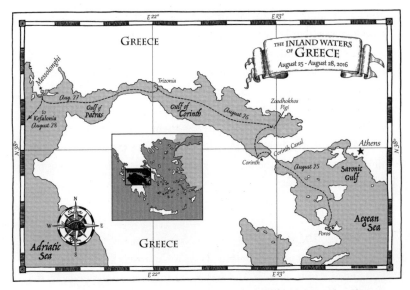

As strong as the wind was on the Aegean side, the canal authority warned us that the Gulf of Corinth was a raging maelstrom. Inside the canal, with steep walls on both sides, conditions were deceptively calm. If it is possible to relax nervously, we did so, waiting for our audience with the angry giant. The moment we got to the west end of the Canal, we found him waiting for us. The Gulf of Corinth was virtually whitewater, with winds over 30 knots. And there was no turning around.

As soon as we left the protective cover of the Canal, we turned south, going with the fierce wind and waves, hoping to take refuge in the Corinth Marina. Once we were inside the breakwater, we quickly realized it was a maze of small, concrete slips where docking our behemoth would be impossible. In one tense moment, the keels touched bottom. Once again, we were caught without a Plan B, except the ultimate Plan B, which was to keep sailing. We considered going all the way back to Galaxidi, but it was late in the day, and we were willing to try anything other than sailing that far on a stormy night.

I studied the chart further, considering a wider range of destinations, and saw a small group of islands called the Alkionides about 15 miles to the north. Facing into the fury of wind and waves with both engines at full throttle, we ran another four hours, finally anchoring in the lee of the island of Zoodochos Pigi as the last glimmers of sunlight faded. The Alkionides Islands are named after the goddess Alcyone, or Halcyon, the mythical daughter of Aeolus, god of the winds. When Alcyone's husband, Ceyx, drowned in a storm, Alcyone cast herself into the sea to join him, and the two lovers emerged from the sea as halcyon birds. Aeolus took pity on them and calmed his winds, allowing them to build their nest in peace. Mythology maybe, but after sailing through this stretch of water twice and experiencing two of the worst days of the voyage, I would have happily traded two hamsters for a halcyon bird.

August 26, 2016
We weighed anchor and continued our westward trek under full sails, hugging the hilly shoreline to starboard to catch just enough of the fierce northerly wind to fill the sails. As we passed openings in the hills, we were assailed by powerful gusts that forced us to reef. Growing tired of reefing and unreefing the sails with the fluctuating wind, we devised a work-around. We set full sails, and when we encountered a strong gust, we simply turned the boat directly downwind. By running at 10 knots in the same direction as a 30-knot blast, we reduced the "apparent wind" to a manageable 20 knots, which allowed us to keep sailing without reefing. As we passed through areas of lighter winds, we worked our way back to windward on a close-hauled tack. In this zigzag fashion, we meandered 50 miles to the island of Trizonia.

Early the next morning, I woke to a ghastly scream coming from the woods on shore. The sound was so eerie that I was not sure whether I had heard it or dreamt it. I lay in bed holding my breath, waiting for another. As I silently took inventory of all the mosquitoes smashed against the ceiling of our cabin, another hair-raising wail erupted from shore. It was a man's voice, and this man was obviously in extreme pain. The prolonged cry started off intense, hit a crescendo, and then quickly faded, as if he were losing a very desperate struggle. If men could give birth, this is the sound they would make. I tapped Valerie on the shoulder to wake her. I have woken her from a deep sleep only three or four times in our marriage because of the danger involved.

"What is it?" she mumbled.

"Shhhh! Listen! Somebody's screaming out there," I answered in a voice revealing panic at the thought of playing a role in a real emergency. My volunteer training in Antibes had covered first aid, but only on mannequins.

Valerie opened her eyes, furrowed her brow, and we both waited in silence. Of course, at this very moment the screaming stopped for a solid two minutes. Then, another edge-of-death, ghastly wail echoed from the woods on shore. I looked at Valerie with fear in my eyes, but also feeling vindicated, and said, "Hear that?"

She rolled over, covered her head with the blanket, and declared "They're goats."

I allowed myself to believe her.

Later that morning, Valerie and I made some quiet one-on-one time with our daughter over breakfast. We were both seeing subtle hints that our little girl was developing into a young woman. Her fourteenth birthday was coming up in a few weeks, and it occurred to us that we had a teenage daughter onboard and we had not yet had a conversation about the birds and the bees. Valerie gave me a knowing glance, turned to Madeleine, and started the conversation.

"Are you staying in touch with any of your friends from school?"

"Uh-huh."

"Do any of them have...boyfriends?" said Valerie, moving quickly into the heart of the discussion. Then came another ghastly shriek from the woods.

"What was that?" asked Madeleine.

"Goats," said Valerie.

"I've never heard a goat like that before," Madeleine said, casting her eyes toward shore, hoping to catch a glimpse of the creature making such a hideous noise.

"We had goats like that on my grandmother's farm," Valerie said, assuring us both that it was indeed merely a goat and not some mythical Gollum-like creature that inhabited dark European woods. The screaming goats made a delicate conversation that much more awkward, so we did what any parent would do and postponed it for another day.

We had another long day ahead of us, so I started the engines while the kids hauled up the anchor. As we drove away, I looked over my shoulder and I finally saw them. A dozen goats had gathered on the rocky shore as if to bid us a bon voyage.

Our next stop was Messolonghi, a town accessed by a 2.5-mile canal that took us to a large, manmade basin deep inland. It seemed the perfect place to enjoy a peaceful night without worrying about the anchor dragging in the strong winds. With the boat tied to a seawall in flat water, we had our best opportunity to send somebody up the mast in a bosun's chair to fix the VHF antenna that had come loose. The antenna had developed a wobble as the boat rolled and pitched, and it would eventually break.

Valerie and I decided that sending one of the kids up the 75-foot mast would be a good experience; neither of us wanted to do it, and they would probably think it was fun. In the interest of running a gender-neutral boat, we chose Madeleine. We wanted to raise a daughter who could hold her own with tools. After some back and forth, with me explaining the concept of "righty tighty, lefty loosey," we hoisted her up the mast. She tightened the bolts and came down a more confident young woman. She might have missed the lesson about the birds and the bees, but she was developing socket wrench skills.

August 28, 2016

We were back in the Adriatic Sea, leaving the mainland astern and feeling very sad that our time in Greece was coming to an end. With its hundreds of islands, coves, beaches, villages, shops, taverns, and ruins, Greece is a sailor's paradise. Our farewell would be the island of Kefalonia, where we would make the jump back to Italy.

Kefalonia is the largest of the Ionian Islands, and it boasts some of the most beautiful beaches in Europe. We were planning on dropping anchor off the coast for one night and leaving for Italy the next morning. But we could not let go of Greece that easily, so we spent another three days exploring the island. We first stopped in the town of Argostoli, where we Med moored to the seawall.

We visited the Drogarati Cave, featuring a natural chamber big enough to host concerts, toured the underground lakes of Melissani on a boat, and buried our toes in the sand of some of Kefalonia's world-renowned beaches. That night and the next day, we ate dinner, breakfast, and lunch at local restaurants, relishing our last opportunities to savor souvlaki, moussaka, gyros, Kalamata olives, feta cheese, dolmas, baklava, and the aromas of coriander, mint, honey, and nutmeg that would forever evoke fond memories of Greece.

After lunch, we cast off from the city dock and drove to the southeast corner of Kefalonia, where we anchored off of Kounopetra Beach. We planned to get an early start the next morning on our long crossing to Italy, and launching from an anchor is easier than launching from a dock. An early departure from a city dock can bring surprises. We might wake up to discover that our neighbors have fastened their dock lines over ours, or a boat that had docked in the middle of the night was blocking our exit. At anchor, all we had to do was start the engines, weigh anchor and go.

13

Islands and Volcanoes

Kefalonia, Greece
September 1, 2016

We woke in darkness, warmed up the engines and the coffee and were on our way by sunrise. The run to Italy was 190 nautical miles, taking us roughly 32 hours. We were shooting for a midday arrival in Rocella Ionica, a small city on the sole of the boot-shaped Italian peninsula. At midnight, we lost our wind and motored the rest of the way across the Adriatic Sea. For those doing the night watch, driving a motorboat or a motoring sailboat is far easier than sailing. There are no sails to trim or strike in heavy weather. For those *not* doing night watch, trying to sleep in the aft cabin, the diesel engine is a noisy roommate one thin bulkhead away from the pillow.

Until we turned west at the Greek island of Ios, we had not set much of an itinerary, preferring to go, literally, whichever way the wind was blowing. As we made our way east, every stop had been a new experience. We felt free to go wherever we wanted and stayed however long we wanted. Once we made the turn west, we had to put more thought into where we were going in the context of where we had already been.

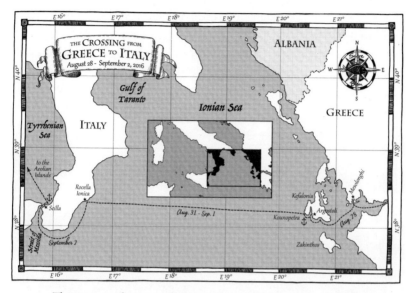

There were other considerations driving the itinerary. Our marine insurance policy stipulated a cruising territory that included the European territorial waters of the Mediterranean and specifically excluded North Africa. We were still free to sail to Egypt, for example, but we would not be insured. Though certain countries, namely Algeria and Libya, and more recently Egypt, present challenges to boat insurers, Tunisia and Morocco historically have provided safe and popular destinations for cruisers. However, in 2015, the year we began our cruise, a spate of terrorist attacks in Tunisia that specifically targeted tourists compelled the insurance industry to rewrite their policies. Those tragedies ultimately played a considerable role in shaping our Mediterranean itinerary. Though we never ceased to appreciate how the European cultures in the Mediterranean changed as we sailed the east-west axis, a trip south to Tunisia or Morocco would have added a new dimension to the voyage.

We also had to consider the refugee crisis playing out on the open waters of the Mediterranean between North Africa and Europe. In 2015, the UN estimated that over a million refugees from North Africa had arrived on the shores of Greece, Italy, Spain, Cyprus, and

Malta, many making the trip in small, unseaworthy vessels operated by armed human traffickers. If we came across an overcrowded refugee boat, the Law of the Sea obligated us to render assistance. Destinations with shorelines that were a short, direct shot from North Africa, such as Malta and the southern coasts of Sicily and Sardinia, were off the itinerary.

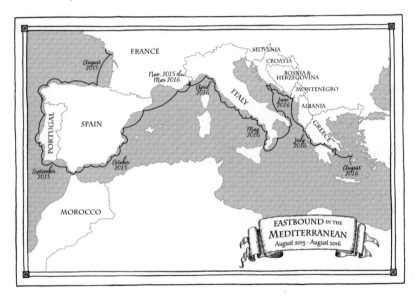

On the eastbound part of the voyage, we chose to sail coastwise along the European mainland. For the westbound leg we decided to run through the middle of the Mediterranean, visiting the larger islands like Sicily, Sardinia, Corsica, and the Balearics, as we hop-scotched our way west. Though these islands are territories of Italy, France or Spain, in terms of culture, history, cuisine and language, they are countries unto themselves. We were also eager to visit the many smaller island groups, such as the Aeolians off Sicily and the Maddalena Archipelago off Sardinia. As island hoppers, we would undertake more overnight passages and spend more time on the open sea, but as a seasoned sailing family, we found more tedium than terror in the prospect.

Islands and Volcanoes

After a day in Rocella Ionica, we continued our run along the southern coast. At the toe of the boot, we made a right turn into the Strait of Messina, negotiated the notorious currents, whirlpools and sea monsters, and dropped anchor off the town of Scilla, virtually in the same spot we had dropped anchor three months prior.

The sun rose behind Castello Ruffo, lighting up the glassy waters of the Tyrrhenian Sea like an inferno. We weighed anchor and set a northwest course for the Aeolians, a group of seven islands north of Sicily, of which two are active volcanoes: Vulcano and Stromboli. Though Vulcano had not erupted in over a century, Stromboli promised regular, sometimes violent eruptions. Eager to catch the next show, we pointed *Sacre Bleu* towards the northernmost island of the group, Stromboli.

Volcanoes are a giant cone with very steep walls, a shape more easily appreciated when they sit on land, their unmistakable profile looming on the horizon like a sleeping giant. Rising from the seafloor with its top poking out of the water, a volcano looks like just another island. One very inconvenient feature is hidden beneath the waves: the sides descend at a steep angle with no flat shelf to set an anchor. The chart of Stromboli revealed one potential anchorage on the northeast corner, but when we arrived, our hopes were dashed by signs on buoys that declared it a no-anchoring zone. (This was a continuous theme in the Mediterranean: Anchoring is frequently prohibited in areas that are most suitable.)

With no place to go, we idled by a steep-walled volcano in the middle of the Tyrrhenian Sea and pondered our next move. Thinking more like lawyers than sailors, we drove past the line of buoys that defined the no-anchoring zone, dropped our anchor, then backed down, letting out enough chain for the boat to be just outside of the restricted area.

This did not sit well with the lifeguard, who witnessed our ruse from the beach. He got into his inflatable motorboat and zoomed out to inform us that even if our boat was not in the no-anchor zone, our anchor was. While Valerie was clashing with the lifeguard, a motorboat roared past, inside the no-anchoring zone, and the lifeguard and the driver exchanged knowing waves. They were clearly friends. Valerie ripped into the lifeguard for insisting that an anchored sailboat posed a risk to swimmers while a reckless, speeding motorboat, driven by one of the lifeguard's friends, posed no risk at all. Sensing the fight was lost, the lifeguard gave up and returned to his perch, where he aggressively twirled his whistle-on-a-string and glared at us.

Stromboli
September 4, 2016

The next morning, we rode the dinghy to San Vincenzo, the principal town on the northeast corner of Stromboli, the "safe" side of the island. The volcano had been silent for three days, but all the tour guides were certain that the next eruption was minutes away. Mount Stromboli's eruptions typically consist of a harmless puff of black smoke, as if controlled by a wizard living inside the mountain who is paid by the chamber of commerce. On the rare occasion of a violent eruption, lava and ash flow away from the town and down a steep embankment into the sea.

Guided volcano tours did not start until 5pm, so we opted for the do-it-yourself tour, grabbed a trail map, and started hiking. I mentioned to Valerie that a do-it-yourself volcano tour sounded like a good start to a bad story, but she brushed off my pessimism, as usual. When we finally reached Mt. Stromboli, the top was veiled in clouds. We saw no reason to hike any farther and settled into an overlook along the ridge to savor the view.

The spillway that runs from the crater into the sea is a barren lunar landscape on a steep slope. Each of us was thinking the same thing as we contemplated the stage from our safe balcony seat: Now would be the perfect time for a violent eruption, the violenter the better, preferably with lots of poisonous gases and flaming lava and flying boulders. We gave it fifteen minutes, but no natural disasters seemed to be in the cards for us that day. Feeling unlucky and endowed with fleeting attention spans cultivated from years of watching television, we headed back down.

Back on *Sacre Bleu* by midday, we weighed anchor and, to get a look at Mount Stromboli from the sea, we charted a course around the north end of the island and down the west coast. We skirted the danger zone indicated on the nautical chart, hoping to see any sign of eruption. As a parting gesture, Mount Stromboli ended its silence in a puff of black smoke belching into the sky above. I turned to Madeleine and William, who were at the galley table immersed in their Nintendo DS consoles, thumbs ablaze, and said, "Hey, guys, look! The volcano's erupting!"

They both glanced up and then quickly back down again, fearing that they had left the Super Mario Brothers in a bad situation. That's when Valerie took the game consoles away.

We hopped to the island of Lipari, the largest of the Aeolians, 35 miles to the south, then Vulcano, the southernmost of the Aeolian Islands, where we anchored in a rocky cove on the northwest side of the island. Vulcan, besides being a fictional race of extraterrestrials on Star Trek, is the Roman god of fire. The Romans believed that the island was the chimney of Vulcan's forge as he fashioned weapons for the god of war, Mars. Though we get the word "volcano" from this island, Vulcano erupts far less frequently than Stromboli (where we get the word for pizza turnover). Nevertheless, whatever is happening beneath the surface of Vulcano, whether it is a workshop of the gods or colossal tectonic plates grinding against each other, provides enough heat to turn the island into a geothermal theme park.

As we approached the shore of Vulcano in the dinghy, sulfur fumes filled the air. Once we landed, we went in search of a hot mud experience and were overwhelmed with options, from a public mud pit where the unwashed masses wallow in sludge, to fancy indoor spas, featuring small tubs labeled with temperatures ranging from 38 to 42 degrees Celsius, where the mud looked edible. Having kids in tow, we opted for the sludge.

A dozen people in the public bath all wore expressions of uncertainty as they sat shoulder-deep in gurgling mud. Once I waded in and sat down, I understood why. Was this enjoyable? Would I develop an appreciation for this mud, or would I develop a terminal rash? I stewed for five minutes, determined it was not going to become more enjoyable and got out. Luckily, the mud bath is only steps from the beach, where the same geothermal activity gives the ocean a kiddy pool warmth.

After a day of marinating in sulfurous mud and swimming in the warm ocean, we made our way back to the boat, where we all took long, hot showers, a luxury we rarely indulged in as a boat family. We had planned to make the 20-mile return trip to Portorosa that afternoon, but after a hot shower and an ouzo, we lost all our motivation and opted to stay in Vulcano. Later that night, as a storm from the north brought strong winds and waves into the exposed anchorage, we decided we would be better off in Portorosa after all, so we departed at midnight. With a 25-knot wind at our backs, we drove through the dark, choppy seas and finally tied up to the dock at Portorosa at two in the morning.

Now for a brief digression on the French language: The French word *décider* translates into the English verb "to decide," but a subtlety in the French is lost in translation. As strictly an intransitive verb, "decide" never takes a direct object. You can decide to leave, but you cannot decide *me* to leave. The French verb décider can be both intransitive and transitive. In French, you can decide to leave, or you can decide me to leave, as in "My wife decided me to leave for Portorosa at midnight during a building gale." In English, we might be tempted to use "persuade" or "convince" to describe this action, but persuading is not the same as deciding. When we decide somebody, there is no discussion.

Portorosa has a service center for marine electronics, so we contacted a technician to help us troubleshoot the autopilot, which was causing the boat to sail erratically. "You've been to Vulcano," he observed as I accompanied him to the bridge. "Yes. How did you know?" I asked. "You smell like sulfur," he said matter-of-factly as he unscrewed the panel to access the circuit board. I smelled the back of my hand, I smelled my arm, I smelled my shirt. I could not smell a thing. Scary.

We departed Portorosa and sailed 50 miles along the northern Sicilian coast, a stark yet stunning stretch of granite cliffs and verdant valleys that resemble Yosemite National Park on an ocean. Squall lines stalked the horizon, casting dark shadows on the water as they lumbered towards the shore. We anchored in a cove off the town of Cefalù just as the squalls caught up to us.

Cefalù is a jumble of white stucco buildings with red clay roofs, bay windows, balconies, overhangs, and terraces. It looks as if a ship that had been moving a village foundered in a storm, and all the village pieces washed ashore. Unique as this Sicilian village was, we had no time to visit because Valerie had a ticket to fly home to Lyon, France, the next day to pay a surprise visit to her family and celebrate her father's 80th birthday. The departure point for Palermo Airport, and the best shelter for the rest of us to bide our time was Castellammare del Golfo, a small city 60 miles farther along the coast.

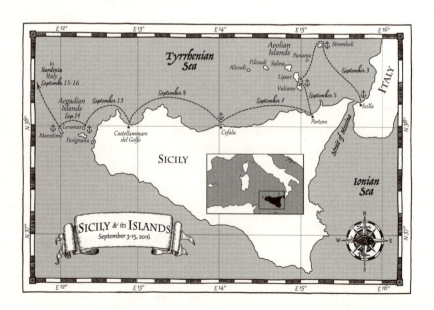

We arrived in the late afternoon and secured a slip with a sweeping view of the town. Castellammare sits at the mouth of a valley that rolls into the sea, walled in by rocky bluffs that break through the green sloping valleys, soaring vertically into the sky. As with so many other towns along this coast, fishing and tourism now support the ancient city, whose storied past includes many American Mafia figures. Before Joe "Bananas" Bonanno and Stefano "The Undertaker" Magaddino ruled the streets of New York, they ruled the playgrounds of Castellammare del Golfo.

Early the next morning, Valerie caught a cab for Palermo Airport. And then we were three.

A newfound sense of aimlessness and bewilderment set in within minutes. "Where does mom put the toilet paper?" "How does the washing machine work?" "Who's responsible for washing the dishes?" Personalities changed and social hierarchies shifted. Madeleine became more talkative, and William no longer napped so much in a remote corner of the boat. They both knew that I was not going to make them do any chores because I had no idea what needed to be done.

We spent the next day in the neighboring Riserva Naturale dello Zingaro, a nature reserve with cliffside trails that run high above the roaring surf. Hiking has always been a favorite family activity, and Valerie did most of the talking during a hike. Now that we were a threesome, an empty, silent volume of air hovered over us like an empty cartoon voice bubble. We were three inward-looking souls hiking a common trail, but it might as well have been three trails. William was especially in his own world and provided an easy target for tricks.

Madeleine and I would stop walking and he would march on and on, lost in a daydream. Seeing my son walking off in a catatonic state, being entertained by whatever show was playing in his head, compelled me to worry that my children were developing into introverts. I became determined to reverse the process. I reasoned that their inward focus was more a product of laziness than of being the offspring of a reticent cartoonist. On the next day's hike, I forced them to tell jokes and stories. I peppered them with questions about their favorite places on the cruise, their favorite food, what they liked about living on a boat, what they did not like, which friends they missed, what they wanted to do when they grew up. Once William started talking, he had the capacity to continue. He simply switched his inner conversation to an outer one. When Madeleine and I tried to converse, it was like playing that favorite birthday party game, the egg-and-spoon relay. It would last one exchange, maybe two, then abruptly end with two faces looking down bashfully.

With Valerie away, I decided it was a good time to take apart and re-grease all nine of the deck winches, an annual practice recommended by the manufacturer. Back home on land, I did not spend one waking moment thinking about preventative maintenance. Who cleans the leaves out of their rain gutters every spring? Not me. Are you supposed to change the air filters in the furnace? Annually? Really? When home is a boat with hundreds of independently operating mechanical and electrical components each prone to failure in its own unique way, at the worst possible moment, with potentially life-threatening consequences, even the most diehard procrastinator must confront the demons of preventive maintenance.

I started with the three winches up on the flybridge. Setting my laptop next to the first one, I watched a YouTube demonstration about disassembling a winch, produced by the manufacturer. Screwdriver in hand, I tried to mirror the technician's every move. His operation went a lot smoother than mine, partly because he was taking his winch apart on a flat, well-lighted tabletop, but mostly because he knew what he was doing, and I had no more business taking apart a winch than performing knee surgery. I removed the top, and much to my surprise, found inside that winch drum hundreds of tiny parts waiting for their moment to break free. The first to take flight was a spring that leaped out as soon as it saw daylight. Paralyzed, I watched it bounce down the first step from the flybridge to the main deck, almost come to rest, drop down the second and the third steps, pick up momentum, hit the deck and roll, and finally settle about a half inch from falling in the water. I looked inside the open winch drum and counted seventeen tiny gears. I retrieved the spring, reassembled the winch, gave up and made coffee.

Valerie arrived the next afternoon, bursting with stories and glowing from the three days she had spent with her family. The dead air was once again filled with voice and emotion and stories about relationships and feelings.

We spent the rest of the day exploring Castellammare del Golfo's streets. Like so many towns that we visited that were off the tour bus circuit, Castellammare was filled with locals going about their daily lives, and it provided us an opportunity to observe Sicilian culture unadorned by tourism. Stores sold groceries, hardware, building supplies and clothing. Patrons at cafes read their newspaper over an espresso. Schoolchildren queued up at the gelateria. Entire families, from the very old to the newborn, gathered around a table for a long lunch at a restaurant. Life is slow paced, and the hustle of tourism is nowhere to be found.

Castellammare del Golfo, Sicily
September 13, 2016

The next morning, we departed for Levanzo, one of the Aegadian Islands off the western tip of Sicily. When we arrived, we found a harbor crowded with work boats. By the look of these timeworn skiffs and fishing boats, the locals did not spend their weekends waterskiing or sport fishing. We anchored outside of town, just off the island's cemetery.

That night, we drove the dinghy to the town dock for a gelato. A small general store served as the island's community center, where young and old gathered to sit and sip, keep an eye on the kids playing in the street, keep another eye on the soccer match on television, and share an evening with fellow Levanzans, a rare breed that numbered about 450. We strolled along the coastal road to the outskirts of town, where we eventually came upon the cemetery near where we were anchored. Like most Italian cemeteries, it was enclosed by a high stone wall with an iron gate. We peeked through the gate at the burial sites, rows of above-ground crypts, many of ornate stone, some shaped like small houses and containing entire families. Hovering in the dark sky like a cosmic nightlight, the full moon painted the stone in a pale blue wash. Valerie tried the gate latch; it was unlocked. We looked left and right, pushed open the creaking portal to the Village of the Dead, and slipped through to the Other Side.

Our wandering eyes were met by the gazes of dozens of moonlit saints and angels frozen in white marble, bearing down on us with mournful demeanors. Were they alive moments before, enjoying their nightly gathering before we interrupted? I put that image in William's head as we started down one of the dark pathways lined with crypts, and he stayed close on my heels the rest of the night. With the glow of our phones, we lit up some of the tombstones and read the inscriptions, most of which featured a photograph of the deceased. Many were elderly, as one might expect, and their inscriptions told stories of long lives well lived. In other crypts lay children and young adults whose photographs caught them in a happy moment when death seemed remote. The departed wore the fashion of their day: frizzy hair and wide lapels from the 1970s, padded shoulders and perms from the 80s, a matriarch from long ago wearing formal dress and an austere expression. By Italian custom, these crypts are reusable; most of the dead are not in their final resting place but are merely passing through. After the lease expires, families may opt to move their loved ones' remains to the nearby ossuary to make room for more dearly departed on this island where space is limited but mortality is unrelenting.

The next morning, we learned that a sirocco was approaching from the south. A sirocco is born as a giant swirl of hot air in the Sahara and Arabian deserts. When it moves north over water, the heat and dust collide with moisture to create "blood rain," as it is called by the Italians because of its ruddy color. The sirocco leaves a thin layer of red dust in its path as far north as Britain—where cars are coated in a fine powder and rain gutters sprout weeds— as far west as the Amazon basin, and as far east as Japan. Over millions of years, this soil transfer has gradually transformed North Africa into a desert while turning Europe into a Garden of Eden, shaping the course of civilizations and changing climates.

The approaching sirocco was on everyone's mind as we passed boats in the harbor on our morning run for bread. We wasted no time departing Levanzo, sailing twelve miles west to the island of Marettimo. There we anchored off Punta Troia, a stone outcrop crowned with a 16th century castle, to get a few hours' rest. At midnight, with the sirocco bearing down on us, we hauled up the anchor and began the 210-mile run to Sardinia, timing our departure to arrive midday.

As the morning sun rose, the southerly wind filled in behind us and *Sacre Bleu* lifted under her sails like a racehorse. The day was chilly and wet, so I lowered the clear plastic and canvas panels and zipped them up, making a watertight flybridge area. This created the most popular room on the boat, and the kids went below to grab their pillows and blankets and settle in for the day's transit. When William opened his cabin door, two songbirds came fluttering out into the salon. The creatures were tiny, terrified, and lightning fast, and they seemed to vanish and reappear at a new perch in the salon whenever Madeleine or William got close. One of the birds flew up into the bridge, where it came to rest on my steering wheel. As the autopilot made small course corrections with the wheel, the bird shuffled sideways to the left and to the right like a lumberjack in a log rolling competition. The bird tried out new perches in the bridge, and even flew around outdoors, circling the mast, but always came back to rest on the steering wheel. Somehow, it sensed that the closest land was still not close enough, and it needed the boat as much as we did.

We sailed into the night, assuming the stowaways would surely be gone by morning, but when I took the watch from Valerie at six a.m., we still had one bird on the steering wheel and possibly another, whereabouts unknown. Light rainsqualls had been pitter-pattering the canvas covers on the bridge all night long, but by sunrise, the weather cleared as the dark profile of Sardinia appeared on the horizon. I sat at the helm, looking into the eyes of my feathered companion, searching for a moment of truth in our relationship, thinking perhaps that I could tame him and train him to eat mosquitos. But then the bird abruptly launched itself through the opening in the Bimini and towards land, never looking back.

After long crossings, the exterior of the boat is invariably caked in sea salt. When we finally make landfall, before we do anything else—before we take a nap or explore—we thoroughly clean the outside of the boat. On our arrival in Olbia, we did the same. The sirocco arrived that night, and by the next morning our thoroughly cleaned boat was thoroughly coated in red dust.

Olbia, Sardinia
September 21, 2016

We spent the day in Olbia waiting for the sirocco to pass, then continued to the northern tip of Sardinia, where the island comes within seven miles of touching the French island of Corsica. The sirocco had been gone less than a day when a mistral arrived, bringing stronger, colder winds from the west. A mistral enters the Mediterranean Basin via the Rhone Valley in France and races easterly until it hits a wall of mountains in the form of two large islands: Sardinia and Corsica. Determined to continue its progress, this mass of angry air tries to squeeze between the two islands, creating semi-regular gale conditions in the seven-mile-wide strip of water called the Strait of Bonifacio. La Maddalena Island sits in a veritable wind tunnel.

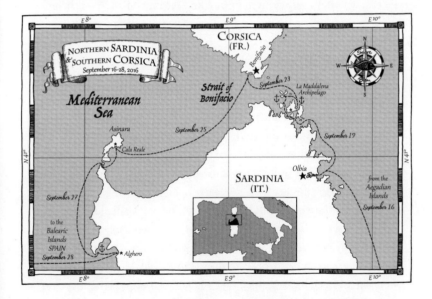

Oblivious to the wind conditions, I saw the island on the nautical chart and thought, La Maddalena ...Madeleine...Hmm...What a nice place to spend Madeleine's fourteenth birthday.

The ride to La Maddalena was wild, bumpy and wet. We had a favorable wind, albeit a strong one, like a bouncer escorting us out of a bar, pulling us along with a lot more force than necessary. In the middle of it all, William discovered the second stowaway bird in his cabin, dead. It was a testimony to the state of cleanliness of William's cabin that a dead animal could go unnoticed for three days. We gave it a burial at sea.

When we arrived at the Strait of Bonifacio, it was clear that no small boats were making the passage to La Maddalena Island. We secured *Sacre Bleu* to a mooring ball on Sardinia, grabbed our wind breakers and boarded a ferry. In the streets of La Maddalena town, the air was calm, so we found an outdoor cafe and celebrated Madeleine's birthday. Lacking a gift, we gave her an apple, with the promise that we would buy her a new Apple computer when we resumed life on land.

More than a year into our cruise, with Madeleine celebrating a second birthday away from home, I could see that boat life was beginning to wear on her. It was a lifestyle that most adults would envy, but not one most teenagers would choose. The never-ending sailing adventure did not offer lasting friendships with anyone but her little brother. Every day was extraordinary, but that only made the ordinary that much more alluring to her—gathering with friends for a sleepover, a game of tetherball on the playground, taking Belle for a walk. Valerie and I could sense that the young woman that was growing up before our eyes was, at times, missing the life she left behind. Still, her eyes perked up when the waiter arrived with an improvised birthday cake: Nutella pizza.

The mistral passed, allowing us to explore La Maddalena's Archipelago of seven large islands, countless small islands, stretches of white sandy beaches and sparkling turquoise water. The tropical feel provided a nice break from the deep, dark, cold Mediterranean we were accustomed to. I strapped on a scuba tank in hopes that the clear waters of La Maddalena had some sea life to offer.

Sacre Bleu carried enough dive gear for two people, but we rarely used it other than to work on the boat below the waterline. In one way, a dive in the Mediterranean is rewarding because the water is crystal clear. However, you will soon discover that there is very little sea life in all that clear water. Centuries of fishing pressure has done its damage, but there's another reason why there are so few fish. A scientist would refer to Mediterranean water as "oligotrophic," meaning it is deficient in dissolved nutrients. The Mediterranean is virtually a closed body of water with very few rivers flowing into it—rivers that bring vital nutrients that feed the microorganisms that form the foundation of the food web. At the biggest point of water exchange in the Mediterranean, the Strait of Gibraltar, there is a net *loss* of nutrients. In all this wonderfully clear water, sea life is hard to find, even with a microscope.

At the northern extreme of the archipelago, we could see the French island of Corsica. France was only an hour's sail away, and the temptation was too great. We were tied up to a dock in Bonifacio that afternoon.

Bonifacio is a jewel of a medieval city, clinging to a white chalky cliff overlooking the sea and protected by stone ramparts to landward. After exploring the town, we zoomed along the coast in the dinghy. We anchored just off a beach and let the kids jump off boulders into the water while we tried to read our books, the parent in us too distracted by our children cliff diving to concentrate. For that one afternoon, we lived up to the glamorous image of life on a boat in the Mediterranean: pristine beach, walled city in the distance, travel-wise children entertaining themselves, parents relaxed in a dinghy. Something was bound to go wrong.

Nothing did. We spent another day in Bonafacio before continuing our westward progress, setting a course for the island of Asinara, on the northwest corner of Sardinia. Asinara had been a penal colony until the 1990s, when it was converted to a national park and nature preserve. What remains from its days as a prison complex is the "village" of Cala Reale, a sprawling campus of mostly abandoned buildings, a park ranger office, and a museum. Asinara means "donkey inhabited" in Italian, and much to Madeleine's delight, the island was crawling with them. We toured this mostly barren island in a rented golf cart, discovering delightful hidden beaches, ever more abandoned prison buildings, and donkeys. Everywhere.

The next stop would be our last in Italy. We were about to make the jump to the Balearic Islands, and the port town of Alghero on the west coast of Sardinia seemed the perfect staging point. 200 miles of open, potentially rough sea lies between Sardinia and the closest Balearic Island, Menorca. The crossing would take the better part of two days.

We found a marina that would allow us to easily provision and get a night of undisturbed sleep. Walking the streets of Alghero, we entered a tiny restaurant off a narrow cobblestone street to savor our last meal in Italy. As usual, the restaurant was empty at eight o'clock, since it was way too early for any Italian to be eating dinner. We told the waiter we were having our last meal in Italy, and he recommended the porceddu.

Speaking in English, he described it as a traditional Sardinian dinner of suckling pig stuffed with rosemary and fennel, roasted in an oven for seven hours to the point where the skin becomes a crispy sheet of bacon. As the words "crispy sheet of bacon" left his mouth, three of us said "yes" in unison. Madeleine always took a no-surprises approach to eating out, so she ordered her usual pasta dish, which was almost always carbonara. With her appreciation for subtlety, I am confident that she will one day write a book called *Carbonaras of Coastal Italy*. We, on the other hand, had a new recipe for the far-ranging cookbook that we would never get around to writing.

14

Cruising to Crossing: A New Plan

Alghero, Italy
September 28, 2016

Leaving Sardinia in the late morning in light easterly winds, we arrived in Menorca early afternoon the next day. We made landfall at Mahón, the capital city of the island and worked our way into an anchorage flanked on both sides by the massive Fortress of Isabel II. Initially built by the Spanish to protect the harbor from the British, it was subsequently enlarged by the British to guard against the Spanish, and further enlarged by the Spanish to guard against the British.

Once the kids had set the anchor, we drove to the city dock in the dinghy, where we enjoyed a casual dinner of tapas and Menorcan red wine. We felt a pang of melancholy being back in Spain, where we started our Mediterranean adventure a year before as wide-eyed, novice sailors. After a couple of rainy days at anchor, touring the town and the fortress, and doing some minor repairs on the boat, we worked our way along the north coast of Menorca, running along the rocky coastline, exploring beaches and towns along the way. On a chart, the coast resembles an old circular saw blade—an irregular jagged edge beaten up over time. Deep coves gave us protected anchorages, and with each stop we went ashore to sample the seafood and the local wines. Once we reached the western end of the island, we made the five-hour hop to Majorca, the largest of the Balearic Islands and the most visited by tourists.

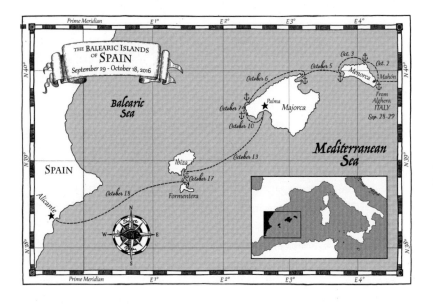

With the wet weather following us to Majorca, we kept moving, driving around Cape Formentor at the northwest corner of the island and continuing west along the rugged north coast. The lofty cliffs, at times several hundred feet high with massive rolling sea swells exploding at their base, were even more beautiful veiled in the mist. On days like this, weekend sailors never leave the dock, yet as cruisers, we often found ourselves at sea in these suboptimal yet sublime conditions. Sailing just two hundred feet from massive waves breaking on shore, waves that with every set released energy comparable to an avalanche, we witnessed the magnificent power of nature from a front-row seat.

We continued along the coast to Palma, the capital city and major port of Majorca. Now on the unprotected west side of the island, we felt the unbridled wrath of the weather system that had been hampering us for the past week. Because of the strong winds and heavy seas, we stayed put in the city marina.

We had always resisted thinking too far ahead on the cruise, but as we drove westward, we would eventually reach the Atlantic Ocean. Then what? A crazy idea kept resurfacing: Why not continue across the ocean?

"Coastal cruising is easy enough," I argued to Valerie, playing devil's advocate. "We're never far from a safe harbor, a cell phone signal, and a grocery store. But crossing an ocean is vastly different. The middle of an ocean is no place for amateurs."

"We're not amateurs," she interrupted. "We've been through bad storms, we've done plenty of night watches, when things break we fix them. We're ready to cross an ocean. It's the same exercise, only longer."

"Maybe we're no longer amateurs," I agreed. "But neither are we the kind of hardcore offshore sailors who could navigate by the stars when all else failed. The open-water legs of our cruise never lasted more than two or three days."

"How long would it take to sail across the ocean?" Madeleine asked, wanting to learn more details about what her parents were getting them all into.

"Three weeks, minimum," I said to Madeleine. She answered with an expression that said, "That's a lot of Nintendo."

"Have you considered this," I said to Valerie, determined to make a point whether I won or lost, "that we've pushed reliable weather forecasts as far as they can go. A transatlantic crossing lasts 20 days, and once committed beyond those three or four days of reliable forecast, vessel and crew are at the mercy of whatever weather appears on the horizon."

"The time to sail west across the Atlantic is just coming up. It's in November. People do it in small boats all the time," Valerie said. Then she added, "It'll be way easier to sell the boat in the Caribbean or the U.S. than in Europe. And we'll probably get a better price."

That tipped the argument towards crossing the ocean. Having sailed *Sacre Bleu* hundreds of miles at a stretch without a serious incident, Valerie and I convinced ourselves we could sail the three thousand miles to the West Indies. But the ocean kept us humble, and we looked into professional guidance for this first crossing.

First-time ocean crossers frequently join a rally of boats organized by a team of veteran sailors. As a flotilla staging in one location, crews spend time together educating themselves, comparing notes, and helping each other get boat and crew prepared for what is considered the final exam of cruising. The rally organizers play an important role, giving seminars, advice on provisioning, inspecting boats for safety, and generally instilling confidence in the skippers and crews. They provide this service on both sides of the ocean but leave the participants to do the crossing on their own.

Veteran sailor and author Jimmy Cornell had an organized rally, the Atlantic Odyssey, leaving from the Canary Islands on November 19. That was eight short weeks away. In our family odyssey we had tried to avoid commitments that required us to be in a specific place at a specific time. If we signed up for the rally, we would have to consider the timing of every leg of the journey from now on.

October 17, 2016

Our estranged friend, the sun, finally showed its face. We set a course for the island of Formentera, the smallest of the Balearics. Today was William's 12th birthday and we were in almost the same place we had been on his last birthday when we had happened across a pod of pilot whales. Unlike Madeleine's birthday a few weeks earlier, the plan for William's birthday was inspired more by convenience than design. We had a friend in Formentera who ran a dive shop, and since both the kids were now of age to become certified divers, this was the time to put them in the water.

As observer diver/helicopter parent, I tagged along with the instructors as we flew through underwater stone archways, along walls filled with coral and through schools of striped jacks. The water in western part of the Mediterranean is richer in nutrients, so sea life is more plentiful. That day, an entirely new world opened up for William and Madeleine. The kids had traveled thousands of miles over a blue surface that kept most of its secrets hidden beneath. Now, they were on the other side, exploring that secret world and seeing the whimsical landscapes and bizarre life forms that their father loves so much.

From Formentera, we made the 90-mile transit to Alicante on the Spanish mainland, arriving at night, as we had exactly a year earlier. Since this was our return visit and we had some maintenance to do on the diesel generator, we did not wander far from the marina.

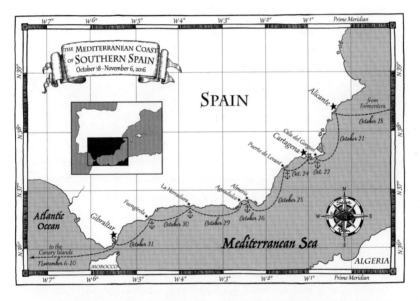

Continuing our westward trek, we sailed another 65 miles to Cartagena, tying up in the same slip we had been in a year earlier. To add to our déjà vu, Sailing for Jesus was also in the exact same place at the city waterfront, setting up for a concert. For old time's sake, we joined the marina potluck dinner that evening, this time with plenty of sea stories of our own to tell.

Departing Cartagena, we and set a course for Aguadulce's large and well appointed port. The basin is lined with restaurants and retail stores, and it looks more like a shopping mall with a parking lot full of boats. Walking about were ordinary people, not marine contractors in coveralls with paint-speckled cell phones, or disheveled cruisers staggering to the shower looking like liberated POWs. We cherished our time in Aguadulce port, eating breakfast, lunch and dinner in restaurants, shopping every square inch of the mall, and satisfying our American craving for retail, a spirit within us that we assumed had died sometime in the course of our life-changing voyage. We managed to resuscitate it in minutes.

October 26, 2016

There happened to be a dive shop in the marina complex, so we signed the kids up for a two-day course to finish the Open Water Diver certification they had started in Formentera. Customers at the dive shop were few, and Madeleine and William had two dive instructors all to themselves. Because business in the marina was also slow, they did their first dive twenty feet from the front door of the dive shop, amongst the empty boat slips. After their epic dive through soaring underwater arches and schools of fish in Formentera, I was afraid the marina dive was going to disappoint them. But at the end of the day, they reaffirmed their love of being underwater, regardless of the view.

That night, in high spirits, we celebrated Valerie's birthday at a family-owned restaurant, receiving personal attention all night long because business there was also slow. Madeleine made her mom a kirigami paper cut-out of *Sacre Bleu* sailing through paper waves and dolphins, and William serenaded her with "Happy Birthday" on the ukulele, still played slowly and tentatively, and abruptly stopping at random moments, but at least he had developed some musical expression and rhythm.

The next day, the kids logged two more dives at a nearby beach and earned their certificates. I used the quiet time on an empty boat to get ahead on my comic strip. My cartooning routine ran in weekly cycles: every week, I drew seven comic strips—six black-and-white daily strips and one larger color Sunday strip. I emailed the batch to my syndicate in New York about five weeks ahead of print publication. That gave my editor time to proofread, fact check, occasionally question my storytelling skills, look for subversive messages, run it by legal, and eventually approve them for the funny pages. Each week during the cruise, the kids drew a cartoon sea animal in the background of my Sunday comic strip. These cartoon extras are memorialized in my books and serve as a secret travel diary for the family: If it's a pink jellyfish, we were in Barcelona.

Since the transatlantic was going to take three weeks minimum, maybe six, and only millionaires can afford high-speed internet in the middle of the ocean, I needed to frontload at least four weeks' worth of comic strips before we started the crossing. Over the twenty years I had been creating *Sherman's Lagoon*, and I had never managed to get even a week ahead of my contractual deadline. For the next five weeks, until we started the transatlantic, I had to double my cartoon output. This was going to be more difficult than crossing any ocean.

Gibraltar
October 31, 2016
Two days and two intermediate stops later, we reached Gibraltar, pulling into Queensway Quay Marina, where we were greeted by our friend, Ian the dockmaster. It felt good to be back in Queensway Quay, where we had christened *Sacre Bleu* so long ago. On the other hand,

there was urgency in the air. Tomorrow was the first of November, and we had to get ourselves and *Sacre Bleu* to the Canary Islands—a 710-mile journey over the open Atlantic—by November 12, when the Atlantic Odyssey seminars started. We were dependent on a weather window to make the four-day trip, and if that meant leaving tonight, so be it. We were venturing into the open ocean, and the ocean made the rules.

But first, we celebrated Halloween Gibraltar style. The streets were teeming with children in costume, but none were knocking on doors and demanding candy from total strangers. The Gibraltarian version of Halloween is more like a good-spirited, costumed block party for children than an unbridled candy giveaway. For Madeleine and William—dressed in skeleton costumes I had bought at Morrisons—this trick with no treat was a scandalous waste of energy. To assuage them, I found a candy shop that sold gummy candy of all shapes and colors, gave them each a budget of ten Gibraltar pounds, and let them load up. This flash flood of candy into their sugar-deprived lives sent them both to their cabins for hours to gorge on blue, yellow and green gelatinous products shaped like insects and reptiles.

The marine forecast for the next five days called for high winds and ten- to fifteen-foot seas between Gibraltar and the Canaries. It takes a day or two for all that energy to dissipate, so venturing out immediately after a storm is almost as bad as going out during a storm. With an idle week on our hands, Valerie decided us to go to Morocco. Early the next morning, we were in neighboring Tarifa, Spain, boarding a ferry to Tangier.

Morocco
November 2, 2016

A French couple who owned a bed and breakfast in Tangier helped us make the most of our stay in Morocco. They arranged for our driver, Mohammed, to meet us at the ferry terminal. Within thirty minutes of landing in North Africa, we were immersed in a frenetic marketplace, or *souk*. Morocco is Francophonic country, but the working language at the souk is English and the official language is Arabic. Valerie's ability to transition a negotiation from English into French without skipping a beat threw some shop owners off balance, but worthy opponents rose to the challenge, changing their game on the fly, like prizefighters. Valerie, however, was just getting a feel for how the game was played in the souk, practicing and not buying.

Mohammed drove us from Tangier to Cap Spartel, the northwest corner of the continent of Africa, with its Moorish-style lighthouse and sweeping view of the white-capped Atlantic. We continued south to the Caves of Hercules, rich with ancient mythology and history, and only ten Moroccan dirhams to get in. We followed a coastal road that ran alongside a wide, sandy beach, empty of people, except for the occasional camel ride operation.

The sailor in me was paying more attention to the churned-up Atlantic Ocean heaving immense walls of water towards us, and the dearth of safe harbors along this stretch of unpopulated coast. If our sailing leg to Tenerife had to be cut short, and we were forced to make landfall in Morocco, where could we do it? The one marina we passed was a simple basin of water walled in by concrete, full of tiny fishing boats, with large breaking waves rolling through the entrance.

Back at our bed and breakfast at the end of the day, we took in the view of Tangier from the rooftop deck. As the sacred words of the sunset prayer echoed over loudspeakers from a nearby mosque, I recalled the church bells of Antibes and the chants of the Orthodox priests in Greece, and I reflected on how our trip had been bounded to the north by Roman Catholicism, to the east by the Greek Orthodox Church, and now to the south by Islam. What a broad swath of culture we have been privileged to experience in these fourteen months.

The next day, we took to the streets of Tangier, wandering in and out of the countless shops that sold handmade goods, and eventually found ourselves in a carpet showroom. There I witnessed Valerie and the shop owner face off over the price of a carpet that I did not even like, though I was too awestruck to say so. It was a clash of titans that lasted over an hour. Both contestants called extensively on their deep arsenal of tactics, with Valerie walking out at one point, and at another, the merchant bringing in the man who wove the carpet. Ultimately, a price was agreed upon and tea was served with smiles all around.

The next morning, we were back on the ferry to Tarifa. For months, we had experienced the gradual, sometimes imperceptible, variations in European culture as we plied the northern Mediterranean coast, at times losing our ability to appreciate its subtleties. Our trip to Morocco was a moonshot only ten miles south, but it made the cruise feel like an adventure again.

Back in Gibraltar, we had a quick decision to make. The three-day weather window that gave us a clear line to the Canary Islands had finally opened. A storm approaching from the Atlantic was about to hit the Moroccan coast, and there was another system forecast to arrive three days after that. The opening was just big enough to squeeze through, and the time to leave was now. Actually, not quite, since the ebb and flow of powerful currents in the Strait of Gibraltar dictated that we should leave at three o'clock the next morning. Why wasn't it ever 8:30, just after breakfast?

Before going to bed, I pulled out our satellite-based communication device, which I had not touched since we crossed the Bay of Biscay, fifteen months prior. With a 710-mile, open-ocean crossing ahead, it seemed like a good time to revisit the owner's manual. We had asked our friend back in the U.S., Paul, to be on call during the four-day trip. He would keep an eye on the weather in the Canaries and warn us via satellite text if the forecast radically changed. He could also receive our distress signal, if it came to that. I tapped out a quick text to him: "Hi Paul, testing our satellite device. Plz confirm recd." Moments later, a response from Paul: "I copy. Fair winds."

15

The Transatlantic: If You're Lucky It's Boring

Stage I: To the Canary Islands
November 7, 2016

At three in the morning, the Bay of Gibraltar was a beehive on a colossal scale: container ships, tankers and freighters in the midst of their 24-hour workday, lit up like Christmas trees, some anchored, others underway. Maneuvering around these behemoths in the dark was tricky. With few reference points in the overcast night, it was difficult to tell how fast they were moving or whether they were moving at all, since a big ship's engines never shut down even at anchor. Boats on this scale do not create a bow wave or a wake when they move slow ahead, but they can still be moving much faster than us. As we came across the first ship in our path, I tried to pass in front. The closer it got, I realized, the faster it was moving, until I was forced to turn abruptly and pass it astern.

As we raced through the Strait, riding the powerful outgoing current, we hugged the northern coast long enough to pick up one last weather report with the mobile phone. Weather forecasts are in a constant state of revision up to the moment the actual weather transpires, at which time the forecast becomes 100 percent accurate. The storm that was predicted to hit the Moroccan coast had slowed down, forcing us to change the sail plan. If we set a southwest course straight for the Canaries, we would run smack into 15-foot waves and 45-knot winds. We would first have to do our westing—sail the western component of our southwest course—to allow enough time for the storm to pass to our south. Eventually we would have to turn south, and since there would be no more weather updates, we would have to guess when to make that turn. This change of plan would add at least a half-day to the transit. Then again, if we tried going through the storm, we might never arrive. Weighing late versus never, we chose late.

Conditions were moderate on our first day as we drove into the open Atlantic under a full mainsail and genoa. By the second day, the wind had climbed to 30 knots, the seas had built to ten feet, and it was apparent that we had ventured too close to the storm. We were cheating the course a little bit to the south, and we were now paying the price. We turned *Sacre Bleu* a little to the right, on a due-west course taking us straight out to sea. At some random point over the horizon, we were going to have to turn left, unless we wanted to land in Nova Scotia.

We kept local "ship time" by retarding the clock (setting it back) an hour every time we crossed into a new time zone, and we took some satisfaction in knowing only a few hundred people were sharing this mid-Atlantic time zone with us. However, on the open ocean, the time of day ceases to have any meaning, and the clock simply becomes a device to inform the crew when they should be on watch, and when they could eat and sleep. Ships of old used a bell system for this purpose. The bell rang every half hour: once at the first half-hour mark, twice after an hour, and so on, until eight bells were struck, when a new four-hour watch began. No clocks were necessary in this little world. The slow rhythm of life—eating, sleeping, cooking, relaxing and standing watch—was driven by bells. After a few days at sea, distinction between day and night begins to blur, and eventually time stands still. Regardless of whether it is a Tuesday or Sunday, if you are not on watch, all that matters is when your watch starts. If you are on watch, all that matters is when it ends.

After two days of sailing due west, we finally turned southwest and were making good speed with a strong tailwind and a following sea. During our year in the Mediterranean, I had surfed our big catamaran through narrow port entries, never feeling confident about my ability to stay in control. These rolling waves in the open ocean finally allowed me to practice my surfing technique. One after another, 15- to 20-foot swells approached us from behind and rolled under us. By leaning into the steering wheel at just the right moment, I could coax *Sacre Bleu* to stay on the crest of the wave and surf down the face. The ride lasted only a few seconds, but like regular surfing, the sensation never got old.

By the third day, my four a.m. watch had become a new part of my life. Sunrise was still two hours off, and though I could feel the big waves slowly pitching the boat as they rolled underneath, the darkness did not yield a clue about the sea conditions except for the glowing white caps rising up like nocturnal predators stalking us from a distance. Sailing into a black void leaves the sea state to the imagination, and the mind inevitably fills that void with danger. Sometimes, when daylight comes, reality can be even more frightening.

The sun rose, revealing a vast seascape of liquid hills moving with the boat, golden light sparkling from their summits. Standing high up on the flybridge, I looked aft at the following sea: a wall of water level with my eyeline, relentlessly chasing the boat but never quite catching it. Any moment, I expected the wave to roll over and flood the cockpit, dragging us under like a sea monster. Just when this seemed inevitable, the stern would gently lift, and the wave would pass harmlessly underneath. The energy in one tiny component of the astronomically powerful ocean is enough to lift the 16-ton *Sacre Bleu* like a peanut. The ocean can provide ships with a gentle ride, or, with a tiny bit more energy it can crush them. With a tiny bit more energy, the ocean can destroy a city. I was witnessing the low end of the ocean's energy scale; the high end is incomprehensible.

As the sun rose astern, I made a pot of coffee and savored the dawn light on the open ocean. It's my favorite time of day in my favorite place. Suddenly, off the starboard bow, I saw a dark shape. It was conspicuous in the busy water because it was moving faster than the surrounding waves. Its appearance was so brief I doubted my eyes. I focused on the spot for another moment, saw nothing further and let my eyes return to scanning the horizon. Then it appeared again: a dark fin just off the bow, swimming along with the boat. Our first dolphin escort of the transatlantic, I thought. The fin carved a steady path through the surface of the water and then shot ahead and disappeared. It was unusual behavior for a dolphin. It was not the characteristic up-and-down motion dolphins display when they swim at the surface. This fin plowed straight through the water like a submarine periscope, then took off like a rocket.

Moments later, not 15 feet off the starboard side, I saw a sight that took my breath away. An enormous underwater shape, light in color, as big as the boat, moving along next to us, matching our speed. As it came closer to the surface, I recognized its sharp beak and slender body as a fin whale, the second largest animal—after the blue whale—ever to live on the planet. It broke the surface, puffed a warm cloud of mist, then disappeared.

I woke everyone on the boat and grabbed my camera. When I returned to the bridge, there was no sign of the 40-ton animal. I looked off the bow and to both sides, scanned the horizon and saw nothing but deep blue water. Suddenly, the whale appeared again in our stern wave! It disappeared before I could lift my camera to snap a shot, then reappeared as a giant underwater shape traveling next to the boat. By this time, everyone was on deck watching as it surfaced and puffed. After ten minutes, the whale finally lost interest in its chance encounter with this alien visitor, launched itself forward with a whip of its tail and vanished into the deep.

Five minutes passed, and we all concluded that the excitement was over. Valerie poured a cup of coffee and joined me on the bridge. I lamented that I had failed to get any decent photographs as I set down my camera and picked up my cup of coffee. Touching our coffee mugs together, Valerie and I toasted this spectacular morning on the open ocean. At that moment, 30 feet off our starboard, the whale raised its massive head completely out of the water, dove forward with a giant splash, and disappeared. I had chosen an inopportune moment to be holding a cup instead of a camera.

That evening, the lights of the Port of Santa Cruz, on Tenerife Island, the largest of the Canaries, appeared on the horizon. The 710-mile trip to the Canary Islands had taken 92 hours, with an average speed of eight knots, which was a very good performance for *Sacre Bleu*. All the surfing paid off, though I had a sore elbow to show for my trouble.

The Canary Islands are not named after birds but dogs (the Latin *Canariae Insulae* meaning Islands of the Dogs), which the Romans found in abundance there when they landed in the first century AD.

They were presumably Labrador retrievers or another breed that could swim well, or, more likely, they had caught a ride with earlier settlers. Spain took possession in the 15th century, and the islands have been Spanish territory ever since. There are eight main islands, and, in terms of size, the archipelago is roughly comparable to the Hawaiian Islands. Like Hawaii, the Canaries are volcanically active, have a tropical climate, boast a dazzling variety of landscapes, and host tourists by the millions.

The Atlantic Odyssey seminars did not start for another day, which gave us time for a tour of Teide National Park. Its active volcano, Mount Teide, is the highest peak that Spain can claim in its territory. The moonscape of the park, with its bizarre rock formations sculpted in a palette of earth tones—monuments that have stood motionless for millennia—provided a stunning antithesis to the hills of quicksilver that had been our home for the last four and a half days.

We spent the next few days attending the Atlantic Odyssey lectures, hosted at the nearby Royal Yacht Club of Tenerife. The presentations covered medical emergencies, storm preparedness, improvising repairs, satellite phone use, provisioning and more. The founder of the rally, Jimmy Cornell, is one of the world's foremost authorities on blue-water sailing, but at times he can be an unapologetic curmudgeon. During one class, he stopped lecturing and called me out for reading my email. Eventually, we all saw the purpose of his no-nonsense demeanor: We're going to make this transatlantic fun, but we won't underestimate its difficulty. Judging from the general discussions between lectures, many of the other crews seemed to be just as inexperienced as we were, and that made us feel better. If we were making a colossal mistake by getting in a small boat with our children and attempting to cross an ocean, at least we were not alone.

Twenty-three sailboats from 12 countries convened in Tenerife for the transatlantic crossing. Of those boats, three were catamarans, and the rest were sloops—single-hulled, single-masted sailboats—between 35 and 55 feet long. Most of the boats were crewed by families: mom, dad, and two or three kids, many of them Madeleine's and William's age, and some even younger. Three of the boats were crewed by younger couples with no kids, two were crewed by retired couples, and one of the catamarans had a hired crew. Over the course of the week, the crews hosted each other on their boats, and we learned as much from each other as from the lectures.

The Odyssey sent staff to inspect each boat, interview the captain, and review a checklist of safety gear and electronics that were a requirement to participate in the rally. Never before had anyone evaluated our boat or our methodology, and I was afraid they were going to identify some fundamental mistake we had been making these past fourteen months of cruising. "You've been flushing your toilet water into the bilge. Did you know that?" "Were you aware that you have your main sheet rigged upside down?" I rehearsed snappy comebacks in my head, but I never had to use them. Since our catamaran was less than two years old, it met all the requirements. It didn't hurt that the boat was French, the inspector was French, and my wife was French. They spent more time talking to each other about the boat than inspecting it.

The trip from Tenerife to Barbados, a little under 2600 miles as the crow flies, was expected to take about three weeks. Unfortunately, sailboats cannot sail as crows fly. Like Columbus, who passed through the Canary Islands on his way to the Caribbean, we were hitching a ride with the trade winds, and that compelled us to sail in a giant southward-bending arc, adding several hundred miles to the trip.

In the late fall, after hurricane season ends and temperatures cool, the North Atlantic settles into a wind pattern driven by what meteorologists call the North Atlantic Subtropical Anticyclone. Informally known as the Azores High, it is a giant, swirling high-pressure system with its center somewhere between the Azores and Bermuda. In the northern hemisphere, high-pressure anticyclones rotate clockwise, opposite of low-pressure cyclones, or hurricanes. The Azores High can be nearly the size of the entire North Atlantic, and, compared to cyclones that come and go and leave destruction in their wake, this anticyclone lingers all winter and rotates relatively peacefully, carrying sailboats across the North Atlantic like a giant merry-go-round.

These transatlantic trades are almost always tailwinds, and the trip can vary from a quiet drift to a terrifying white-knuckle sleigh ride, depending on how well established the Azores High happens to be. In Columbus' day, long-distance sailing ships were built specifically to ride trade winds, with square-rigged sails that allowed them to run downwind. For them, getting anywhere that wasn't downwind was a lot trickier.

Running downwind, the three catamarans would have the speed advantage. Unlike a monohull that usually carries tons of ballast in its keel to keep it upright, a catamaran is lighter, so it doesn't sink as low in the water. (Technically speaking, a catamaran has less wetted surface area.) Because cats drag less boat through the water, they are generally faster than equivalent-volumed monohulls. Of the twenty monohulls, the longest, at 55 feet, would move through the water faster than the shortest, at 35 for a variety of reasons. Naval architects speak of "hull speed"—the theoretical speed limit of a displacement boat, a number that is proportional to its length; longer boats are theoretically faster. However, boat speed is more nuanced than that. In recreational sailboats, there is frequently a tradeoff between volume and efficiency: more interior living space usually comes at the cost of a less-streamlined hull. To achieve that optimal interior volume that boat buyers want, shorter boats generally have greater compromises in hull design than longer boats. Also, longer boats are heavier and present a more stable platform to the wind, which helps sail aerodynamics.

For our crossing, we would pick up the Azores High in the Canaries at the three o'clock position, initially sail south and gradually turn west until we were sailing due west at the six o'clock position. At this point, we would be about halfway across the ocean but much farther south. This arced route adds 400 to 600 miles to a straight-line crossing, but it is still faster than trying to sail a straight line through the middle of the Azores High because anti-cyclones, like cyclones, have a calm eye, and in the case of anti-cyclones it can stretch hundreds of miles.

Tenerife's Marina Santa Cruz has been the launch point for transatlantic sailboats for decades, and a tradition has evolved over time. The concrete bulkhead where the floating docks connect to land is covered with small works of art painted by the boat crews, with boat names, crew names, logos, and other images worked into every square inch of available wall space. On painting day, brushes and paint were shared amongst the crews, and by the time we got the chance to paint our signature smiling fish on the wall, we were using flashlights well into night.

Only a day remained before the start of the crossing, and there were still a lot of preparations ahead. I hired a mechanic to perform the routine maintenance on the two main engines and the generator, changing oil and filters, and of course, filling the fuel tanks for the 2600-mile trip. Mechanically, we were good to go. Atlantic Odyssey required robust satellite communication for downloading weather reports and communicating with the rally organizers. Our texting device was not up to the task, so we rented a bigger and better satellite phone that we arranged to have delivered to us in Tenerife.

Provisioning was a mammoth exercise, but the stores in Tenerife are accustomed to catering to transatlantic sailors, and they sell in bulk. Valerie went on a shopping spree that took her to farmers markets, specialty boutiques, butcher shops and grocery stores. She returned to the dock with an entourage of porters carrying roughly 40 bags and boxes of groceries that had to be unwrapped, sorted, and stowed. Provisioning for a three-week ocean voyage consists of more than just buying a lot of groceries. One must think in terms of 21 breakfasts, lunches, and dinners with all the ingredients that are needed and none that are not. There is no sense bringing a jar of salsa across the ocean if you're not serving tacos.

Before stowing any food, it had to be removed from its original packaging and transferred to reusable containers. This eliminates not only trash but also insects, since many insects lay their eggs on the outside of packaging, particularly cardboard. To further minimize bugs, all fresh produce is thoroughly inspected and rinsed. Refrigerator and freezer space is scarce on a boat, so many foods we might refrigerate on land were not refrigerated. For example, we purchased eggs at the farmers market instead of the grocery store because eggs can go weeks without refrigeration as long as they have not been washed or refrigerated at any point in the supply chain. Drinks were made from instant or concentrate; no bottles or cans were taken aboard, with the exception of beer and wine. An emergency supply of drinking water was stowed in large plastic jerry cans in case the water tanks got contaminated or the water maker failed. Finally, our rod and lures would provide a potentially unlimited supply of fresh fish.

With provisioning and meal planning done (including for the hamsters), maintenance on the engines performed, fuel and water tanks filled, emergency water jugs loaded, first aid kit inventoried, spare parts—impellers, fuel filters, fuses and batteries—packed, software updated, the boat was ready. More difficult was getting our lives ready for dropping out of civilization for three weeks or more. Bills had to be paid, emails sent, comic strips drawn, Instagrams posted, and a quick call made to mom and Valerie's parents wherein we showed a confident face so they wouldn't worry. The Atlantic Ocean beckoned.

Stage II: The Big Hop
November 19, 2016

It's not a race.

That was the mantra of boat crews and rally organizers alike during the week we spent together—we few, we happy few, we band of sailors—attending lectures, hosting happy hours and helping one another prepare. It could have been the subtitle of the rally—The Atlantic Odyssey: It's Not a Race.

Oddly enough, it started like a race, with a starting line, a committee boat and the blast of a gun. The rally organizers set up the starting line just outside the mouth of the harbor and informed us that the rally—not the race—started at 11 a.m. I suspected the race format was a device to get rid of us all in one stroke so the race organizers, having done this a few times before, could avoid spending days coaxing the reluctant, one boat at a time, into that big ocean.

And we were off, with all 23 boats starting the transatlantic within fifteen minutes of each other. We had faced many empty horizons before, especially over the past months of island-hopping in the Mediterranean, but this one was different. This horizon would stay empty for at least three more weeks—that's if we kept up our speed, the electronics kept us on course, we didn't encounter a significant rig failure or hit a floating container and sink. We were venturing into the high seas: a part of the planet administered by no government and controlled by no authority. Soon, we would be nobody's responsibility. This three-weeks-or-more passage was far and away the most dangerous sailing we had ever attempted, and for most of it we would have only ourselves to rely on.

The wind was 15 knots out of the northeast, which put us on a gentle broad reach in moderate seas. It was pleasant sailing. At noon, I coaxed the satellite phone into downloading a weather map. The technology worked on the first try, which was encouraging. As the Canary Islands sank below the horizon astern like a great leviathan, all was well.

The first day on the ocean, most of the boats stayed in visual contact, with two or three outliers that set a course farther south.

"What do they know that we don't?" I asked Valerie.

"Probably a lot," was her spontaneous answer.

The next morning, we were alone. The fleet had literally scattered to the wind. "What does *everybody* know that we don't?" I wondered again.

In the dozen or so lectures we attended, I could never summon the courage to ask that curmudgeon Jimmy Cornell the one fundamental question that had been burning inside of me all week: Which way do we sail? The answer seemed too obvious: Go west, you idiot. Everyone else must have been equally intimidated because the topic never came up. "Let the wind show you," was the Yoda-like counsel from many of the other skippers. Following this advice, we kept the wind directly behind us, and whenever the wind shifted, we altered course accordingly.

Every day at noon, Greenwich Mean Time, we connected to the satellite and downloaded the weather forecast from NOAA, as well as the positions of the other boats from the race organizers. This data download brought our daily moment of reckoning. Madeleine was tasked with copying the latitude and longitude of the other boats and plotting their positions on a paper chart. She dug into her art supplies and selected a different color magic marker for each boat. After the second day, all the boats were still within about twenty miles of each other, which was reassuring. We had strayed to the north of the fleet and were sailing a more direct course to Barbados, while most of the boats were sailing farther south, following the established trade route that had been bringing sailors to the New World for centuries.

The weather map we downloaded every day, a synoptic chart, is a simple representation of wind and atmospheric pressure, the only two weather variables that really matter to sailors. The charts are updated every six hours by the U.S. National Oceanic and Atmospheric Administration, or NOAA, but downloading them once a day proved adequate. The map's black-and-white, low-resolution format is deceptively minimalist to allow for easy downloading at sea, yet it packs a lot of information. For the experienced eye, this chart can conjure up a complete mosaic of the weather systems prowling the North Atlantic, including wind strength, precipitation, sea state and more. For the inexperienced, it is like trying to read the entrails of a goat.

Little arrows on the map depict the wind direction, with the barbs representing wind speed in increments of ten knots. For example, an arrow with three and a half barbs represents a 35-knot wind. Atmospheric pressure gradients are presented by lines called isobars. High- and low-pressure systems show up as clusters of concentric isobar circles with the letter H or L in the center. The Azores High, with a big H in the middle, stretches across the North Atlantic on most fall and winter days. Systems with circles that are closer together, resembling a knot of wood, indicate steep pressure gradients with stronger winds.

With each map download, I was on the lookout for any system with an L in the middle and a lot of tight circles around it. That would be a strong low-pressure system. That would be a storm.

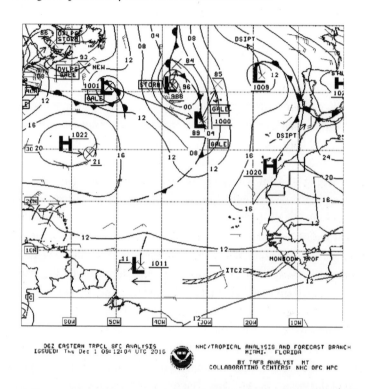

NOAA synoptic chart we downloaded Dec 1, 2016, that shows storms and gales to the north and calm in our latitudes, with the Azores High completely dissipated.

The daily NOAA download also included a text component. Written in capital letters, the text report could make a calm day seem treacherous. Whenever I read the text, in my mind's ear I heard a screaming, panicked voice: LIGHT WINDS WITH SEAS LESS THAN 1 FT! Even more terrifying, the so-called HIGH SEAS FORECAST issued by the NWS NATIONAL HURRICANE CENTER—already enough trigger words to alarm anyone—provided weather forecasts by sector, starting with the northernmost part of the North Atlantic, which in late November is a freezing, storm-ridden hell. Every day, my official NOAA weather forecast opened with words like GALE-FORCE WINDS WITH SEAS 25 TO 30 FT. My stomach sank whenever I opened a new report on my laptop screen. Then I would quickly scan down to the bottom of the page to find the southern latitude forecast that applied to our position: MODERATE WINDS WITH SEAS 5 FT. In all-caps, it was still frightening.

By day three, the fleet had scattered farther, with some heading due south, leading us to suspect that they were planning a stop in Cape Verde, an island nation off the coast of Senegal. The weather map told us that the Azores High was going strong, a little too strong, and we were seeing 25-knot winds and towering waves. Since the boat was moving at 10 knots straight downwind, our apparent wind was a more manageable 15 knots, but it was still a wild sleigh ride through the rough seas. Night watch was particularly terrifying, and as a precaution, we reefed the sails before sunset to make them smaller. Even with reefed sails, *Sacre Bleu* moved like a rocket ship through the starry night. I gazed up at the moon, bright and clear, and on its dead-calm surface I could make out dark patches called "lunar seas." The sea here on earth was anything but calm.

As we were sailing along on the fourth day, we heard a snap and saw that the outhaul—the line that holds the mainsail to the outboard end of the boom—had broken. The mainsail fluttering like a flag, uselessly. Fixing the outhaul proved easy enough, but not ten minutes later we heard another snap and watched helplessly as the code zero—the big foresail—slowly collapsed into the water in front of the boat. Before we could react, we sailed right over it and wrapped it around the keel. Two major failures in minutes! At this rate, we would have to abandon ship before dinner. Then I remembered what Cornell had mentioned in one of his lectures, almost as an aside. If, over a three-week ocean crossing, the boat pitches and rolls once every few seconds, then during the voyage the boat will have to tolerate hundreds of thousands of cycles. Things will inevitably break.

The code zero is an indispensable sail that provides most of the power for driving the boat downwind, so it had to be fixed quickly. First, we had to stop the boat dead in the water and haul the sail back onboard like a massive fish. This took an hour. Then came the hard part: fixing the line that broke—the halyard. That meant somebody had to go to the top of the 75-foot mast and rerun it through the mast from top to bottom. This time, that somebody going up the mast to do the repair was me.

It sounded like a problem on a trigonometry test: If a boat with a 75-foot mast is rolling in 15-foot waves, what arc does the top of the mast swing? I never found out, because about halfway up the mast, I was already swinging in the bosun's chair like a tetherball, fifteen feet to each side, so we aborted the attempt. For the rest of the afternoon, we crawled along with just the mainsail. Once conditions were calm enough to try again, I used a jury rig of safety lines that made the operation much slower but kept me from swinging. Code zero and outhaul fixed, we continued into the setting sun.

November 24, 2016

Today was Thanksgiving, but it did not occur to any of us until after dinner. Dinners on the boat remained family sit-down affairs, with all of us at the table, me positioned eyes forward looking through the forward window of the salon while the autopilot drove. Valerie did most of the cooking, not so much out of old-fashioned tradition but because she had created the meal plan and provisioned accordingly. Some of the other rally participants prepared all their meals in advance and froze them in Ziplock bags; we considered this highly organized approach for about a minute. Lunches were typically sandwiches or pasta and fruit. Dinners on *Sacre Bleu* were prepared from scratch with frozen beef or chicken, long-shelf life vegetables, like potatoes or carrots, and a glass of wine on most nights. In our coastal cruising days at anchor, we would typically finish a bottle over dinner, but at sea we kept our alcohol consumption down because emergencies could happen at any moment, and we all had to be on our game. Other boats went no booze for the crossing; we tried this for a day. The kids cleaned up after dinner, and afterwards, the boat switched to a night routine—Valerie and I watched the helm and the kids stayed inside until the sun rose the next day, when we would start it all over again.

November 27, 2016
Eight days and nearly a thousand miles into the ocean crossing, the wind died, forcing us to start one of the engines. The sea was flat and featureless in all directions. We were skating across an infinite mirror that reproduced the sky in every detail. Fuel was not a concern yet; we started with enough to drive roughly a third of the way across the ocean, and we had used very little so far. With the flat water and the drone of the diesel engine, the monotony reached a level I had not thought possible. As I sat at the helm waiting for the end of my watch, time, like the sea and the air, seemed to stand still.

When I describe an ocean crossing to non-sailors, I always reference a film—not *White Squall* or *Master and Commander*, but *Groundhog Day*. Over the past eight days, every morning at precisely five minutes till four, I woke, ate a bowl of cereal and climbed up to the flybridge to take the watch from Valerie. For those four hours I simply sat and watched night turn to day, which was a different light show every morning. On the eighth morning, alone on the flybridge shortly after taking the watch, I wondered whether I had eaten breakfast or whether my recent memory of eating breakfast was from the previous morning. I put the boat on autopilot and went back down to the galley to look for evidence, but since I always washed, dried, and stowed any dishes I used in case we hit rough water, I knew there would be no evidence. I did not feel any sensation of having eaten or not eaten, so, just to have something to do, I ate a bowl of cereal, possibly my first of the day, possibly my second. I can guarantee the sandwich I ate for lunch exactly six hours later was my only lunch because I had witnesses.

On day ten, conditions were still dead calm. The ocean and the sky were one as clouds and sun appeared above and were reflected below. As terrestrial animals in a busy landscape, we are so accustomed to focusing on specifics that when we see emptiness, its beauty often escapes us. The immensity surrounding us could never be captured in any photograph. It did not look like the earth I knew. Gliding along the top of a polished surface that extended to infinity in all directions made me feel more like a space explorer than a sailor.

The latest satellite weather map indicated that the Azores High had disintegrated into a swirl of light puffs and gentle breezes blowing every which way. Fuel was becoming a slight concern since we had now burned through about a quarter of it.

Based on the daily downloads of the positions of the other boats, it appeared we were in the lead (though it was not a race), and that we were taking the most direct route to Barbados. Truth be told, the autopilot was driving us in a straight line, trade winds be damned. This strategy would take us closer to the calm eye of the Azores High, whenever it reestablished, but since the doldrums stretched across the entire Atlantic, and we were motoring, we figured we might as well follow the most direct route to Barbados. Another catamaran, *JoJo 1*, was about 50 miles behind us. Most of the rally participants did not have the luxury of motoring long distances and had to rely on the predictable trade winds farther south. But even those winds had vanished, and the entire rally was becalmed. When the anticyclone reestablished itself, we might find ourselves smack dab in the eye, but for now, our strategy seemed logical.

To pass the time on watch, I took to reading the user's manual for the electronic navigation system and discovered that the autopilot could be set to drive the boat on a great-circle route instead of a straight-line route, a feature that is useful only in the open ocean. Had I known this earlier, we could have shaved a hundred miles off the crossing. Why did I wait 15 months to read this chapter?

At sea, everyone struggled with the yoke of boredom in different ways. The kids had gotten into our hard drive of movies and were watching one after another when they weren't doing their schoolwork. I did not discourage this activity because in addition to *Space Balls* and *Vampire Academy*, they were watching classics like *Ben Hur* and *Lawrence of Arabia*, which, I reasoned, instilled some cultural literacy in them. About midway through the crossing, the hard drive broke, forcing the kids to return to their projects: kirigami for Madeleine and Legos for William. The kids stood watch together during daylight hours, a task that involved keeping an eye out for other boats and making sure the sails were correctly trimmed. Boat traffic was nonexistent. As for sail trim, since we were always sailing dead downwind, when the wind shifted, rather than adjusting the sails, we would alter course slightly until the sails filled properly again. Sailing the boat was usually an easy, one-person job.

Valerie kept her responsibility as head chef, preparing the dinners, keeping a close eye on food quantity and also when during the cruise it should be eaten. When she was not on watch or preparing a meal, she was usually in the aft cockpit reading a book. When I wasn't on watch, I tried to work at the desk in our cabin, but staring at a computer screen in a windowless room would frequently make me seasick. Otherwise, I puttered around the boat looking for something that might have broken or was about to break.

The temperatures for the entire voyage were mild, even at night, and we rarely needed any covering beyond a T-shirt and shorts except when it occasionally rained. This made the flybridge the most popular place on the boat. Frequently, all us were on the flybridge in hopes of seeing something—another boat, a floating object, a whale—that might break the monotony.

We had a nobler purpose to our horizon scanning beyond fighting our boredom. With the help of the rally organizers, we joined a pair of citizen science projects that was enlisting sailors to help with observations in the open ocean. The seabird project had us photographing any bird we happened to see and noting the position and date of the sighting. This involved taking two photos: one of the bird and one of the instrument panel. We snapped photos of birds on about a dozen occasions, many of them over a thousand miles from land. We later sent the photos to the organization and received a very detailed email from a biologist identifying the species—albatrosses, petrels, arctic terns—and speculating on the bird's migration habits. I had no idea there were birds in the middle of the ocean. How they cope in a storm is anyone's guess. Our knowledge of life out here in the middle of the ocean is informed mostly by passing snapshots from non-scientists like us.

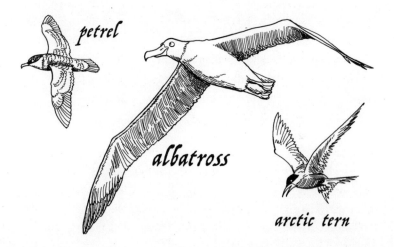

In our second citizen science project, sightings were not so gratifying, for we were logging all the marine debris we came across. Again, a digital photo log was easiest and most useful. In the middle of the ocean, as with virtually everywhere else on the planet, we found plenty of trash, some of it frighteningly big. Although we did not encounter a shipping container—the nightmare of every ocean sailor—we did sail past large wooden crates, an industrial-sized propane tank, and a lot of plastic.

As we approached the midway point of our crossing, sailing over some of the deepest parts of the ocean, I wondered what the world 20,000 feet below us looked like. We had been sailing over the relatively flat Canary Basin, but we were approaching an underwater mountain range called the Mid-Atlantic Ridge. The longest mountain range on the planet, it marks the collision between two continents. Its peaks rival the Rocky Mountains, rising over 12,000 feet from the seafloor, yet still thousands of feet below the waves. Under us were mountains that had never been touched by sunsets, vast canyons that had never been hiked, and mighty summits that had never been scaled. In these valleys roamed migrating whales, giant squid, and the occasional nuclear submarine. On these slopes lived alien creatures that had adapted to the absence of sunlight, freezing temperatures, and crushing water pressure. It is a world as alien and hostile as any in our solar system, and yet, life exists. In fact, life might have originated there.

Technology that rivals the Apollo missions is required to explore this mountain range. Two years earlier, I had seen that world firsthand from the portholes of the deep submersible vehicle *Alvin*. At the base of the Florida Escarpment, in the Gulf of Mexico, two miles deep, I looked up at a sheer cliff that rises thousands of feet in a vertical face. I was surrounded by sea creatures that had evolved in the complete absence of sunlight; creatures that use the chemical energy of deep-sea hydrothermal vents the same way plants use solar energy from the sun to grow; creatures that compelled scientists to rethink the origins of life. I hope to see the day when we turn on the lights in this alien world and get to know this part of our planet better. We have mapped the surface of the moon in far more detail than the bottom of our oceans.

As we sailed in water over four miles deep and more than a thousand miles from any shore, I pondered the scenario of sinking. Because Monohulls carry tons of ballast in their keels, they can sink like a rock. Catamarans, on the other hand, are relatively light, and their double-layer hulls are very buoyant. If *Sacre Bleu* were to put a hole in her hull, from, say, hitting a floating container, she would sink slowly and maybe not entirely. Nevertheless, with a flooded boat, we would be forced to grab the ditch kit (a prepared kit containing an emergency radio, flashlight, and a few jerry cans of fresh water), deploy the EPIRB that would alert a rescue organization to our predicament, and transfer everyone to the emergency life raft. Unfortunately, the middle of the ocean is beyond the range of any rescue helicopter, so we would have to wait in our life raft for the closest commercial ship to get the call and divert from its route to come find us, which could take days.

I also considered the scenario of losing crew overboard. This was a particular fear at night when rescue is virtually impossible. We always clipped our tethers into the jacklines—webbing that ran the length of the boat—when we were on deck after sunset. At the end of the watch, in the brief moments at night when I was unclipped on deck, I would look over the edge into the black void and ponder falling off. The proximity of the danger terrified me; it was like standing near the ledge of a skyscraper.

At noon Greenwich time on the eleventh day, as usual, we downloaded the positions of the other boats in the rally. As Madeleine plotted them, we saw that *Jojo 1* was right on our tail and the two of us were well ahead of the rest of the fleet. Rohan, *Jojo 1*'s Tasmanian skipper, was evidently aware of our position too, because he hailed us over the VHF radio just minutes later. Elated to hear a new voice, and one with an Australian accent, we fell into cheerful banter and continued the exchange for twenty minutes before Ro, a high school principal in his land life, got around to mentioning in a polite, roundabout way that they were running low on water. It seemed that one of his hired crew had left a faucet running all night. I could see his eyes rolling as his words came over the radio. We had been running our engine for three full days, and that also allowed us to run our water maker, a reverse-osmosis process that required power from the engine. Our water tanks were full, so we offered to help.

We were close to the geographic center of the Atlantic Ocean—1,100 miles from Africa, 1,400 miles from the Caribbean, and only eight miles from each other when Ro contacted us. In minutes, we were rafted up and shuttling jerry cans of water over the decks in bucket brigade fashion as Ro carefully poured the freshwater into his holding tanks. In all, we gave *JoJo 1* about 150 liters of water, which our water maker could easily replace in a few hours. Ro reciprocated our gift of water with cold cans of beer, of which this all-male crew from Australia and Germany had an abundance. Since the seas were dead calm and we had time to kill while the freshwater was being transferred, the event evolved into a swim party. How often does one run into a friend in the middle of the ocean?

Ro's crew bounded into the water first, like children, and they were spontaneously joined by Valerie and our kids. Pool toys came out, more beer cans popped, and everyone relaxed as much as they could while treading water. I seemed to be the only one who was intimidated by the idea of swimming over an abyss. Once Valerie was back on board I dove in from high atop the coach roof. Surprisingly, the water was bathtub warm. I hit the water and kept going, extending my dive a few feet deeper. I stopped, opened my eyes and slowly spun around, awed by the deep blue infinity in every direction. Swimming with 20,000 feet of water beneath me was both exhilarating and eerie.

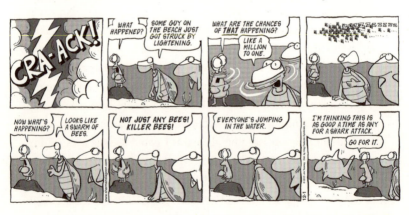

Great white sharks like my comic strip character Sherman get all the media attention, but for the most aggressive animal on the planet my money is on the oceanic white tip shark. It is a relatively small shark with oversized, rounded fins that make it look more like a plush toy than a ruthless killing machine. As the name implies, its home is the open ocean, where opportunities to eat are few and far between. In short, they can't afford to pass up a meal—any meal. As our merry band of sailors treaded water in the middle of the ocean, our legs dangling below, I imagined what an oceanic white tip shark might make of the sight. This apex predator's last meal might have been a Nike running shoe, and that was eleven days ago. Since then, she has been swimming through clear, blue, empty ocean. Suddenly, we come into view: "Do my eyes deceive me? Is that a forest of chubby meat sticks? Pinch me, I must be dreaming."

I should have known better than to worry about sharks. Open-ocean fishing fleets that answer to no authority, plying the lucrative shark fin trade, have managed to render sharks nearly extinct. The greatest danger we faced that afternoon were sunburns.

With the fresh water transfer complete, we parted ways, leaving Ro and his crew in this nondescript location in the middle of the Atlantic Ocean: 19°11.084' north latitude by 37°04.065' west longitude.

On the twelfth day, the wind returned. It started as a light breeze astern, and by midday it was filling our sails and pushing *Sacre Bleu* through the water at six knots. I shut down the diesel engines, and for the first time in three days we could hear the sound of sailing: the placid trickle of water flowing around the hull and the strain of the rigging as the breeze stiffened. We did not realize how intrusive the relentless growl of the engines had been until we shut them off and no longer had to shout at each other to communicate. For the next two days the wind, always dead aft, drove us at a steady pace during the day, easing slightly after sundown, making for carefree night watches.

The stars were our companions during night watches, when the sky in midocean is a stargazer's paradise. Not only are planets and the hazy band of the Milky Way in sharp relief, so are satellites plainly visible as they race across the sky. Meteors became an ordinary part of our evenings, and we no longer pointed them out when they streaked by. Meteorites, the kind that make it all the way to earth impact, still warranted a mention. On Valerie's midnight-to-four watch, she witnessed a flaming projectile with a luminescent tail drop out of the sky and disappear in the wink of an eye. No other crewmember could corroborate the account, but she said it was close enough to hear the splash.

On day 14, the winds strengthened, pushing *Sacre Bleu* from behind with more and more force. Despite this, she refused to go any faster. Her theoretical hull speed played a role, but also, water resistance increases with speed, and like skydivers, boats reach a terminal velocity —a point where the forces pushing it forward are offset by the forces holding it back. Once a sailboat hits its maximum speed, the wind stops making it go faster and turns its attention to breaking it. *Sacre Bleu*'s rig and sails were groaning under the force of the wind as they tried to pull a 16-ton boat through the water faster and faster but couldn't. I stood at the stern wanting to admire the rooster tail of a wake we were leaving behind, but all I could do was look up at the rig and worry.

The wild sleigh ride did have its benefits. I looked over Madeleine's shoulder as she plotted the daily positions of the rally participants. We were still the lead boat. I shouted "Yeah!" "It's not a race, Dad," she responded, refusing my fist bump.

On day 16, we lost our lead to that water-stealing bastard, Ro, in *JoJo 1*, who probably just faked being out of water to make us turn around. "It's not a race anyway," I said in a huff after Madeleine revealed our second-place position.

On day 18, we encountered a continuous line of isolated squalls that appeared as discrete, dense storms wandering the seascape, whipping up white caps beneath. With the squalls meandering in all directions, and the boat sailing in one direction, it was inevitable that we would cross paths with one of the pummeling downpours, forcing us to furl the sails and close the hatches. In daylight, the squalls did not intimidate much. Under a shrouded night sky, however, the rumble of distant thunder and the flash of lightning brought worry. Somewhere out there was a monster we could no longer see or outmaneuver.

On day 19, just as I was taking the 4 a.m. watch from Valerie, the lights of Bridgetown, Barbados, rose up from the horizon. Valerie

The Transatlantic

went below to get some sleep, leaving me alone on the bridge to savor the last few miles of our ocean crossing. After three weeks under the bluish light of distant stars and the moon, the amber, incandescent glow of Bridgetown marked the commencement of our reentry into civilization.

Suddenly, the wind died. When a cooler breeze filled in from a different direction, I knew what was coming next. I rushed down to wake Valerie, but by the time I returned to the flybridge, both sails had jibed and the boat was racing off course. In the span of a few seconds, the wind accelerated to over 40 knots and shifted 90 degrees, pinning the jib against the rigging with such a force that it was impossible to take down. I started the engines and tried to reorient the boat so that the wind was coming from straight ahead, which would lift the sail off the rigging and allow us to lower it. We eventually succeeded in striking the sails. After 20 minutes of pummeling rain, it was all over. We had just crossed 2,600 miles of ocean and the most violent weather of the entire journey struck us within view of the lights of Barbados.

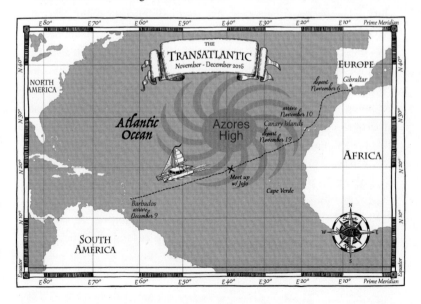

December 9, 2016
We arrived off Bridgetown with the two other catamarans in the rally, *JoJo 1* and *Element*, in the early hours of the morning. Vessels entering Barbados are required to register with customs and immigration at the Bridgetown Shallow Draught Port. We dropped anchor and waited for the port to open.

I was exhausted, proud and a little melancholy about it all being over. Part of me had expected more of an adventure, and the other part of me was relieved at the dullness of the crossing. Either way, we had crossed an ocean. Similar to our decision to embark on the cruise itself, Valerie and I accepted the challenge of the transatlantic knowing that potential dangers lurked, but with the right preparation we could minimize them. Luck played a role, as it does with every endeavor in life, but our plan did not rely on luck. Madeleine and William—at the ages of fourteen and twelve—have an achievement in their young lives that few ever attain, and we hope the perspective they gained from crossing an ocean will make other ambitions seem more achievable.

Valerie and I had considered flying our children to Barbados and hiring a crew for the crossing, like responsible parents. The horrific scenarios that played out in our imaginations bolstered the argument not to expose them to three weeks of open-ocean sailing. But after 15 months in the Mediterranean, through storms and anchor draggings, deck swabbing and night watches, we were a crew and a family, and crossing the ocean had to be done together. Now, each of us had a feeling of accomplishment and a new appreciation for the vastness of the planet in an era when distance has become inconsequential in our daily lives.

Over the next 24 hours, most of the rest of the fleet arrived, with each crew looking similarly exhausted, relieved, and proud. Of the 23 boats that began the crossing, 21 finished within three days of our arrival. One stopped at Cape Verde for repairs, and one would not arrive for another two weeks.

16

The Caribbean: Island-Hopping South

Barbados
December 11, 2016

Crews and rally organizers gathered at beachfront restaurant to celebrate, compare notes, trade contact information. The organizers, including Jimmy Cornell, who had flown in, were there to provide a recap of the transatlantic and praise us all for a job well done. The fleet had encountered no major storms, and there were no serious injuries or breakdowns. Only after arriving in Barbados did a catamaran crew discover that one of their two rudders had fallen off and was somewhere on the bottom of the Atlantic. After our extraordinary accomplishment, most of us in the restaurant were feeling a sense of relief, pride, and… what now?

First came farewells. The four of us bid farewell to Ro and the crew of *JoJo 1*. We said our goodbyes to the crews of *Element*, *Careka*, *Venus*, and *Itchy Foot*. Together, we had touched a remote part of our planet where few have ventured.

Some of the crews would venture west through the Panama Canal and into the wide-open Pacific. Others would explore the Caribbean, and still others would leave their boats and fly home to resume their lives on land. For most of us, it would likely be the last time our paths crossed. But one never knows with cruising.

With the transatlantic finished, we found ourselves a year and a half into the cruise wondering how much of our land lives we had left to return to. Once we had been gone a full-year cycle without showing our faces at the neighborhood picnic or the holiday party, we were officially out of sight *and* out of mind. For the first time in the cruise, we were at a stopping point with no plan.

After we had cleared customs, we left the government dock in Bridgetown and dropped anchor a few miles away in Carlisle Bay. Surrounded by turquoise water and swaying palms, we had a frank discussion about the plan moving forward. We were not the same family that set out from Les Sables-d'Olonne sixteen months earlier. Madeleine and William were not the children who built sand castles on the beach that first week in Isle de Ré. For Valerie and I, this was just another window of time in middle-age, but for Madeleine and William, we knew, these years were formative, and they would not get them back. Valerie and I understood the sacrifices they were making—no friends, no school, no sports—and we were prepared to end the cruise.

Valerie spoke her mind first, declaring that she could not get enough of life on the boat and could keep going for years. Besides, she reasoned, why go home now? Winter was just beginning, and the next five months up north were going to be cold and miserable. We had a perfectly good boat outfitted exactly to our needs, and we knew how to sail it. Here in the Caribbean, much more so than the Mediterranean, the kids could swim, snorkel, scuba dive, learn about the ocean and be outdoors. Besides, dropping the kids into the middle of a school year presented its own problems socially and academically.

"I'm not having as much fun as you are," Madeleine said, directing this barb at Valerie. At 14, Madeline missed the things she loved more than she loved sailing. "All my friends are going to a concert this weekend," she lamented, looking at her cell phone, "and I'm not. But," Madeleine conceded, "I also feel like things are different back home," She would be in eighth grade if we were living in Annapolis, and for many, eighth grade is a year of change. Her friend groups had shifted. Some friends had moved to different groups and different schools, and others had moved out of town. The world she left no longer existed.

"Most of all, I miss Belle," she said. "If we could find a way to get Belle down to the Caribbean, maybe," Madeleine said, "we could keep going." Bringing Belle with us on our return to the Caribbean seemed like a reasonable condition, so we promised to try our best. "No Belle, no cruise," Madeleine announced, feeling she'd gained her ground.

At 12, William was still a happy-go-lucky boy not yet showing any signs of teen angst. He looked forward to returning to a life on land, where he had more choices. He longed to compete in soccer, be a Boy Scout, go on sleepovers and play video games. "I would just like to be normal," he declared. Yet, he seemed willing to adjust to whatever we threw at him. We persuaded ourselves, and him, that we could find ways to keep him happy afloat for another six months.

As for me, I was producing *Sherman's Lagoon* just as easily on the boat as I had in my studio in Annapolis. From a career perspective, I was doing fine. I also recognized this moment in time as an opportunity that would never come again. The kids were still young, my job was very portable, it was the start of new chapter in the cruise, and the boat was in ship shape. When would the stars ever again be this aligned?

Over one short family gathering, we devised a plan that would make everyone happy. We agreed that we would spend the next two weeks in the Caribbean, then fly home to celebrate Christmas in Annapolis. After the holidays, we'd extend the family adventure until the beginning of hurricane season, which was officially June 1. By then, we promised the kids, not to mention our insurance company, we would be back home. This timeline would return us to land life at the beginning of the summer, giving the kids a couple of months to adjust before starting school. The beginning of summer is also the best time to sell a boat. The plan finally fell together.

For the next few days, we played in the aquamarine waters of Barbados, snorkeling, paddle boarding and scuba diving with the kids for the first time in the cruise. The family adventure had already shifted to water-oriented activities. Valerie had arranged to leave *Sacre Bleu* in a large marina on the neighboring island of Martinique while we flew home for the holidays. The Marina de Marin, one of the biggest in the Caribbean, had all the services we needed to do the required maintenance on the boat. Meanwhile, we'd enjoy a French island, with a huge selection of food and wine shipped in from the mother country.

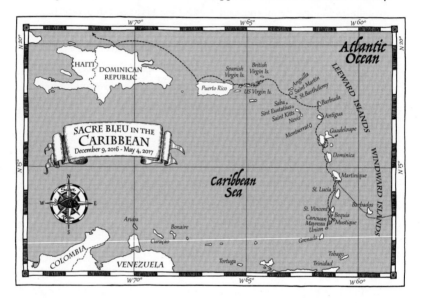

Martinique
December 13, 2016

As we hoisted the mainsail and left Barbados astern, we were sad to bid farewell to so many new friends and acquaintances. We knew that it was unlikely that we would pass through Barbados again as we wandered the Caribbean. Of all the islands that form the Caribbean crescent, Barbados is the most difficult to sail to because it lies the farthest east in a part of the world where the wind blows continuously *from* the east. To sail to Barbados from its closest neighbor, St. Lucia, is to fight headwind and waves through 75 miles of open ocean.

The same winds that make Barbados difficult to sail to make it easy to sail from. Our 120-mile broad reach to Martinique took a mere 13 hours, with *Sacre Bleu* groaning under the force of 25-knot winds from the starboard quarter filling her sails. The wind was still whistling through the rigging when we entered the Marina de Marin, and even after all the tight Mediterranean dockings I was still very nervous about nudging *Sacre Bleu* through the narrow marina fairways in such a strong crosswind. Once the dock lines were secured, I relaxed, knowing that we would not have to leave the slip again for weeks.

Our plan to return home for Christmas had one complication. Two, actually. Two small, four-legged, furry complications. What to do with Snowball and Squirt, the hamsters? I was of the opinion that hamsters are rats with good marketing, and they would be fine with a banana peel and a hunk of moldy cheese for the three weeks we would be gone. Valerie looked into hiring a hamster sitter, but we did not know anyone at the marina well enough to trust them with the keys to the boat and the lives of two beloved pets. The plan shifted to bringing the hamsters home to Annapolis.

Valerie discovered three obstacles to our plan. First, none of the airlines servicing Martinique allow live animals. Second, airport security would not allow a live animal to pass through screening. And third, although U.S. Customs allows pets into the country, the paperwork is formidable, a statement from a veterinarian is required, and passage is not guaranteed. Valerie read that part of the Customs website out loud: "Passage is not guaranteed." Silence filled the cabin. We looked into classifying Snowball and Squirt as emotional support hamsters, but that did not pass the laugh test. On one hand, we had two children who were not going home without their hamsters. On the other, we were up against the airlines, airport security, and U.S. Customs. To make this work, we had to get creative, not to mention break a few regulations.

We sat around the dinner table formulating all the moving parts to the Great Hamster Caper. Getting Snowball and Squirt through airport security would be the hard part; getting them on the flight would be easy.

First, we would need a fence. "Let's get William to do it," Valerie and I agreed. Rather than put the hamsters in a carry-on bag and send them through the X-ray machine, where their little skeletons would show up on the monitor, William would walk through the metal detectors with the hamsters in his pockets. Good, but not perfect. Being a Boy Scout, he was incapable of telling a convincing lie, and that was worrisome. Another potential problem was that hamsters squirm a lot.

Madeleine, the aspiring veterinarian, observed that hamsters take a while to boot up from sleep to squirm, so if we kept them calm until the last minute, we would have minimal squirm at security. To keep them relaxed, the kids built two temporary cages from ice cream boxes small enough to fit in their backpacks. Each cage consisted of a one-gallon cardboard box with a plastic lid. Holes were punched in the lids to provide air for the little stow-aways. The children furnished each box with the appropriate bedding so the hamsters would relax until they went into William's pockets.

If the hamsters were discovered at security, I would pretend not to know anything about it and scold the kids for trying to sneak the hamsters onto the flight. The kids would throw a crying fit, and I would hand the hamsters off to Valerie, who had booked her flight a day later than ours so that if anything went wrong at security she could take the hamsters back to the boat and work on an alternate arrangement. We rehearsed it all the night before and once more as we rode the cab to Martinique International Airport.

At the airport, we cased the security lines and transferred the hamsters from their makeshift cages into the two pockets in William's cargo shorts. I took my place in the security line first, followed by William, then Madeleine. As the line inched along, with people fretting over their shoes and belts, I grew impatient. Finally, I passed through the metal detector and turned around to coach William. As he was about to step through, the woman running the detector asked if he had anything in his pockets. I looked down in horror at the squirming lump in each pocket of his cargo shorts. I caught William's eye and signaled no with a shake of my head. With his hands now in his pockets, he looked the woman in the eye and said no. She motioned him through, and it was over. That was one small step for a child and one giant leap for two hamsters.

Just when we thought we were in the clear, the man running the X-ray scanner waved us over. There was something suspicious in William's backpack. The jig is up, we thought. The security agent unzipped it, pulled out the two makeshift hamster cages and set them aside, oblivious to their purpose. He then removed two tangerines and an apple and held them up for the woman at the scanner. "It's just fruit," he said. "You're okay," he said to us, and returned the fruit. We waved goodbye to Valerie, who was watching tensely as the drama plodded along. I sent William to the boys' room to transfer the hamsters back to their cages, and then we settled in to wait for our flight. The plan was working. The bad news was, from this point on, we did not really have a plan.

The flight was uneventful, partially because I shut down the kids' plan to feed airline peanuts to the hamsters. I did not want to explain to the flight attendant that we had lost something on the plane, and could she please make an announcement to have everyone to look under their seats for a hamster.

Once on the ground at Baltimore-Washington International Airport, the one final obstacle lay before us: The United States Customs and Border Protection Agency.

I was a frequent business traveler in an earlier life, and I had always made a point never to lie to Customs. Powerful authorities and petty infractions can be a dangerous combination, and the cover-up can be worse than the crime. U.S. Customs probably doesn't care much about Cuban cigars coming into the country, but they really hate it when travelers try to put one over on them. Also, like William, I am a terrible liar.

With a hamster in an ice cream box in each of the backpacks of the young and innocent-looking contraband runners, we proceeded to U.S. Customs. I scanned my passport in the automated declaration kiosk, and four questions appeared on the screen:

1) Are you carrying any commercial merchandise or currency over $10,000?

2) Do you have any articles to declare in excess of the duty-free exemption?

3) Have you been close to livestock outside the U.S.?

And the final catchall question:

4) Do you have any fruits, vegetables, plants, insects, meats or meat products, dairy products, animals or animal/wildlife products, disease agents, cell cultures, snails, soil; or have you visited a farm/ranch/pasture outside the U.S.?

I said no to the first three questions and yes to the fourth. The kiosk spit out a ticket with three checkmarks and one "X." We proceeded to the Customs agent, where I handed him the passports and the ticket.

"I see you answered 'yes' to question four," the agent declared. A tense moment passed while he studied his computer monitor. "Are you carrying any food with you?"

"Food? Yes! Why, yes we are!" I said eagerly. "William, show him." William reached into his backpack and worked around the hamster cages to reach the two tangerines and the apple. He showed the fruit to the Customs agent, who promptly said, "You're good to go."

Smelling the fresh air of freedom, we hurried to baggage claim, where we still had to confront the Beagle Brigade: dogs that can detect the faintest scent wafting from the most trifling object buried in the biggest suitcase the instant it enters the baggage claim area. I had a feeling that live hamsters get their attention. Valerie had mastered the art of evading the Beagle Brigade during her numerous entries from France carrying luggage crammed with cheese and sausages. We knew how to handle the Beagle Brigade. "Stay together, and if we see a beagle, we split up and I'll distract it," I said as I scanned the room frantically. Fortunately, our luggage popped out early, so we grabbed it and made a straight line for the airport exit.

One last Customs agent sat between us and daylight, collecting the declaration forms at a desk just before the exit door. As we moved towards him in deliberate haste, singularly focused on the exit, a voice rang out: "Sir, can I see your declaration form?" Another customs agent had appeared out of nowhere. Startled, I gave her the form, and the kids and I exchanged nervous glances as the agent studied it. "Sir, are you carrying any fruits or vegetables with you?" she asked.

"William, show her your fruit," I said. He pulled out two tangerines. "And the apple," I added, to make us look extra transparent.

The agent confiscated the fruit and sent us on our way. We walked past the last agent, and I triumphantly said to the kids, "They never asked if we had hamsters."

Home for the Holidays
December 16, 2016

We had rented our house in Annapolis for the first year, but it was now vacant and waiting for us, cold and dark. I barely had time to turn up the thermostat before Madeleine pleaded with me to pick up Belle. We drove to Adam's, thanked him profusely, and welcomed Belle back into our lives.

Valerie arrived the next day, and we resumed our former lives without skipping a beat, filling the refrigerator, unpacking the winter clothing, shopping for Christmas gifts and decorating the house. I visited my mother at the assisted living center. Time had not left much of a mark on any of our neighborhood friends, but mom had visibly aged. My father's possessions were still evident all over the house, and she spoke of him as if he was going to walk into the room any minute.

In my life on the boat, I had not had much time to reflect on his passing. Or rather, my life was in such flux that I did not fully process that he was gone until I returned to the version of my life where he played a role.

The holidays came and went with the usual excess. When Madeleine and William's friends returned to school the first week in January, I monitored the kids' emotions closely, and neither seemed upset about not getting on the bus every morning for Annapolis Middle School. As a family, we had grown comfortable being outliers.

Madeleine's friend Amelia, who had taken care of Hamster Number One, the late Munchkin, agreed to foster Squirt and Snowball. Now that our two hamsters were U.S. residents, our attention turned to bringing Belle back to Martinique. Our airline flew dogs only on direct non-stop flights, so Valerie rebooked our tickets so that the two legs were separate trips. We had two "non-stop" flights with a stop in between, where we had to claim Belle and re-check her. The pieces were in place to continue the cruise. We packed our bags, emptied the refrigerator, lowered the thermostat, walked out of our empty house, locked the door and caught a ride to the airport.

Return to Martinique
January 23, 2017

I am always anxious when I return to the boat after being away for an extended period, so I was relieved to come back to a boat that was exactly the same as we had left it. My wife, on the other hand, who had spoken in French to a half dozen contractors, leaving them precise instructions about repairing specific items, was furious to come back to a boat that was exactly the same as we had left it. Not a lick of work had been done. The good news was that we could now watch over the contractors' shoulders, keep them off their cell phones and make sure they did the job right. The bad news was that we would have to stay put until all the work was complete, which was going to take another week.

Task number one and two for getting a dog used to living on a boat is, well, going number one and two. Valerie had read up on all the tricks cruisers use to entice their pets to relieve themselves in the correct spot when nature calls. We even paid good money at a pet store for a spray bottle of dog urine that was supposed to give the designated spot that certain *je ne sais quoi*, but Belle did not fall for it. Being a bird dog, she was fussy about her urine odors. We tasked Madeleine with the responsibility of training her, and we turned our attention to bird-dogging the contractors to do their work. After a few days, Madeleine had trained Belle to pee near the bow, where we could easily rinse the deck. Belle's number twos continued to appear in random locations on the boat, leading to extended dinnertime discussions about why dogs have two different approaches to these two seemingly similar operations.

St. Vincent and the Grenadines
January 25, 2017

While the contractors finished working on the boat, we made a cruising plan. We had until June 1, a little more than four months. Our starting point in Martinique put us roughly in the middle of the Caribbean's two island chains: the Windward Islands, extending about 250 miles to the south, and the Leeward Islands stretching 250 miles north and another 250 miles west. Also on the way home was Puerto Rico, the Dominican Republic and The Bahamas. We would have to continuously sail a northerly course to get to Annapolis, but we weren't ready to head north just yet. The Windward Islands beckoned.

We started late in the morning for the 30-mile run to the first island south, St. Lucia. When sheltered by the steep hills of the islands, the winds coming off the ocean are deceptively gentle, but the stretch of sea between the islands is exposed to the full force of the open Atlantic. These between-island stretches were the most dreaded segments of our Caribbean island-hopping.

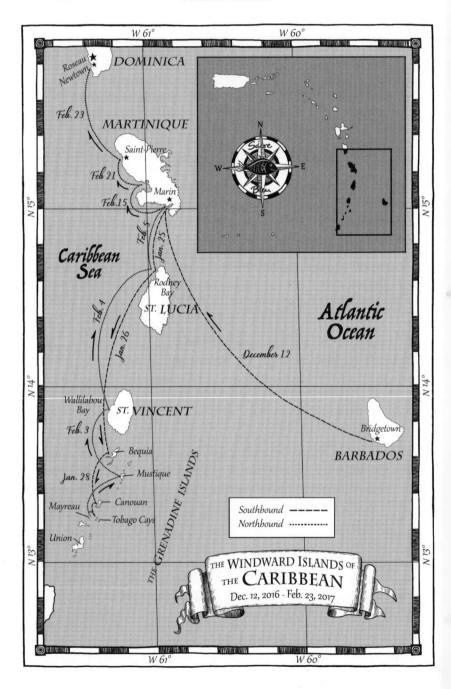

Our stop in St. Lucia would just be for the night, for we wanted to start our exploring at the farthest point south and gradually work our way north. We anchored in Rodney Bay, and left early the next morning, continuing farther south past St. Vincent to Bequia. Now that we were in the Caribbean, with its myriad of countries and borders, with a dog no less, arrivals were more complicated.

Bequia is part of St. Vincent and the Grenadines. As a new arrival, we were required to display our yellow Q for quarantine flag (a nautical tradition since the days of yellow fever) and clear customs. Valerie, always the optimist, loaded the dog onto the dinghy and drove herself to the customs dock with ship's papers in hand, where she was promptly told to take her dog and leave the country. In the end, we resigned ourselves to a short visit on shore in Bequia while Belle stayed on the boat.

The next day, we continued sailing farther south to Canouan, a Grenadine Island with barely enough real estate to fit a town, an international airport, and an 18-hole golf course. The dog police on Canouan seemed more relaxed, so we let Belle play on the beach with the kids while Valerie and I tried the Canouan beer.

Our ultimate destination as we drove farther and farther south was the Tobago Cays, a group of five tiny islands in the southernmost part of the Grenadines. The Tobago Cays Marine Park is a 1,400-acre snorkeler's paradise featuring shallow water with a white sandy seafloor and coral reefs populated with tropical fish that resemble swimming candy. But the relentless winds from the east were particularly fierce that day and the water was too rough to spend the night on anchor. After a brief stop and a swim, we took refuge in Salt Whistle Bay, off the close-by island of Mayreau, population: 271.

February 1, 2017

Our long journey north began today with a 20-mile run to Britannia Bay, Mustique. Officially one of the Grenadine Islands, Mustique is entirely privately owned but allows visitors. Over the years, Mustique has become a refuge where the rich and famous, from Mick Jagger to

Tommy Hilfiger to British royals, have a second home or perhaps a fifth. In fact, during our visit, I thought I saw Mick Jagger wearing a dark pair of sunglasses and a baseball hat. I spent a lot of time explaining to the kids who he was and why that was a big deal. After I saw another Mick Jagger, my enthusiasm waned. Back on *Sacre Bleu*, we introduced the kids to music by the Rolling Stones, starting with one of my favorite albums, *Some Girls*.

The next morning, we continued north to Wallilabou Bay, St. Vincent. Remotely located and hemmed in by steep hills and dense jungle, Wallilabou Bay is the location for the opening scenes of the first *Pirates of the Caribbean* movie, *Curse of The Black Pearl*. What remains of the production is a Potemkin pirate village and a makeshift museum with photographs of the frenetic two-week shoot that took place there.

Our entry into Wallilabou Bay was a stark contrast to our arrivals in chic Bequia and Mustique, where nobody seemed to notice a 45-foot catamaran dropping anchor. In Wallilabou, we were greeted by a flotilla of local entrepreneurs, some offering fresh produce, others offering to help moor the boat. We could have easily—a lot more easily—fastened our own lines to the mooring ball, but in the interest of stimulating the local economy, we paid a young man in a canoe $20 to do it for us. I had nothing but twenties in my wallet, and I was confident that a request for change would have produced a smile and a shoulder shrug. While we got the mooring assist, the fresh produce vendor laid his entire inventory on the deck of our boat, inching the fruits and vegetables closer to us one at a time like checkers pieces. Seeing a worthy opponent, Valerie stepped in and a haggling duel commenced. In the end, we traded a half dozen mangos and a large bunch of very green bananas for another $20 bill.

That night we watched *Curse of The Black Pearl*, but we saw nothing in the film that resembled Wallilabou Bay. Through the wizardry of camera angles, a few well-placed set pieces, and digital post-production, our anchorage was unrecognizable. Even this tropical paradise needed a layer of make-up to play in a Hollywood movie.

The sailing was relaxing and the seas were calm as we moved from St. Vincent to St. Lucia to Martinique, in the lee of the islands. We could have played solitaire on the deck. However, as we made the hops between the islands, the conditions were reminiscent of the most difficult early days of the transatlantic. Swells towered overhead, wind howled through the rigging, waves crashed over the bow, and the spray was relentless as we fought to keep the boat pointed in the right direction. The rough conditions had become routine for us, but as I sat on the flybridge I was not prepared for the sight of the family dog squatting on the bow, doing her business, ears blowing in the wind, oblivious to the danger. A panicked Madeleine rushed forward to rescue her, prompting me to rush forward to rescue Madeleine.

With Belle onboard, Madeleine had more purpose in her day. In nearly every anchorage, she would run Belle to shore to stretch her legs and be a dog for a while. This involved loading Belle in the dinghy, starting the outboard, driving off, choosing a landing point, landing the dinghy, and reversing the process. Madeleine was not only happier with Belle on the boat but also more confident, enjoying the responsibility that Belle brought into her life.

17

The Caribbean: Island-Hopping North

Back to Martinique (Again)
February 15, 2017

We had settled into a routine that was very different from our lives in the Mediterranean. We were spending more time in remote anchorages and less time on shore. Our boat was built to be off the grid, and we were finally there. With a generator, solar panels, and a water maker, we could stay in any remote anchorage as long as we wanted. We were also engaged in more outdoor activities: swimming, scuba diving and paddle boarding. We had evolved into a real seagoing family from the family that once drove from one quaint Mediterranean village to the next in search of better gelato.

As we worked our way up the west coast of Martinique, we ran across the occasional boat we recognized from the Atlantic Odyssey. These chance meetings happened far more frequently than I would have expected, and they made me appreciate how few of us are wandering the world in a sailboat. As time went on, at any given anchorage, we came to recognize many of the boats around us. The entire cruising community seemed to be made up of only a hundred lucky souls.

As we approached the northern end of Martinique, the weather forecast brought the threat of a major storm that forced us to find a secure anchorage. The shallow waters off the beachfront town of Saint-Pierre offered the best prospect for the night, so we dropped anchor about 500 feet offshore. To make sure the anchor was properly set, I put on snorkeling gear, dove 30 feet to the sandy bottom and looked at it up close.

The wind and waves were furious that night, and we were unable to sleep as *Sacre Bleu* rose up and down with the incoming surf. Valerie and I anxiously sat in the dark salon, feeling like we were stuck on an elevator, slowly moving up and down, looking out the windows to make sure the town lights had not gotten any closer. I was thankful I dove the anchor, but considering the forces at play that night, I was still skeptical about its ability to keep us attached to the loose sandy bottom. When I dove it again the next morning, the anchor had plowed a 30-foot-long trench in the sand.

With the morning light, we discovered we were the lucky ones. On the shore, a 36-foot ketch was lying on its side like a beached whale, a Danish flag still proudly fluttering at its stern. The crew was frantically pulling belongings out of the boat and laying them on the beach to dry. They were living the nightmare that had haunted me the entire cruise. Having lost the battle, they were methodical about the surrender, carefully arranging the ship's galley items in neat rows in one part of the beach, clothing and personal effects in another, sails and rigging in another, their lives and shattered dream on display for all to scrutinize.

We devoted the next day to exploring Saint-Pierre. As with Herculaneum in Italy, a pleasant beach town had sprung up around the charred ruins that told the story of a tragic past. The twin-spired cathedral was one of the few structures to survive the 1902 volcanic eruption that destroyed the town.

The Zoo de Martinique was a short hike out of town. There, we saw an impressive collection of native birds, butterflies, lizards, and monkeys, all reproduced in plush miniature in the zoo gift shop, where we spent at least half our time. The woman who ran the shop suggested we visit the Neisson Rum Distillery for a quintessentially Martiniquais experience. I thanked her very much and asked how we might find a taxi or Uber. Without a second thought, she gave us her car keys. Her random display of kindness left us all speechless. She earned a place on my list of people that I have met whom I think about when I need to remind myself that selfless generosity still exists in the world. The idea of driving a borrowed car on unfamiliar, winding mountain roads to visit a rum distillery did not seem like a good idea at first, but she persisted, so we accepted. That afternoon, at the open-air Neisson Rum Distillery, deep in the forested hills, a soft-spoken guide made the process of turning sugarcane into rum seem like alchemy. Later, we returned the car, thanked our new friend with a bottle of rum, and returned to *Sacre Bleu* with fond memories of the people of Martinique.

Dominica
February 24, 2017

Continuing our island-hopping north, we arrived on the southern tip of Dominica in the afternoon, taking a mooring ball off Newtown, a suburb of Roseau, the capital city. We tied the dinghy to a dock that was missing most of its planking and walked tightrope-style into an abandoned building and then out the door into a noisy sidewalk filled with pedestrians and food vendors. In the frenetic street, we found a cab driver who was more than happy to give us a tour of the island.

The next morning, we slipped the mooring and made our way up the coast to Portsmouth on the north end of the island, anchoring in Prince Rupert Bay. There, we found a more traditional Dominica: artisanal fishing boats, street vendors, an easygoing vibe, restaurants and beach clubs. The Indian River is the principal attraction here, with its mangrove-lined banks providing a home for snakes, lizards, butterflies, water birds, and parrots. As we wound our way through the dense jungle in the dinghy, we made use of Valerie's almost supernatural powers of observation: a tree frog here, a snake there, a butterfly

The Caribbean: Island-Hopping North 285

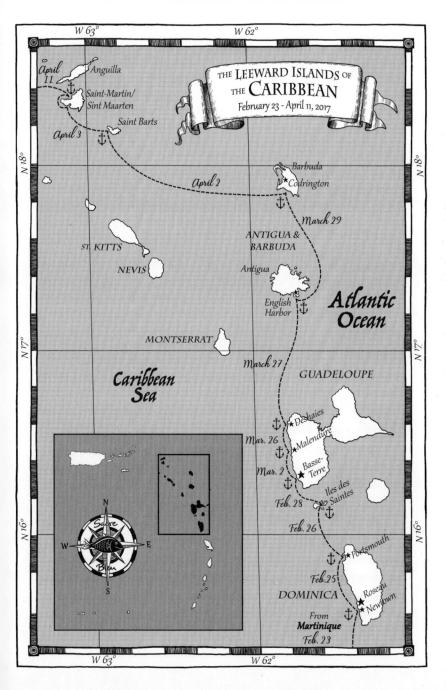

over there. She can see right through their camouflage, and I suspect animals are irked by that. I imagined them saying, "Damn. How'd that woman see me?"

Guadeloupe
February 27, 2017

It was Shrove Monday on the Christian calendar, making tomorrow Shrove Tuesday, also known as Mardi Gras in other parts of the world. Islanders who are practicing Catholics use this time for last indulgences before Lent begins on Ash Wednesday. These three days mark the climax of the Caribbean carnival season, culminating in a grand parade and the burning of King Vaval, a 30-foot-tall totem made of wood. Carnival is an event not to missed, and we were told that the best one in the entire Caribbean was just up the west coast of Guadeloupe in the capital city of Basse-Terre.

There was no protected anchorage off Basse-Terre and we had no choice but to anchor outside of the breakers off the beach. I was not comfortable leaving *Sacre Bleu* in such an exposed location, so I spent most of my time onshore glancing down the beach to check on the boat while Valerie and the kids shopped for costumes. If the anchor dragged in that easterly wind, I thought, *Sacre Bleu* would end up in Venezuela.

On Tuesday morning, the streets of Basse-Terre were choked with hundreds of costumed people organizing themselves into groups and eventually into a parade. The procession of marching bands, dance troupes—women wearing enormous hats with feathers, flowers, and beads, floats, jugglers walking on stilts and young men cracking whips—went on for over a mile. The parade meandered through the streets from one end of the city to the other, lasting all day and well into the night. By early evening, we returned to our quiet boat, which was, much to my relief, still anchored down the beach.

Ash Wednesday arrived, bringing a different complexion to Basse-Terre. Whereas the theme on Shrove Tuesday was bright colors, sparkle, and feathers, the theme on this first day of Lent was black and white. The celebration was visibly toned down, so we stayed late into the night and even joined the parade at one point. The musicians and dancers had worked glow sticks into their costumes, and as darkness fell on Basse-Terre, the parade route resembled a luminescent green river, its banks ebbing and flowing with the music. At the end of the parade route stood Vaval, King of the Carnival, awaiting his sacrifice. We took our leave in the dinghy as Vaval went up in flames, watching the final act of Carnival from our inconspicuous home bobbing in the dark waves offshore.

March 2, 2017
We were now five weeks into our Caribbean cruise, and in terms of miles covered, we were about where we wanted to be. As in the Mediterranean, we preferred not to follow a strict itinerary; we wanted to be able to drop anchor and stay a week wherever we felt the urge. Continuing our steady northerly trek, we planned to spend the month of March exploring the Leeward Islands, which stretched 250 miles north and another 250 miles west. Around the first of April, we hoped to turn that corner and sail west into the Virgin Islands and on to Puerto Rico and the Dominican Republic. For the month of May, we hoped to be in The Bahamas. The passage from the northern part of The Bahamas to Annapolis would take a week or two, getting us home in early June.

From Basse-Terre, we sailed north to Plage de Malendure, a popular beach midway up the west coast of Guadeloupe known for its black sand. While I was on the helm, I saw what looked like a bright white submarine passing quickly across our bow, port to starboard, about five feet under the surface. I threw the helm to port, anticipating a collision with the mysterious object. When I looked to starboard, I saw an enormous adult humpback whale, ten feet across, surfacing close enough for me to step off the boat and onto its back. The leviathan ignored us and kept swimming, apparently in a hurry to be someplace. Later that day, we heard a distress call over the radio from a sailboat that had hit a humpback whale and needed a tow. We were only a few feet from that same fate; *Sacre Bleu* was still a lucky boat.

Applying our no-itinerary philosophy in Plage de Malendure, we dropped the anchor and did not pick it up again for three weeks. The anchorage was secure, there was a fine selection of bars, restaurants and adventure outfitters on shore, and the grocery store had its own dinghy dock. The adjacent Jacques Cousteau Underwater Reserve provided ample diving, and with the help of a local dive shop, the kids logged their first night dive. On shore, we went on rock-climbing in the jungle, visited the bird sanctuary, and lived on island time, which still passed quickly.

Madeleine and William took advantage of our two weeks of sedentary life to gain experience at snorkeling and scuba diving. We sent them on several more dive trips with the local dive shop, and when they didn't have a tank strapped to their backs they were snorkeling the coral reefs near the boat. The land excursions provided welcome variety to our offshore lives. After a day of rock climbing in the jungle, the kids had found renewed purpose to our travels. The laid-back atmosphere of Malendure also allowed Madeleine to take Belle on frequent beach walks. Both girl and dog seemed to have adjusted well to life on the water.

March 26, 2017

We were running along the coast of Guadeloupe when another whale appeared in our path. Similar to the first, this adult humpback swam off the bow, its white underbelly visible just below the surface of the water. The whale was swimming with the boat this time, so no frantic course correction was needed. It surfaced now and then, blew some spray into the air with a loud puff, and continued its escort. We cut the engines to see if it might consider lingering with the boat, but this whale also seemed to have an urgent appointment and just kept going.

With all the whale watching, we were running out of daylight, so we opted to stay in Guadeloupe for one more night. We had already cleared out of Guadeloupe customs, but after three months in the Caribbean and zero interventions, as opposed to our weekly boardings in Europe, we were becoming relaxed about authority. We anchored off Deshaies, a beach town set inside a protected cove. As we strolled the main street, we passed a whale-watching company with photos in the window of startled tourists pointing at whales from the deck of a tour boat. "So what?" said William. "We almost hit one." I gave him a thumbs up. I was proud that our whale-watching experience included a lot more excitement, even some moments of terror, and we didn't pay a dime for it.

Soon after we anchored, a neighboring boat told us about the resident bottle-nosed dolphins that swim through the anchorage every day. Sure enough, the next morning, three dolphins swam by the boat. We all jumped in the water with snorkeling gear and caught up to them. Madeleine, a particularly good free diver, followed the animals all the way to the bottom, nearly 30 feet deep.

Our time in Guadeloupe began with Carnival—a cultural explosion of music, dance, art and religion—and ended in a tranquil encounter with dolphins. During our time in between, Madeleine and William became confident divers. As we slowly worked our way north, we were beginning to appreciate the subtle variations that the Caribbean offered. Our next stop to the north would bring distinct change as we left a French island for a former British colony.

Antigua and Barbuda
March 28, 2017

We left Deshaies midday and, after a between-island crossing that brought strong winds and choppy seas, we arrived in English Harbor, Antigua, just before sunset. Antigua and Barbuda are two islands that form one country, but they could not be more different. The nation is a member of the British Commonwealth, and while Antigua is very British and monied and endowed with resorts, Barbuda is undeveloped and sparsely populated. The small number of resident Barbudans are mostly descendants of freed slaves, and they dwell in modest homes on modest plots of land. The two islands are also different geologically. Antigua resembles most of the rest of the Caribbean island chain, with hard coral shorelines and high scrubby hills, while Barbuda is low-lying with a stunning white sandy beach perimeter surrounded by sparkling, clear shallow water and protected by an outer perimeter of pristine coral reefs. Barbuda should have been dropped in the Bahamas, where it would have fit in perfectly.

Of the two islands, I was more fascinated with Barbuda because it is considered a forbidden destination in the sailing world. The cruising guides warn approaching skippers to time their arrival for when the sun is high in the sky because any reflection on the water creates a grave risk of hitting one of the many coral reefs that surround Barbuda like mines. The island has very little in the way of tourist infrastructure, and as a result, it does not host many visitors from sea or by air. Spending a few days there seemed like a perfect plan, assuming we could get there without sinking the boat.

Barbuda first appeared on the horizon as a dark line of trees and a brilliant white beach. Then the ominous dark patches of water, jagged coral heads that lurk just below the surface, came into view. As we approached, the wall of coral looked so continuous that it seemed impossible to get close enough to the island to drop an anchor. A handful of other sailboats had settled close to shore on the other side of the reefs, and we concluded there had to be a way through. Valerie stood at the bow, scanning the water immediately ahead, giving me hand signals as we negotiated the uncharted obstacle course. We finally reached clear shallows, and the kids dropped the anchor in sand between the reef to seaward and the breaking waves on shore.

I looked down through 30 feet of gin-clear water, following our chain all the way to the anchor clearly visible on the flat sandy bottom. Four or five stingrays puttered around slowly, moving in and out of the shadow of the boat as a school of yellowtail snapper swam through. I sized up our destination: wide empty beaches, swaying palms, and not a touch of humanity in sight except for two other sailboats. We could call this home for a while.

We threw our dive gear in the dinghy and drove over to Coco Point, where we snorkeled through forests of elkhorn coral and swam with eagle rays, nurse sharks, and schools of small tropical fish in vivid colors that created a kaleidoscope effect in our dive masks. Madeleine devoted most of her dive to following a timid porcupine fish with an awkward, box-shaped body. It dashed from one crevice to another, peering out of its hiding place with large, wide-set eyes that gave it an almost-human expression of fear. How did nature come up with so many different designs for making a living on a coral reef?

The next day, we visited Codrington, the only development on the island dense enough to be considered a town. We strolled the unpaved streets, past similarly sized homes, by the Holy Trinity Primary School to the office of tourism. There, the woman behind the desk recommended that we take a tour of the frigate bird sanctuary. Our animal-loving kids gave it an enthusiastic approval, so we asked when the next tour was leaving. A man in his sixties with coffee-black skin and white hair stepped forward, introduced himself as George, and announced that the next tour was leaving whenever we wanted. We spent the afternoon in George's skiff, darting around Codrington Lagoon at breakneck speeds in water that looked ankle deep. I had an uneasy feeling that we would hit bottom at any moment, and we would all be launched into the water. George obviously knew the lagoon well, and he also had an ornithologist's understanding of frigate birds, which seemed to outnumber humans on this island.

George explained that frigate birds, with their enormous wingspans, can spend most of their day aloft with little effort, giving them the ability to soar across oceans.

"Why do they have inflatable red throats?" Madeleine asked. George answered that it was how the males impressed the females.

"How weird," was William's reaction. Was he talking about inflatable throats or impressing females?

While the birds that call Barbuda home prefer to wander thousands of miles, the people here seem content to stay put, and after our four-day visit it was easy to understand why. Barbuda seems to offer a very egalitarian existence in an idyllic setting.

After sailing north since February, we turned northwest from Barbuda, setting a course for the French island of Saint Barthélemy, or St. Barts, and then on to Saint Martin. From there, we turned west towards the British Virgin Islands, rounding the corner of the Caribbean.

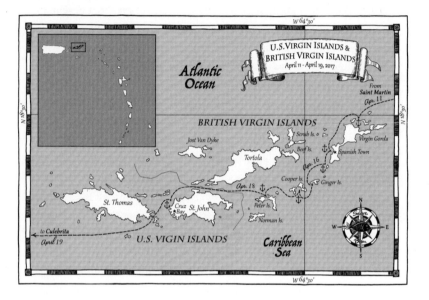

The British Virgin Islands
April 11, 2017

On open ocean legs, we frequently mounted a deep-sea fishing rod on the stern and trolled for whatever kind of fish consider that part of the world home. Far offshore is a tough neighborhood for sea life: the fish are big and aggressive, and they're angry and uncooperative by the time you land them on the boat. As opposed to fishing on a lake or a river, in the deep sea you're catching animals that could catch you. On our way to the BVIs, for example, we landed a barracuda. Situations like these are why we owned a pair of chain mail gloves. We knew better than to keep the barracuda because their flesh contains a toxin. I carefully removed the lure from its toothy, snapping maw with long needle-nose pliers before throwing it back in the water. Later that day, we caught a painted mackerel. Within minutes, Valerie had reduced this two-foot, pearlescent blue-and-yellow torpedo of a fish into a large bowl of ceviche and two filets, and everyone filled up. We even let Belle indulge in a plate of fresh mackerel, which she inhaled.

Fifteen minutes later, Belle threw up. A strange tingling sensation in my fingers set in a couple hours later when we were anchored off Spanish Town, on the island of Virgin Gorda. William came down with a violent stomachache, Madeleine said that she had a "weird" sensation when she drank cold water, and Valerie complained that when she was washing the dishes she could not distinguish cold water from hot. The dog, for her part, was feeling fine.

The symptoms, as varied and strange as they were, all added up to dire news: We were suffering from ciguatera fish poisoning. Our senses of touch, taste, and smell were miswired, and we all felt like we were gestating aliens. Hot showers felt cold, ice cream tasted salty, and wearing clothing was painful. This illness is commonly associated with eating barracuda, but we were learning the hard way that many other large predatory fish, including painted mackerels, carry ciguatera. In a process called bioaccumulation, small fish feed on an algae growing on the coral reef that happens to be a neurotoxin, and they accumulate the toxin in their flesh. As bigger fish gobble up the smaller fish, they too accumulate toxin in their flesh. These toxins do not harm the fish, but humans (and dogs, apparently) can become gravely ill when they insert themselves into the food web. According to an online reference, "The symptoms can last from weeks to years, and in extreme cases as long as 20 years, often leading to long-term disability, but most people do recover slowly over time." Thank goodness the children got it when they were young.

The ciguatera symptoms lasted a few more days, returning intermittently for weeks afterward. With everyone on the boat ailing, we established an easy itinerary, drifting from Virgin Gorda to Ginger to Cooper to Peter Island. It was high season in the BVIs and anchorages were crowded, so we avoided the popular spots and favored areas the charter sailboats were not authorized to go.

Because we never bothered with the paperwork to bring Belle into the BVIs, we left her on the boat when we went ashore. Belle suffered from separation anxiety and leaving her alone caused her to go into howling fits. To address this problem, we developed a routine that allowed us to vanish without her noticing. Just as we were getting ready to leave, William would hide a dog treat deep in the boat—say, under a pillow in one of the cabins—while Madeleine kept Belle distracted. Being a nose-oriented bird dog, she would spring into action as soon as we let her go, sniffing every nook and cranny in search of her prize. While Belle was busy locating her liver-flavored quarry, we quietly slipped into the dinghy, drifted far enough away to discretely start the outboard, and zoomed off. Belle would eventually find the treat and eat it and not give us a passing thought until we reappeared. That was the plan, and it worked, repeatedly.

Anchored off Peter Island after dinner ashore, we returned to find an empty boat. Belle was gone. The four of us did not quite know what to do or where to start looking. We scanned the dark water in all directions and saw nothing but the lights of other boats anchored nearby. The beach was not far, but not close either, and Belle would have had to know to swim in that direction to have any hope of surviving. We shouted into the darkness, calling her name, becoming more despondent as each minute passed. Our pleas were answered with silence. Madeleine broke into tears.

Valerie and I thought the worst, but to the kids we told a different story. "I'm sure she made it to shore," Valerie said.

"Somebody probably found her on the beach. Now, she's going to live the good life in the islands," I said.

Our children were not buying it. More silence filled the night air. Then a voice in the darkness rang out: "Do you own a dog named Belle?"

"Yes!" We shouted back to a neighboring boat.

"We have her over here!" the voice said. Belle had abandoned ship, swam for the nearest light, and managed to jump onto the transom of the neighbor's boat, materializing from the darkness like a tail-wagging sea monster. Luckily, she was wearing tags, so when the crew on the other boat heard us calling, the mystery was solved.

Puerto Rico and the Virgin Islands
April 19, 2017

On this noteworthy day, *Sacre Bleu* entered U.S. waters for the first time, anchoring off Cruz Bay, St. John, U.S. Virgin Islands, where we cleared customs. We would not idle in our native waters for long. To avoid the formalities and duties required to officially import *Sacre Bleu*, we registered as a visiting boat. We were eager to get to our special place, which was now only 25 miles farther west, so we spent only one night at anchor and departed early the next morning.

Five years earlier, on our first experience as a boating family, we had chartered a similar catamaran out of Puerto Rico and ventured twenty miles east to a group of islands few Americans have heard of and even fewer realize are U.S. territory: the Spanish Virgin Islands. There, through sheer beginner's luck, we stumbled onto the perfect little Robinson Crusoe island of Culebrita. Part of the larger Culebra National Wildlife Refuge, Culebrita is one square mile of an uninhabited paradise that features six beaches, a cove loaded with sea turtles, tidal pools teeming with tropical fish, trails winding through the hills, hidden ponds and the ruins of a Victorian-era lighthouse. We shared the anchorage with an American family who had just finished a multi-year cruise. Their boat was outfitted with a wind generator and solar panels, bow and stern anchors, and numerous other modifications that allowed them to sail to the ends of the earth. On the evening of our arrival, they dinghy'd over to our boat with a homemade pie and a bottle of wine, and we spent the rest of the night enraptured by their stories of adventure. That night, the seeds for our family cruise were planted. Now, we were the veteran world cruisers passing through Culebrita near the end of our voyage in our ocean-rigged, sea-worn vessel.

After two wonderful days in Culebrita, and three more exploring the other Spanish Virgin Islands, we reached the mainland of Puerto

Rico. Sailing past the imposing Castillo San Felipe del Morro, which has stood watch over the harbor for 400 years, we worked our way into San Juan harbor. According to our rough itinerary, we had another ten days to visit Puerto Rico and the Dominican Republic. We had visited San Juan before, so after spending a day visiting the Castillo and strolling through town, we continued west to Aguadilla, a popular surfing destination on the northwest corner of the island. There, we rested up for our 240-mile crossing to the port of Luperón, Dominican Republic. We were running out of the time we had allocated to spend in the Caribbean, and we fought the urge to stretch the itinerary further. We had made a commitment to Madeleine and William to be home by June 1.

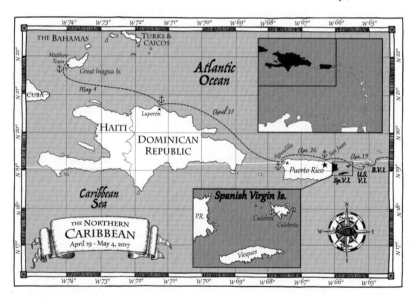

The Dominican Republic
April 27, 2017

We arrived in Luperón before sunrise, and, since the cruising guide warns entering vessels "to strictly follow the buoys that mark the narrow entry channel," we hove-to and waited for daylight. The morning light revealed a small river mouth on the beach that did not appear big enough to lead anywhere. I double-checked the chart to be certain we had the right river mouth, and indeed we did. We were back in the Western system of "red, right, return," so, when I saw the first buoy, a red nun (conical buoy) appearing as depicted on the chart, I passed leaving it on our right-hand, or starboard side. The next buoy was a green can (cylindrical buoy), as depicted on the chart, so we left it to port. The next buoy, depicted on the chart as green, was in fact not a green can but a red nun. Should we leave it to port or starboard? I guessed the port side and we ultimately made it into the harbor without running aground.

Entry formalities for the Dominican Republic include Immigration, Customs, Agriculture, and the Navy. The cruising guide instructed us to anchor in the harbor, display the Q flag and wait for the Navy. Three men in blue jumpsuits eventually showed up in a skiff. They approached a little too fast and bumped into our boat hard. Their military demeanors momentarily changed from serious to sheepish, as if to say "Sorry, but things like this happen when you're conducting important business." Instead of hitching their dinghy line to our stern cleat, the way a proper sailor would, they tied a granny knot to the swim ladder. The three of them awkwardly climbed on board and looked around like children in a candy store, sizing up the luxury and volume of *Sacre Bleu*. They repeatedly implied we must have a lot of money to be able to own such an impressive boat. They warned us that the entry procedure is time consuming, but for a small fee they would be willing to expedite us. We refused to take the hint, feigned stupidity, and thanked them profusely for all their kind words. Before they left, I asked one of the officers about the entry buoy that was red instead of green. He explained that the green buoy was carried away by a storm, and since they had run out of green buoys they replaced it with a red one.

The remaining entry formalities were still unfinished, so we went ashore and found the customs and immigration offices, a group of buildings that appeared impossible to access because they sat on the other side of a culvert full of stagnant water running the length of the block. At one time, apparently, a bridge spanned the water, but the planks were missing and all that remained were two narrow steel beams. With ship's papers in hand, Valerie and I scaled one of the beams like a tightrope, heel before toe, crossing the 15-foot chasm, trying not to look down. Safely on the other side, we cleared customs, a process that turned out to be uneventful with no bribery involved.

We spent a fun-filled week in the Dominican Republic, visiting historical monuments from Columbus' first voyage, hiking the jungle trails, and learning about the ex-pat life from a friend who had moved there a year earlier. When it was time to be on our way, we had to perform all the formalities again to depart the country. We walked the narrow beam once more and filled out all the clearance forms, then returned to the boat and waited. All that stood between us and the Bahamas was a visit from the Dominican Navy.

The same contingent arrived in their skiff and climbed aboard. Since we had a long crossing ahead of us, in the interest of time, I got right to the bribing. Valerie was ready to dig in and spend another night in Luperón before giving them a Dominican peso, but I just wanted to be on our way. The older, more senior officer played the role of the facilitator: "I don't want anything myself. I'm only asking for them," he said.

Without discussing it with Valerie, I presented each of the two younger men with a bottle of cheap wine we had just purchased at a grocery store in town. Valerie's eyes turned to fire when she saw what was unfolding. The two men were clearly disappointed as they were expecting a monetary tribute more fitting with their status as naval officers. With the bribe irreversibly set into motion, a ritual ensued: "Take it as our gift," I implored. They were obliged to say no at first, and I had to insist. We not only did we have to bribe them, we had to make them feel good about taking it. Seeing in our demeanor that the negotiation was over, the younger officer picked up the bottle of wine, and the two of them slinked back to their dinghy, dragging out their departure in hopes of creating another opening to negotiate. As they drove off, we reflected on our week in the Dominican Republic. It is a beautiful country, and we looked forward to returning when it is under new management.

18

The Bahamas: The Ultimate Infinity Pool

Great Inagua
May 4, 2017

After a 30-hour crossing, we dropped anchor off Matthew Town, Great Inagua Island, at midday. *Sacre Bleu* was the only boat in sight. Just the morning before, we were anchored in the muddy Bay of Luperón, surrounded by mangroves, in a veritable floating village of boats with jury-rigged awnings, television dish antennas and potted plants. Here in The Bahamas, looking down through crystal clear water on coral reefs, fields of seagrass and the sea animals wandering through it all: a school of yellowtail snapper here, a barracuda there, a sting ray just below. Bahamian water is like no other on the planet. It's a clear window into what is usually a mysterious and opaque world.

Great Inagua, the southernmost island in the Bahamas, is a quiet outpost that is rarely visited by cruise ships or tourists. The Morton Salt plant is the biggest operation on the island, with its sprawling evaporation ponds and the World's Tallest Mountain of Salt, glowing white in the Bahamian sun, with enough elevation to make a decent ski run.

The customs office in Matthew Town is a one-room affair reminiscent of a small-town post office. Inside sits the one-and-only

Customs and Immigration officer responsible for keeping the entire southern border of The Bahamas secure. We did not choose to enter The Bahamas through Great Inagua for this reason; we just got lucky. Why? Because we had yet another international smuggling operation to pull off.

The Bahamas has some of the strictest regulations regarding pets, and Belle was not allowed to enter without a certificate of health from a veterinarian. Since we were already anchored in Bahamian waters, a visit to the vet was not in the cards. We elected to go with our tried-and-true strategy of diving in headfirst and improvising. Ready, fire, aim! We all entered the customs office, and I let Valerie talk to the Customs agent. From a distance I watched Valerie fill out the necessary forms and pay the entry fee. Then she walked right past us and out the door, and we quickly followed without saying a word. "There was no place on any of the forms to declare a pet, so I didn't," Valerie said once we were outside. It was another one of those lies of omission, like "They never asked if we had hamsters."

We had the entire month of May to explore this nation of 700 islands. Continuing our slow northward trek from Great Inagua, we sailed to Long Island over water that was dark blue, almost black. As we rounded the north end of Long Island and entered Calabash Bay, the water abruptly changed to the color of a swimming pool. We had just passed over an underwater cliff that rose from a depth of 12,000 feet up to the Great Bahama Bank, a sun-dappled shallow plain of white sand as far as the eye can see. Only from the deck of a small boat can one appreciate just how shallow and expansive this stretch of clear water is. As we glided over miles and miles of tabletop-flat sea bottom, dappled with geometric patterns of sparkling sunlight, I saw sharks, rays, barracudas, and other big, dark shapes darting away in a flash, startled by our shadow.

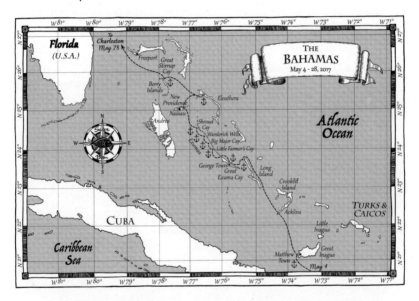

The seafloor in The Bahamas is like a desert, with sands continuously shifting, building up shoals and carving out channels. Here, nautical charts are of little use. The safest way to navigate is by stationing a crewmember on the bow to assess water depth based on color. Water that is 15 to 20 feet deep appears as medium aquamarine blue. Water that is the palest of light blue is still five or six feet deep, just enough to float *Sacre Bleu*. We found we could navigate in any water as long as it was not white. Dark patches indicate coral reefs. Since red and yellow light is quickly absorbed by water, deeper reefs appear black, while shallower, more dangerous reefs show their true browns, reds, and yellows. Like a token on a giant game board, we moved about, our path determined by colors.

After 32 hours of sailing, we dropped our anchor into the medium aquamarine blue water of Calabash Bay on the west side of Long Island. That evening, while I was sitting on the flybridge watching the sunset, it occurred to me that I was living a cliché. I was on my yacht in The Bahamas. For most of my adult life, being on my yacht in The Bahamas represented the ultimate in wealth and accomplishment. "If only I had bought stock in Apple Computer back in the day, I wouldn't be here, I'd be on my yacht in The Bahamas." Now I was. I didn't feel any different.

Long Island
May 9, 2017

After a day of snorkeling in Calabash Bay's clear waters, we continued to Great Exuma Island, anchoring near George Town so that I could take advantage of its airport to make a quick trip home. Valerie and the kids not only had a large town close by but also were anchored a hundred feet from a beach bar that somehow managed to tame giant stingrays into eating out of your hand. I was confident they would not get bored for the three days I was gone.

The intent of my trip was to purchase boat supplies that were either impossible to find or extremely expensive in The Bahamas. Valerie figured that if I was bringing back half a suitcase full of hard-to-get boat supplies, I might as well fill the other half with hard-to-get groceries. On my return trip, my largest of large suitcases, the type so massive it can only be rolled, was full of fuel and oil filters, drive belts, zinc anodes, and other boat supplies, while the adjoining half contained two heads of iceberg lettuce, frozen steaks, an assortment of French cheeses and Rice Krispies cereal. As I approached Bahamas Customs, I was asked if I had any food items. Of course, I said "yes," but I tried to say it as nonchalantly as possible. It didn't work. When the customs officer opened the suitcase, the only words he could find were "Oh, Lord." I managed to talk my way out of the situation with only a stern warning, assuring him that it was all for personal use and we would not sell any of it.

Back on board *Sacre Bleu*, we were eager to see the rest of the Exumas, a group of islands that includes the Exuma Cays Land and Sea Park, a marine reserve with even more pristine anchorages, dive sites and hiking trails on shore. We followed the island chain north to Little Farmer's Cay, and for the entire 45-mile trip, we drove over water that was six feet deep, leaving a slim 18-inch clearance between our keel and the sand. As we sailed along at eight knots, I could not stop worrying about the anomaly—a rock or a hill—that might rise more than 18 inches from the bottom, but all of that worrying was for naught. The bottom was flat as a parking lot.

Near sundown, with several more miles to go, we encountered violent squalls. With no sunlight, it was impossible to gauge the water depth ahead of us, so we stopped dead and drifted, anxiously assessing our next move. The squalls continued, with strong wind and driving rain, and night began to fall, forcing us to act. We consulted three different charts: the ship's electronic system, an iPad application, and a paper chart. None of the charts even remotely agreed, so we inched our way forward, praying that we would not run aground. We finally found water suitable for anchoring and stopped for the night. The squalls passed, a starry night opened up overhead, and a warm breeze blew gently over the deck. It was another day on the boat that touched all the emotions, from bliss to terror and back again.

Our next stop in the Exuma island chain was Big Major Cay, which has become a global tourist attraction in recent years. Here, and only here, can visitors witness the unique juxtaposition of sparkling aquamarine water and feral hogs. These swine are not shy. When visitors land on the island, to get a jump on their rivals for food, they will swim out to meet the arrivals. As pigs paddle over the surface of the clear water, harmless nurse sharks glide below, bringing two animals together that should never cross paths in nature. The larger pigs bully their way into the line-up, pushing the small pigs aside like bowling pins as they throw their snouts into an approaching dinghy.

We had read that when landing a dinghy on Big Major Cay, always bring an offering of food scraps and a jerrycan of water as the pigs are especially in need of drinking water. Madeleine, our aspiring veterinarian, drove the operation with military precision, slicing and preparing all our fruits and vegetables that were past their prime and loading them in Tupperware containers. Like many a military operation, however, our Plan A did not survive first contact with the enemy. The pigs rushed our dinghy, and the panicked kids jettisoned all the food hoping to draw the pigs away from the boat. The lead hog vacuumed up most of the floating scraps, the smaller pigs scattered in pursuit of the sunken bits, and the sharks watched from a safe distance. We all quickly exited the dinghy when the smallest pig jumped in. Fortunately, we left the dog on the boat and avoided adding a third species to that unnatural mix.

Certain cruising communities in The Bahamas could be described as permanent in location but transient in membership. For example, off Stocking Island near George Town, where we sat on anchor for a week, a community-designated boat in the anchorage broadcasts a VHF radio show twice a day that includes the weather report, a reading of items for sale by other boaters, activities and happy hour gatherings. When this boat departs, another amateur DJ takes over. On Big Major Cay, we stumbled on a sailing community that gathers on an inconspicuous stretch of beach permanently set up as an unofficial clubhouse, with tables, hammocks, a tiki bar and a fire pit.

Just a little farther north at Warderick Wells, inside the Land and Sea Park, another sailing community is building an art installation of sorts. At the top of Boo Boo Hill, passing sailors add a piece of driftwood with their vessel's name to an ever-growing sculpture. Madeleine made a day's work out of creating our contribution: a scrap of driftwood with *"Sacre Bleu* 2017" painted on it. Conscious that we were part of a greater collaborative work, we tried a dozen different places before settling on just the right location. In the end, no spot seemed ideal and we had to force ourselves to just pick a place. That is the way with most art; it is not finished, it is abandoned.

Exuma Cays Land & Sea Park
May 20, 2017

On this bright, cloudless morning, I went scuba diving with Madeleine and William. As the three of us were paddling along the wall of a coral reef, we were joined by the biggest barracuda I have ever seen, and I have seen a lot of them. Even taking into account that objects appear bigger through a dive mask, this fish looked like a small submarine with a jaw full of crooked dinosaur teeth that had evolved to rip flesh from bone while a frightening musical score played. I signaled to the kids to start making our way back to the dinghy, which was anchored about a hundred feet away. As I gestured "you go first and I'll follow," I could tell by the look in the eyes of this fish that it understood scuba diving hand signals and it was coming along too. The barracuda followed, its toothy maw inches from my swim fins, as we covered that long hundred feet. When we reached the dinghy, we quickly jumped in. I had been ocean diving most of my life, frequently with barracudas and large sharks, but this was the first time any animal had advanced on me. Days later, a local explained that barracuda had grown accustomed to being fed by spear-fishers and would follow the divers back to their boat where the divers cleaned their catch. Evidently, the barracuda was not being aggressive, but these subtleties are hard to read with their limited facial expressions.

Just when I thought The Bahamas could not offer any more exquisite combinations of clear water and white sand, we stumbled on Shroud Cay, our last stop in the magical Exuma Land and Sea Park. While all the islands of the Exuma Cays might look the same on a chart, each is unique in some surprising way. About three miles end to end, Shroud Cay is pierced coast to coast by clear-as-air, sandy-bottomed aquamarine rivers teeming with ocean wildlife. For tropical fish, sea turtles, rays, and sea birds, these ribbons of saltwater are merely extensions of their ocean homes. We explored the island's interior in the dinghy, at one point getting lost in the confusion of tributaries. "That's a hawksbill sea turtle!" Madeleine cried, pointing to a juvenile the size of a dinner plate. "They have a pointy nose," she added, anticipating that I was about to question her identification skills.

Nassau
May 25, 2016

The Atlantis, Paradise Island Resort in Nassau could not be more different from the Exumas, but with two children on board, we couldn't just sail by it. Madeleine and William had exhibited an adult-like patience and curiosity over these many months of travel, and it was time to cut them loose at this world-famous waterpark so they could be children for a day. Both kids were in their bathing suits before we had finished tying up to the dock. "The Power Tower is the place to start," William declared, as he surveyed a map of the waterpark with furrowed brow, like a general going into battle.

We tied up in the resort marina and found ourselves on an alien planet of luxury and excess cast in pink concrete. Its constructed beaches, manicured gardens, and shark-filled aquariums were a pale imitation of the real Bahamas we had left behind. If boats had feelings, *Sacre Bleu*, after taking us to so many exquisitely authentic destinations, would have broken her dock lines and sailed away. "It's a lot of pink," Valerie observed as she reluctantly stepped off the boat.

The waterslides have names like Leap of Faith, The Abyss and The Drop, and I discovered the hard way that they are designed for teenage bodies. I reluctantly followed William over the edge of The Drop, where I went into a free fall that ended in a dip engineered to gently arrest the plunge without breaking bones. I heard my spine crack, blacked out briefly, and floated slowly to the end of the ride in convulsions. For the remainder of the day, I watched the kids plummeting down waterslides and racing back to the queue, over and over again, from the safety of the tiki bar.

For real thrills, on our last day in Nassau, I wanted Madeleine and William to experience sharks up close. In my comic strip, *Sherman's Lagoon*, Sherman the shark defies the public image of these animals being mean and aggressive; Sherman is lazy and unambitious. I wanted to show the kids that sharks, with few exceptions, are not like their public image; they're more like Sherman. A dive operation called Stuart Cove's offers excursions that bring people and sharks together in one place. We put on scuba gear, went offshore in a dive boat, and dropped to a depth of 40 feet, where 20 to 30 large Caribbean reef sharks swam in circles around us. The kids were frightened at first, but they soon realized that the sharks were less interested in them than in the fish the divers were handing out. The sharks swam by, sometimes within inches, giving us a chance to admire these wild predators up close.

May 27, 2017
The days were passing quickly, and our time in The Bahamas was coming to an end. The next morning, we continued our northward trek, sailing 55 miles in near-perfect conditions to the Berry Islands.

Sacre Bleu lifted out of the water and kicked up a giant wake behind her twin hulls as the westerly breeze filled her sails. It was a fitting last day of sailing in foreign waters for us. Early the next morning, we would set a course for Charleston, South Carolina, and soon after that, home to Annapolis. Anchored by Great Stirrup Cay, we relished our last moments in these magical islands, using flash cards to identify the fish—yellowtail parrotfish, trumpetfish, hogfish, great barracuda—gliding beneath us.

After nearly two years, our expat sailing life was coming to an end, and *Sacre Bleu* had been a lucky boat through it all. From her launch in Les Sables-d'Olonne to her baptism off Rome, from crossing an ocean to dodging coral reefs in the Caribbean, she delivered us safely to every destination. To make it this far, we needed more than luck; we had to become not only skilled sailors but also adept travelers. Overcoming our fear of the unknown was fundamental to both.

The run from the Berry Islands to Charleston was 455 nautical miles, putting us on the U.S. mainland on the last of May, a day before the official start of hurricane season. We were running about a week late on our commitment to be home June 1, but the kids had been enjoying these past few weeks, and none of us was counting the days. The weather forecast called for light winds, and if the forecast was wrong, we were prepared for rough weather. A several-hundred-mile leg through open ocean had become routine for us. Our watch system now included the kids, and everyone knew their roles and responsibilities. William still had to be reminded to do his watch, but he was willing and able once he took the helm. Madeleine had become a reliable deck hand and could operate almost every system on the boat. If all else failed, we always had the modern convenience of an SOS button on our satellite device. As a family and a crew, we now felt like we could go anywhere.

19

Homeward Bound

The Eastern Seaboard
May 30, 2017

A hundred miles off Charleston, Valerie saw a cluster of peculiar shapes in the water. Black, round and smooth, like the top of a Weber grill, a half dozen of these mysterious orbs sat motionless on the flat sea. We altered course slightly to get a closer look and discovered that they were pilot whales spy-hopping to get a better look at us. As we approached, the whales dove under and gave us a gesture with their tails that I interpreted as a whale insult. We got closer, and they swam around and huffed and puffed, snorting vapor out of their blowholes, clearly perturbed by our presence. Once we had sailed far enough away, they popped their heads out of the water again and kept an eye on us until we were safely distant. We were clearly not welcome in that gathering.

Under a continuous easterly wind, we sailed a broad reach the entire three-day, 455-mile crossing to Charleston without tacking once. The sailing was so easy I was considering training Belle to do a watch. We had never been to Charleston, so for us it was yet another foreign port that we were excited to visit.

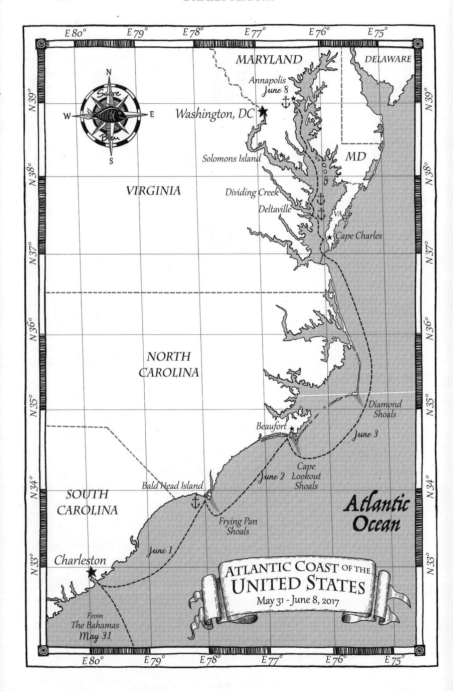

As we strolled the palm-lined streets of downtown Charleston, and Valerie and I considered the merits of renovating an old townhouse and using it as our get-away for long weekends in the winter. We were already contemplating life after *Sacre Bleu*, which was both exciting and sad.

Between Charleston and the Chesapeake Bay there would be precious few safe harbors. In Europe and the Caribbean, we could improvise our sail plan by stopping at whatever port or anchorage we happened to be near at the end of the day. Now that we were up against the long stretches of ocean sailing in the so-called Graveyard of the Atlantic, there would be no more improvising.

We identified two ports-of-call between Charleston and the Chesapeake Bay that fit our sail plan: Bald Head Island, NC, and Beaufort, NC. These stops split the 450-mile trip into three manageable segments, none requiring more than one night's watch.

Besides the dearth of safe harbors along this stretch of coast, we also faced three notorious hazards to navigation: Frying Pan Shoals, off Cape Fear; Cape Lookout Shoals, off Cape Lookout; and Diamond Shoals, off Cape Hatteras. As in The Bahamas, the sand shifts continuously in these shallow areas and charts are useless. The official NOAA chart of Diamond Shoals contains a chilling note: "Hydrography is not charted due to the changeable nature of the area. Navigation is extremely hazardous to all types of craft." Summer hurricanes, winter nor'easters, unpredictable shoals, not to mention prowling Nazi U-boats had all claimed their share of vessels and crews in the Graveyard of the Atlantic.

We reached Bald Head Island, North Carolina, at midday, anchoring in the Cape Fear River. Bald Head is a community of mostly second homes flanked by a marshy nature reserve to the west and magnificent beaches to the east. We explored in a golf cart, which, along with the tennis courts, golf course, and near-perfect landscaping, made us feel like we had landed in a enormous country club. For me, this was by far the easiest day of our two-year cruise; *Sacre Bleu*'s anchor was safely buried in mud in the Cape Fear River, it was a beautiful late-spring day, and we were in a culture I intimately understood. It was an easy day but, in a sense, a sad day as well. After 20 months wandering the unfamiliar, we had reached the familiar. Our adventure was coming to an end.

That afternoon, we left for Beaufort, about a 20-hour run. Between us and Beaufort lurked our first navigational hazard: Frying Pan Shoals. As we left the mouth of the calm Cape Fear River and entered the choppy Atlantic Ocean, I instinctively wanted to turn north and follow the coastline. However, the chart, not to mention all the locals at the marina, implored us to continue sailing southeast, straight out to sea, about 18 miles, and then turn northeast when we saw the buoy that marked the safe channel through the shoal waters.

Sailing 18 miles in the wrong direction was going to be a frustrating start to a 110-mile trip. The detour would add three or four hours to the leg, and worse, it would take us far offshore. About ten miles out, as we carefully sailed parallel to Frying Pan Shoals, I saw a cluster of large white shapes on our port side. At first, I took it for a group of sport fishing boats gathered around a hot spot, the way they do in the Chesapeake Bay when charter captains get to talking over the radio about where the rockfish are biting. This might be our shortcut through the shoal, I thought to myself.

As we approached, the depth sounder warned me that the seafloor was rising quickly from 80 feet to 15 feet. We were out of sight of land but in 15 feet of water! To my horror, I realized that the large white shapes were not fishing boats but enormous standing waves breaking against each other, forming what looked like a tempest inside an acre of sea, a phenomenon that occurs when big ocean swells meet shallow water. I quickly threw the wheel over and put *Sacre Bleu* back onto a southeast course.

We arrived in Beaufort, North Carolina, the following morning.

That afternoon, we took a carefree stroll around Beaufort, a seaport with southern charm and three centuries of history. Our never-ending fascination for the morbid led us to the Old Burying Ground, a cemetery with graves dating back to the early 1700's.

Many of the gravestones described sea captains, military officers, and unfortunate travelers, by land or sea, who intended to pass through but ended up staying for eternity. One grave had been turned into a shrine of sorts, the stone ledger covered with flowers, notes, toys, shells, junk jewelry, and other trinkets deposited by visitors. In letters chiseled in weathered stone, the headstone bluntly proclaimed "Little Girl Buried in a Rum Keg," leaving us all fighting over the brochure to learn the gory details. "She died on the ship returning from England. Her father had promised her mother that he would bring their daughter back home, which he did, albeit inside a rum barrel." I wondered how that conversation went: "Honey, we're home... Good news and bad news."

We departed Beaufort the next morning, safely rounding Cape Lookout Shoals and setting a northeast course for Cape Hatteras. This next leg measured 220 nautical miles and would take 36 hours. It would be our last night watch on *Sacre Bleu*, and in some ways the most stressful. At midnight, we would be sailing over Diamond Shoals, the most treacherous of the three shallows, with shifting sands that have been foundering ships for centuries. Since wind, waves, and depth are unpredictable in these waters, both Valerie and I stayed on deck until the shoal water was safely behind us.

The Chesapeake Bay
June 4, 2017

Sacre Bleu left the salty ocean for the last time and entered the brackish waters of the Chesapeake Bay. As we crossed the invisible line marking this final stage of the cruise, I thought of a similar line we had crossed 20 months earlier: the Pillars of Hercules, marking our entry into the Mediterranean. We had covered 12,000 miles since, traveling at the speed of a jog. Even at that pace, the trip was going by too fast.

The city of Norfolk, home to a large naval base, loomed on the congested western shore. A nuclear-powered aircraft carrier lumbered out of the James River, dwarfing the tugboats restraining its movement.

We instinctively gravitated towards the less-developed eastern shore and found the town of Cape Charles, Virginia.

As we walked down Mason Avenue, I felt as if I had walked back into the 1960s. The two-story red brick buildings with aluminum awnings all looked like the world of my childhood, at least as I vaguely remember it. At the back of Watson's Hardware, a circle of metal lawn chairs accommodated customers who could just sit and talk and not buy a thing. Madeleine said she felt like she was in a time machine. It occurred to me that I had reached an age in which the world of my youth was mostly gone except for pockets like this.

The next morning, we sailed 30 miles up the Bay to Deltaville, Virginia, off the Piankatank River on the western shore. Like so many tributaries off the Bay, the shores of the Piankatank are lined with modest homes on large parcels of land with sweeping green lawns rolling onto marshy shorelines. We anchored off the Fishing Bay Yacht Club, where just three years earlier Madeleine had won a medal in a sailing regatta. At that time, we never dreamed we would be passing through again as a cruising family. Those days of driving the kids around every weekend from one sporting event to another seemed so distant.

Just 20 miles up the western shore, we wandered into Dividing Creek, carefully following the buoys that mark the narrow channel to Hughlett Point, where we dropped anchor. There, the five of us, Belle included, spent the day exploring the sandy beaches, tide pools, and marshes of the nature preserve. Like so many of our stops in the past two years, this exquisite patch of earth is easily accessed by boat and difficult to access otherwise, so we had it to ourselves. I was reminded of other boat days when we were alone in a wonderland: on Delos, among the ruins of an ancient Greek city; in the company of a fin whale in the middle of the Atlantic Ocean; zooming through the crystal-clear inland rivers of Shroud Cay. Sailboats have been taking people to new places for thousands of years, and despite innovations in travel that have brought us planes, trains, automobiles and more, when I look back on the extraordinary places I have been, a sailboat has taken me to most of them.

We woke to clouds and drizzle. As we left the shelter of Dividing Creek and returned to the Chesapeake Bay, heavy winds and seas battered us, forcing us to reconsider our plan. We hoped to crisscross the Bay, from western to Eastern Shore and back again, visiting hard-to-reach Chesapeake landmarks like Tangier and Smith Islands, but the forecast called for more heavy weather over the next week, so we reluctantly set a course for Annapolis.

June 8, 2017
The dome of the Naval Academy chapel appeared on the skyline as we rounded Tolly Point and entered the Severn River. Sailing dinghies clustered like a kaleidoscope of butterflies, slowly worked their way around the race marks in Annapolis Harbor. We lowered *Sacre Bleu*'s sails—an exercise we would perform for the last time as a family—found a mooring ball in the harbor, fastened the bow lines and shut down the engines.

We spent our last night together on *Sacre Bleu* playing "Timeline," a favorite board game from our winter in Antibes. William had evolved from never winning to winning his share, and he was on his way to another victory. Madeleine had grown accepting of her little brother occasionally getting the better of her, and she even eked out a compliment for him.

The next morning, we docked *Sacre Bleu* in a local marina. After 12,615 nautical miles, 32 countries and territories, and 672 days, we were home. Instead of our usual arrival drill of provisioning and exploring, we packed up, cleaned up, and moved out. It was an unceremonious end to a two-year adventure. We stepped off the boat and onto the dock, crossing that last invisible line back into our old lives, but our old lives were nowhere to be found.

Afterword

In the years leading up to the cruise, Valerie and I convinced ourselves that a moment would arrive when all the moving parts in our lives would fall into place and we could finally set out on our long-planned adventure. A time would come when we were secure enough in our careers, when the kids were the right age, when we had enough money in the bank, and when we were finally expert sailors—only then would we fulfill our dream of exploring the world on a sailboat. But stars never align so neatly. As time passed, the certainty of our lives became increasingly more attractive than the uncertainties of venturing so far from the familiar and the comfortable. Ultimately, it took the irrational act of giving up it all up to embark on a journey with unknown consequences.

Even if we could rationalize the journey, there was no logic in doing it in a sailboat—a complicated, high-maintenance, slow form of travel—and spending two years winding our way along the coastlines of foreign countries, subject to storms, accidents, breakdowns, and other unpredictable elements. But in a life driven by pragmatism, comfort and economy, sometimes irrational choices bring us our most meaningful moments. Had we been able to travel faster, had it been less difficult and less risky, had we a road to follow and a fixed itinerary, the voyage might have been just another rose-tinted tourist experience instead of a life-changing journey.

Almost every day, we started from a position of vulnerability: navigating foreign waters, on a boat we hardly understood, at the mercy of forces beyond our control. By the end of the day we had done something we had never tried before: climbed a 75-foot mast in the open ocean or placated an obstinate customs official or fixed a generator. The work was always less than perfect, but good enough to get us to the next day, when we could wake up a little wiser and go a little farther.

We were well into our cruise when we discovered that most of the fears we brought with us were unfounded. Foremost, we feared being newcomers in an unfamiliar place. But as we passed through countries and cultures, and crossed paths with so many other people along the way, as we bought provisions or asked for advice, as they helped us fix an outboard or loaned us their tools, we came to realize that the spirit of helping complete strangers is alive and well. We found generosity daily, whether it was a fisherman sharing his catch, a woman lending us her car, or local sailor inviting us to his yacht club for dinner.

We also feared the elements. Wind and waves pack astronomical forces, and boats are mere trifles in their path. We never lost our respect for the weather, and our itinerary was always subordinate to the forecast. We were occasionally caught in heavy seas, and it was at these times that I most appreciated having a catamaran with two engines, not so much for the horsepower but for the redundancy. We ultimately calmed our fear of the elements, but it took some very frightening rites of passage, such as the storm off Rome.

Whales, sharks, and other sea life also ranked amongst our fears. Our first live encounters with these creatures were intimidating, but we quickly realized that nature was not out to get us. The fin whale that escorted us during the Atlantic crossing could have easily broken our boat in half. The humpback we almost hit off Guadeloupe could have done serious damage. The barracuda we retreated from in The Bahamas turned out to be too human-friendly for its own good. If nature were out to get us, it could have finished the job when we were still living in caves. Even the ciguatera fish poisoning we contracted from a painted mackerel faded completely after several months, with none of us suffering any aftereffects.

We learned that our fear of crime was also unwarranted. Frequently, we were the biggest, fanciest boat in most ports on both sides of the Atlantic. Almost every night we left our cockpit and dinghy open to the world, cluttered with dive equipment, electronics, fishing gear, and other desirable, useful, and easily portable valuables. In the two years we cruised, not a single item was stolen from us. We ventured miles offshore and along remote coastlines into parts of the world, where, for all practical purposes, there are no laws. We never felt threatened by any of the vessels that came near us.

The U.S. flag on our transom was a catalyst for countless friendly introductions. If there were people along the way who harbored hostility towards us because of our nationality, they did not make it known.

Living on a boat made us all more conscious of scarcity. Food, water, ice, battery voltage, diesel fuel, propane, cell phone minutes, and printer paper were always in limited supply, and we were constantly finding ways to conserve. When we washed dishes on the boat, we never left the water running. When we made a cup of tea, we used enough energy to heat up only one cup of water and no more. Little efficiencies add up on a boat, and we became accustomed to a world of just enough.

In the time spanning August 2015 to June 2017, much happened in the world, from Britain voting to leave the European Union to the U.S. presidential election of 2016. We missed live media coverage of it all, getting our news in short, slow drips when we could find internet access. The cruise was an unintentional two-year media diet, and in retrospect it was good for our mental health.

When I first stepped off *Sacre Bleu* in June 2017, I was intimidated by what lay ahead—just as intimidated as I had been when I stepped onto *Sacre Bleu* two years earlier. My appointment book was empty, but when I looked at its blank pages, I saw opportunity. I did not rejoin my old boards of directors, I did not bother renewing my club memberships, and I even stopped making independent films. Instead of retreating to familiar ground, I devoted my energy to diversifying *Sherman's Lagoon*. Currently I am working with a writing team on a stage musical and with a production team on a children's television program, both based on the comic strip.

Many people have remarked that since I draw a cartoon with an ocean theme, living on a boat must have provided me with an endless source of inspiration. That is true, but not in the way one might expect. I incorporated very little of our on-the-water experiences directly into my underwater comic strip. However, living in a fiberglass box with my wife and two children for 22 months provided enough material to last the rest of my career.

The cruise changed us in many ways. As a family that spent 22 months together on a boat, relying on each other to complete another leg of the journey, we became tightly bound. The traditional pecking order of father, mother, older sister, and younger brother was flattened under the demands of offshore cruising, requiring all of us to take turns as captain, crew, navigator, and cook. We brought these sensibilities back to our land lives, and we have a healthier family for it.

As I write this, we are in the throes of a pandemic. From lockdowns to remote learning to the virtual office, when we got the mandate, our family embraced these unprecedented lifestyle changes without losing a beat. Home schooling, virtual work, and living in close quarters had been part of our daily routine for two years on *Sacre Bleu*.

The relentless presence of others within arm's length and earshot forced us all to redefine the meaning of private space as a frame of mind instead of a physical reality. During lockdown, our old ways quickly fell into place, and we found a way to work separately together. We had no idea that those good times on *Sacre Bleu* would prepare us so well for the bad times ahead.

In our time afloat, what shaped Madeleine's and William's characters most was not the privileges of life on a boat—not the travel and the adventure—but its limitations. Madeleine created a diverse collection of art with the limited supplies we could fit in a small cupboard. William taught himself to play the ukulele and piano, and improvised building projects long after his conventional toys got old. Every day, they had to confront their own boredom in a world with only occasional access to electronics. Free from peer pressure, social media, television, and other distractions and influences, their development was driven by their own interests, curiosity and creativity. In short, they had time to discover their own versions of themselves at a very critical time in their lives.

Madeleine's pursuits required focus and patience. On the boat she had the luxury of uninterrupted time to explore projects at her own pace. This aspect of her personality did not change. In fact, she became a more mature version of her younger self: introspective yet engaged. In other ways, Madeleine did change. She found confidence fixing the antenna at the top of the mast, making solo runs in the dinghy, and standing a night watch. As she grew, we realized Madeleine is not timid: she is a young woman who holds strong opinions and does not waste words. Holding her own in family discussions, she developed directness, wit, and the ability to defend her ideas to a tough crowd.

William benefitted most from the limitations that boat life imposed. The opposite of Madeleine in many ways, William needed to be in an environment where he had few alternatives. We took a boy who was prone to losing himself in video games for hours and handed him a ukulele. Surprisingly, the ukulele filled the void in his life that video games left. Once he developed the basic skill of forming notes, music provided instant feedback, endless hours of entertainment, and the opportunity for slow, steady improvement.

Valerie and I were just as worried about our children's readjustment to life on land as we had been about their initial adjustment to life on a boat. For two years, their sense of normal consisted of sailing into a new port in a foreign country almost every day, where they might swim with dolphins, jump off a 30-foot cliff, ride camels on the beach, or see a prince. Would the world after *Sacre Bleu* seem boring for these two teenagers? Reality proved to be just the opposite. The world they came back to, so delightfully normal, provided the exact ingredients that had been missing in their lives: classmates, teachers, team sports, social gatherings, and driving cars were all part of their new adventure.

Because they were so well traveled, we were also concerned they might have become too cultured for their own good. At their friend's pizza party, would they declare that the pizza in Rome was better? For better or worse, they rarely spoke of the cruise to their friends, preferring topics where there was commonality: girls, boys, music they liked, teachers they did not. Conversely, the only person on the planet with whom Madeleine or William did have this commonality, with whom they could have this conversation, was each other. This shared experience will always keep them close.

We did not lose our love of boating. During the summer of 2017, we continued to take *Sacre Bleu* on short cruises on the Chesapeake Bay. By the fall, with the kids starting school and the weather turning cold, we realized that our time with *Sacre Bleu* had come to an end and we sold her. As a family, we look forward to more cruises when Madeleine and William are older. We keep a list of destinations we would like to visit—the cruises we planned but never did, like the Galapagos Islands and the South Pacific.

The summer of 2017 brought tragedy to the Caribbean when two Category 5 hurricanes, Irma and Maria, struck days apart, reshaping that region forever. As we grieved for the victims, we counted our blessings and reflected on the role that luck and timing played in our voyage. Just a few months before the hurricanes hit, we had been in Dominica exploring the Indian River, in Barbuda touring the frigate bird sanctuary, in the BVIs watching the sunset at Bitter End. These islands and so many more were devastated and have yet to recover. As we followed the horrors of the storms, the people and places that were so fresh in our memory were in our thoughts and prayers.

August 2017 brought the passing of Snowball the hamster, and later that fall, Squirt gave up the ghost. Born in a pet store in A Coruña, Spain, and adopted by two American children, they traveled the Mediterranean, crossed an ocean, were smuggled into the United States past the watchful eye of Federal authorities, and were laid to rest on a hillside overlooking the Chesapeake Bay. If hamsters could write memoirs...

On Thanksgiving night, 2017, Belle died at home in Madeleine's arms. Belle had been fighting cancer, and near the end the veterinarian recommended that we put her down. She seemed not to be in pain, so we let nature take its course, and it quickly did. We had plucked Belle from a rescue shelter at the age of six. She spent three happy years with us, though she probably would have preferred a rug and a rawhide bone to a Caribbean cruise.

As a family and crew, we made it through the storm off Rome and the tedium of the transatlantic. We kept company with the second-largest animal to ever live and swam in water four miles deep. We witnessed Pope Francis lead a ceremony for a thousand worshippers, heard the call to prayer from a distant mosque and watched King Vaval burn. We experienced the joy of Italian hot chocolate and the misery of ciguatera. In a way, we're still out there. In the Greek Islands or The Bahamas or the middle of the Atlantic Ocean, our dream still sails. In the times ahead, whenever we seek solace even for a brief moment, we will always have a place on the deck of *Sacre Bleu*.

Jim Toomey
Annapolis, Maryland
December 2021